The Smithsonian Guides to Natural America

THE SOUTH-CENTRAL STATES

The Pacific
Northwest
WA
OR

The
Northern
Rockies
MT
ID
WY

The
Northern
Plains
ND
SD
NE

The
Far
West
NV
CA
UT

The
Southern
Rockies
CO

KS

The
Southwest
AZ
NM

Okla

Texas

HI

The
Pacific
AK

MN

WI

MI

The Great Lakes

The Mid-Atlantic States

Northern New England

ME

VT NH

NY

MA CT RI

Southern New England

IA

The Heartland

IL

IN

OH

PA

NJ MD DE

MO

KY

WV

VA

The Atlantic Coast

Arkansas

Central Appalachia

TN

NC

•ma

Missis-sippi

AL

GA

SC

Louisiana

The Southeast

FL

The South Central States

THE SOUTH-CENTRAL STATES
TEXAS – OKLAHOMA – ARKANSAS
LOUISIANA – MISSISSIPPI

THE SMITHSONIAN GUIDES TO NATURAL AMERICA

THE SOUTH-CENTRAL STATES

TEXAS, OKLAHOMA, ARKANSAS, LOUISIANA, MISSISSIPPI

TEXT
Mel White

PHOTOGRAPHY
Jim Bones and Tria Giovan

PREFACE
Thomas E. Lovejoy

SMITHSONIAN BOOKS • WASHINGTON, D.C.
RANDOM HOUSE • NEW YORK, N.Y.

Front cover: Avery Island, Louisiana
Half-title page: Green heron
Frontispiece: Briarwood preserve, Natchitoches, Louisiana
Back cover: Armadillo; strawberry pitaya cactus; painted bunting

THE SMITHSONIAN INSTITUTION
SECRETARY I. Michael Heyman
COUNSELOR TO THE SECRETARY FOR
BIODIVERSITY AND ENVIRONMENTAL AFFAIRS Thomas E. Lovejoy
DIRECTOR, SMITHSONIAN INSTITUTION PRESS Daniel H. Goodwin
EDITOR, SMITHSONIAN BOOKS Alexis Doster III

THE SMITHSONIAN GUIDES TO NATURAL AMERICA
SERIES EDITOR Sandra Wilmot
MANAGING EDITOR Ellen Scordato
SERIES PHOTO EDITOR Mary Jenkins
PHOTO EDITOR Sarah Longacre
ART DIRECTOR Mervyn Clay
ASSISTANT PHOTO EDITOR Ferris Cook
ASSISTANT PHOTO EDITOR Rebecca Williams
ASSISTANT EDITOR Seth Ginsberg
COPY EDITORS Helen Dunn, Karen Hammonds
FACT CHECKER Jean Cotterell
PRODUCTION DIRECTOR Katherine Rosenbloom

Library of Congress Cataloging-in-Publication Data
White, Mel
  The Smithsonian guides to natural America. The South-Central
States—Texas, Oklahoma, Arkansas, Louisiana, Mississippi / text by
Mel White; photography by Jim Bones and Tria Giovan; preface by
Thomas E. Lovejoy.
      p.   cm.
  Includes bibliographical references (p. 250) and index.
  ISBN 0-679-76479-8 (pbk.)
  1. Natural history—Southern States—Guidebooks. 2. Southern
States—Guidebooks. I. Bones, Jim. II Giovan, Tria. III Title.
QH104.5S59W495 1996
508.76—dc20   95-51226
                                                 CIP
Manufactured in the United States of America
98765432

How to Use This Book

The Smithsonian Guides to Natural America explore and celebrate the preserved and protected natural areas of this country that are open for the public to use and enjoy. From world-famous national parks to tiny local preserves, the places featured in these guides offer a splendid panoply of this nation's natural wonders.

Divided by state and region, this book offers suggested itineraries for travelers, briefly describing the high points of each preserve, refuge, park, or wilderness area along the way. Each site was chosen for a specific reason: Some are noted for their botanical, zoological, or geological significance, others simply for their exceptional scenic beauty.

Information pertaining to the area as a whole can be found in the introductory sections to the book and to each chapter. In addition, specialized maps at the beginning of each book and chapter highlight an area's geography and geological features as well as pinpoint the specific locales that the author describes.

For quick reference, places of interest are set in **boldface** type; those set in **boldface** followed by the symbol ❖ are listed in the Site Guide at the back of the book. (This feature begins on page 257, just before the index.) Here noteworthy sites are listed alphabetically by state, and each entry provides practical information that visitors need: telephone numbers, mailing addresses, and specific services available.

Addresses and telephone numbers of national, state, and local agencies and organizations are also listed. Also in appendices are a glossary of pertinent scientific terms and designations used to describe natural areas; the author's recommendations for further reading (both nonfiction and fiction); and a list of sources that can aid travelers planning a guided visit.

The words and images of these guides are meant to help both the active naturalist and the armchair traveler to appreciate more fully the environmental diversity and natural splendor of this country. To ensure a successful visit, always contact a site in advance to obtain detailed maps, updated information on hours and fees, and current weather conditions. Many areas maintain a fragile ecological balance. Remember that their continued vitality depends in part on responsible visitors who tread the land lightly.

C O N T E N T S

PREFACE

The south-central states—Texas, Oklahoma, Arkansas, Louisiana, and Mississippi—are natural America's crossroads: a richness of flora and fauna from east and west, north and south. This is not, however, the only way I think of them.

For me they evoke such memories as an anticipation-charged wait in the mist and dark of a tallgrass prairie with Molly Boren (whose husband's name is honored by an Oklahoma nature trail) until I first heard the boom and then saw the leaps of greater prairie chicken males displaying. I recall the sight of fluttering technicolor as migratory songbirds made landfall on a Louisiana chenier, the lazy meander of the Pedernales River near the LBJ Ranch, and flocks of the now-recovered brown pelican off artist Walter Anderson's beloved Mississippi Gulf Islands. The south-central states also remind me of my first donation to conservation (a paltry amount but significant for a college boy) to preserve the Attwater prairie chicken.

The prairies are one of natural America's most changed ecosystems, and healthy examples survive only here and there. In Oklahoma, the Nature Conservancy's Tallgrass Prairie Preserve now boasts re-introduced bison. Yet in many ways the joys of the prairie ecosystem are its grasses, deep-rooted and invulnerable until the advent of John Deere's plow. Big bluestem, little bluestem, switchgrass, Indiangrass, and others, each in itself is a botanical work of art. And then there are the wildflowers. One can imagine, however, that in its original horizon-to-horizon expanse the tallgrass prairie could spell peril; it was easy to get lost in grasses taller than a person, and raging prairie fires must have been nothing short of terrifying.

Almost as reduced (90 percent) from their original extent are the glorious bottomland forests of the south-central watercourses. Fortunately concerted efforts have been and are being made to protect what remains of these magnificent hardwood trees in a number of national

---

PRECEDING PAGES: *Sunrise limns a canyon in Texas's Big Bend country, where the Rio Grande has carved a spectacular series of sheer-walled chasms.*

wildlife refuges such as Oklahoma's Little River, Arkansas's Felsenthal and White River, Louisiana's Tensas River (the last place ivory-billed woodpeckers were seen in the United States) as well as the Pascagoula River Wildlife Management Area in Mississippi.

The loss of bottomland forest is part of this century's far-reaching alterations to the hydrology of the Mississippi. Never totally tameable, the great river is for the moment kept from following its natural direction into the Atchafalaya Swamp. (See John McPhee's gripping 1989 account of this subject in *The Control of Nature*.) As a consequence, the Mississippi now acts more and more like a continental-scale firehose, spreading silt out into the Gulf of Mexico, where it cannot nourish the floodplains, and virtually eliminating Les Isles Dernieres, which previously protected the coast from storm surges. Nonetheless wetland riches survive in Louisiana, which harbors 40 percent of the nation's marshlands—as well as the considerable ornithological spectacle of Avery Island, astride its salt dome.

Geologically, the south-central portion of natural America is also rich. El Capitan in Texas's Guadelupe Mountains is the world's largest (albeit fossilized) coral reef. Salt domes abound, and in Dinosaur Valley State Park near Fort Worth ancient footprints reveal a predatory dinosaur stalking its prey. Windblown loess formations contour the landscape, and an abundance of caverns (with attendant bats) seems woven into underlying limestone formations. And, at Arkansas's Crater of Diamonds State Park, you can try your own luck at finding a gemstone.

Looming large in this part of natural America is—inevitably— Texas. After all, it is the only state that Roger Tory Peterson felt merited its very own field guide. Here is Big Bend National Park, with more bird species than any other, and Padre, the world's largest barrier island. There are shortgrass high plains, mixed-grass rolling plains, canyons, caves, Texas Hill Country, and the 84,000 remaining acres of once extensive (3.5 million acres) Big Thicket. The Gulf shores are a primary place to see Kemp's ridley sea turtles in this country; the Houston toad occurs in only seven (admittedly Texas-sized) counties. In Texas the lucifer hummingbird pollinates the ever-so-much-larger century plant (the

---

OVERLEAF: *A rare dusting of fresh snow coats the spiny yuccas in the Chihuahuan Desert of Guadalupe Mountains National Park in western Texas.*

latter's 50 years to flowering indicates only modest exaggeration if one uses the scale of two), and least grebes and buff-bellied hummingbirds inhabit the lower Rio Grande. Santa Ana is the place for relatively exotic tropical birds such as the chachalaca; that funny black cuckoo, the groove-billed ani; and the pauraque, a whippoorwill relative. In addition, the Lone Star state is the scene of continuing conservation drama—the whooping cranes at Aransas; the struggle (once again looking positive) over the Balcones Canyonlands, home of the rare golden-cheeked warbler and black-capped vireo; the wildlife spectacle of as many as 100,000 sandhill cranes at Muleshoe National Wildlife Refuge.

The south-central region has lost the ivory-billed woodpecker and the red wolf in its original form. It has been a long time since the sighting of an Eskimo curlew, and that small denizen of the old-growth longleaf pine forests, the red-cockaded woodpecker, is endangered. Indeed, much has changed since Thomas Nuttall characterized the Ozarks as a "vast and trackless wilderness of trees." Yet there is still captivating native wildlife to be seen here, whether the fleet-footed pronghorn, the exotically colored roseate spoonbill, or a town of busy prairie dogs interacting in what Washington Irving termed their "pigmy republic."

First and foremost, this region of vast skies is a place for soaring birds: Harris's, red-shouldered, Swainson's, and ferruginous hawks; aplomado falcons; Mississippi and white-tailed kites. This part of natural America may boast the largest state—Texas—and the one Rodgers and Hammerstein has led us to know requires an exclamation point—Oklahoma!—but for me it is above all home to birds that perform spectacular aerial pirouettes. With this book and Mel White's knowledgeable text as a guide, I hope you too may experience the indescribable joy of spotting a scissor-tailed flycatcher, its long feather pennants adrift in the prairie wind.

—*Thomas E. Lovejoy*
Counselor to the Secretary for
Biodiversity and Environmental Affairs,
SMITHSONIAN INSTITUTION

LEFT: *A roseate spoonbill flaunts the pink plumage that makes it one of the Gulf Coast's most admired species. Seriously endangered earlier in the century, spoonbills have staged a modest but encouraging comeback.*

COLORADO

KANSAS

Canadian *River*

Amarillo

NEW MEXICO

Lubbock

Wichita
Falls

Fort
Worth

El Paso

Guadalupe Mtns

T E X A S

Colorado R.

AUSTIN

Rio Grande River

San Antonio

MEXICO

SOUTH-CENTRAL
STATES

50   0   50 Miles

50   0   50 Kilometers

INTRODUCTION

INTRODUCTION:
THE SOUTH-CENTRAL STATES

A s the rising sun lights the rocky slopes of the Chisos Mountains, a roadrunner sets off across the west Texas desert in search of lizards still torpid from the night's chill. In Oklahoma, where it's already full daylight, a bull bison shakes its shaggy head and begins to browse amid tall grasses and wildflowers on the rolling prairie. Another night of hunting finished, an ocelot curls up amid thick vegetation in the Rio Grande Valley to sleep through the heat of the day as a gaudy green jay scolds from an acacia above. Deep in a "holler" of the rugged Arkansas Ozarks, a black bear finds a patch of ripe huckleberries and settles in for a feast, while in Louisiana a red-cockaded woodpecker methodically probes for insects in the bark of a tall pine. Farther east, in Mississippi, warming air stirs the ancient psyche of an alligator; the massive reptile slides down a muddy bank into the swamp and swims silently toward a bustling heronry to lie in wait—just in case one of the nestlings above makes a fatal misstep.

On a spring morning in the south-central United States, all the disparate elements of a vast range of ecosystems are conducting business as usual: the hunters and the hunted, the many-legged and the no-legged, the big and furry, and the small and slimy. Few other regions of the country can match the diversity of these five states, which encompass habitats as different as bottomland hardwoods in the Mississippi Valley, High Plains in the Oklahoma Panhandle, subtropical brushland in south Texas, and white-water rivers in the heavily forested Arkansas mountains.

Manifestly and indisputably, the south-central states are where East meets West. The most significant aspect of this transition is moisture. In Louisiana, annual rainfall can top 60 inches, whereas El Paso gets less than 10 inches of precipitation in an average year. The regimens imposed by those statistics are undeniable: Southern bayous overtop their

---

PRECEDING PAGES: *Snow dots the pines in the Arkansas Ozarks, and water-skiers on Beaver Lake have given way to wintering ducks and loons.*

RIGHT: *The Glass Mountains of northwestern Oklahoma were named for the shimmers of sunlight that reflect off its exposed gypsum outcrops.*

banks each spring, sharing their rich silt with the bordering lands and favoring water-tolerant trees; in west Texas, plants have learned to poison each other to reduce competition for every precious drop of water.

In the zone where eastern and western species meet—the Texas Hill Country is a good example—the result is a fascinatingly varied landscape: Bald cypresses line riversides west of San Antonio while mesquites grow on the surrounding hills; eastern bluebirds nest near western canyon wrens; fox squirrels cavort in the same woods as ringtails. Similar combinations occur in the Big Thicket of northeast Texas and the mountains of Oklahoma, where America changes from the moist East to the arid West.

Although in this part of the country temperature is less important than water as a determining factor in the environment, extremes vary considerably with latitude. The entire area can be very hot in the summer; winter stays mild on the Gulf Coast (and downright sultry in south Texas), but the "blue norther" winds that roar across the Texas and Oklahoma panhandles bring bone-chilling conditions and frequent blizzards.

The south-central states offer visitors scenery as grand as any in

ABOVE: *The rugged-looking dunes of Texas's Padre Island National Seashore are in fact quite fragile formations, easily destroyed when careless hikers trample the vegetation that holds them together.*

North America. Few sights can match the awesomely deep river-carved canyons of Big Bend National Park and the massive face of El Capitan in the Guadalupe Mountains in Texas, or the lonely beauty of white-sand barrier islands off the Mississippi coast. Equally impressive, in their own ways, are the incredibly fecund Atchafalaya Swamp in Louisiana, the fall-foliage colors of deciduous woods in the Arkansas highlands, and a herd of bison thundering across the Oklahoma prairie.

Other scenes invite—and amply repay—more contemplative observation: the prolonged, but lethal, enticing of prey by an insectivorous pitcher plant in a Mississippi savanna; the complex cycle of sea life in a coastal marsh, where so much depends on the fragile balance of fresh, brackish, and salt water; the annual passage of migratory songbirds across woods and fields; the early spring appearance of wildflowers in the Ozark Mountains, where hepatica, bloodroot, crested iris, bellwort, trout lily, and Solomon's seal light the still-brown slopes like candles in

OVERLEAF: *In rolling Texas Hill Country, a lush meadow of colorful wildflowers—including contrasting swaths of red paintbrush and yellow wild chicory—blossoms at Palmetto State Park near Gonzales.*

LEFT: *Sunset burnishes the moss-hung bald cypresses growing in Arkansas's mirrorlike Enterprise Lake. The leaves of this deciduous conifer turn reddish brown in fall and drop off each winter.*
RIGHT: *The chuckling call of the southern leopard frog, a familiar sound across the region, is unnaturally stilled when wetlands are drained for agriculture.*

a shadowed room. And no one who has sat quietly and watched the antic activities in a prairie-dog town can ever again consider the northwest Texas grasslands boring—even though they're among the flattest and most treeless places on earth.

As in too many other parts of the world, nature has suffered significantly in sections of the south-central states where cities have expanded, land has been cleared for crops and livestock, swamps have been drained, and forests have been converted into tree farms. Prairies, which attracted settlers because they required no draining or clearing, may have lost the most. Only a tiny portion of Texas's original 12 million acres of blackland prairie remains in natural condition, and Arkansas's Grand Prairie and the Cajun Prairie of southwest Louisiana are also greatly diminished.

The rich bottomland soil that supported great hardwood forests in the Mississippi River valley is equally productive of cotton, soybeans, and winter wheat. Some counties in east Arkansas have lost 95 percent of their natural woodland—and with it one of the world's richest ecosystems, described by early explorers and hunters as a "paradise" of wildlife. In western Arkansas, streams that once ran free and crystal clear have been dammed to create huge reservoirs, delighting water-skiers but eliminating habitat for smallmouth bass, river otters, mussels, and dozens of other species. In south Louisiana, the coastline is eroding at an alarming rate, partly because levees keep rivers from spreading land-building silt and partly because man-made canals have disrupted protective natural restraints on water flow.

Nonetheless, conservation success stories dot the map of the region, and in each of the five states parks and refuges invite visitors to enjoy America's natural heritage. The proposed wildlife corridor in Texas's lower Rio Grande Valley, for one admirable example, will restore habitat vital for birds, mammals, and reptiles unique in the United States. Although political slogans have superseded environmental considerations in the Texas Hill Country, significant areas may yet be set aside to protect such endangered species as golden-cheeked warblers and black-capped vireos. State and federal agencies have acquired important waterfowl wintering grounds in the Cache and White River drainages in east Arkansas, and several of the region's national forests are showing new environmental awareness in their management programs.

Oklahoma's Tallgrass Prairie Preserve will re-create the natural conditions of this once-vast grassland habitat, including bison grazing and regular controlled burning. Bald eagles, ospreys, and brown pelicans—all fish-eating birds harmed by pesticide use in past decades—are making encouraging comebacks throughout the region. The American alligator, which suffered a serious decline in the 1950s and 1960s, has made its comeback; it boasts especially healthy populations in the swamps of Louisiana. The whooping crane—one of the most famous, and most precariously rare, of the country's endangered species—continues its slow recovery, wintering at Aransas National Wildlife Refuge and nearby coastal areas of Texas. Thousands of birders visit Rockport each year in hopes of glimpsing this majestic bird—a symbol of America's commitment to preserving its natural diversity.

Although no one will ever see a Carolina parakeet again, or most likely an ivory-billed woodpecker or Bachman's warbler either, places such as Aransas, Big Bend, and the Atchafalaya Swamp offer refuge to other beleaguered species, from glamorous picture-postcard stars like mountain lions and swallow-tailed kites to lowly mussels, shrubs, and salamanders.

More and more, people are realizing that classifying one species as more "valuable" than another is presumptuous and shortsighted. Similarly, wise travelers know that these five states offer intriguing sights beyond the best-known and most popular destinations. Texas's Guadalupe Mountains National Park and Padre Island National Seashore and Arkansas's Buffalo National River deservedly attract visitors with their beauty, recreational offerings, and ecological importance, but many smaller, less-publicized sites can be just as rewarding. The Tunica Hills of Louisiana; Lost Maples State Park in Texas; Rich Mountain, on the Arkansas-Oklahoma line; Tishomingo State Park in far northeastern Mississippi; Caprock Canyon State Park in west Texas; Village Creek State Park on Crowleys Ridge in Arkansas; the Crosby Arboretum at

Three faces of natural Texas: The long-billed curlew (left) nests on the rolling short-grass prairies of the Panhandle; the tiny green kingfisher (top right) patrols streams in the Rio Grande Valley and the Hill Country; the elegant pale gray scissor-tailed flycatcher (bottom right) is often spotted on fences or power lines on the open western plains.

Picayune, Mississippi; Briarwood nature preserve in northern Louisiana; Salt Plains National Wildlife Refuge in Oklahoma—all these and many others are well worth a trip of a few hours or a few days.

No place in the south-central states is far from at least a sampling of the wild world. Even the great urban areas of Dallas, Houston, New Orleans, and Tulsa embrace parks and nature centers where flowers bloom and birds sing for anyone who takes the time to leave the malls and freeways and enjoy them. And at the other extreme, places still exist—in the Ouachita Mountains of Oklahoma and Arkansas, in the Big Bend backcountry, on Gulf Coast barrier islands, in the pine forests of Louisiana—where, in the words of Mississippi painter-naturalist Walter Anderson, "the world of man is far away and so is man."

Lace up a pair of hiking boots, throw on a day pack, and head down a trail in one of these out-of-the-way places to discover experiences as enduring as the land itself: to see pronghorn racing across the prairie or hundreds of shorebirds wheeling over the surf; to hear a screech owl call or a coyote howl; to smell witch hazel in the woods or run a hand over rock a billion years old. This area offers enough of natural America to keep any curious traveler busy, and happy, for a lifetime.

TEXAS

T E X A S

Texas is big. Speaking ecologically, geographically, politically, or sociologically, the Lone Star State's sheer acreage overshadows all other considerations. It stretches as far south as Miami, as far north as North Carolina, as far east as Minneapolis, and as far west as Albuquerque. Texas contains counties bigger than Connecticut. Its elevation ranges from sea level to 8,749 feet; it encompasses humid temperate forests and arid deserts, subtropical scrub and Rocky Mountain conifers.

For the naturalist, this vast expanse means a great diversity of habitats—a catchphrase indicating that there's a lot to see here. So much, in fact, that a visitor could get a fair sampling of America's outdoors without ever crossing the borders of Texas. (Such exploration would entail a considerable journey, though: A drive from the Rio Grande Valley to Big Bend and the Guadalupe Mountains, up to the High Plains, across the prairies to the Piney Woods, and down the Gulf Coast again would cover, at a rough estimate, nearly 3,000 miles.)

Texas pride and tall tales are infamous, but the braggadocio is based on fact. What other state could be home to alligators and elk, ocelots and prairie chickens, sea turtles and aspens? Texas contains the world's longest barrier island and largest fossil reef. It includes some of the youngest land in North America in the Gulf Coastal Plain, and some of the oldest in the Llano Uplift, or Central Mineral Region,

---

PRECEDING PAGES: *The magnificent escarpment of the Sierra del Carmen rises across the Rio Grande from Tornillo Flats in Big Bend National Park.*

where rocks up to three billion years old are exposed. Vertical cliffs of river-carved canyons in west Texas rise 1,500 feet tall, and expanses in the Panhandle are among the flattest places on earth.

So diverse is the state that of the handful of legendary birding hot spots in America, Texas boasts three: the Gulf Coast, with its waterbirds and spring migration "fallouts"; the Rio Grande Valley, with its Mexican specialties; and Big Bend National Park, home to avidly sought rarities and an astonishingly long cumulative species list. National wildlife refuges in Texas—among them Anahuac, Aransas, Laguna Atascosa, and Santa Ana—are immensely popular destinations, magnets for both birds and the travelers who come to see them. The state's notable species range from egrets and golden eagles to the Colima warbler of the west and the tiny buff-bellied hummingbird of the south. Even visitors with no interest in birds can hardly fail to notice the spectacular flocks of gulls, terns, and shorebirds that frequent the coast's beaches and mudflats.

As in most other places, the conservation story in Texas mingles disappointment and success. Nearly all the state's once-extensive tallgrass prairie has been lost to crops, grazing, and development, and only relatively small, noncontiguous parts of the Big Thicket of east Texas have been preserved. The beautiful Texas Hill Country west of Austin, home to the endangered golden-cheeked warbler, is the focus of a sometimes bitter struggle as conservationists work to create ecological preserves in an area valued by farmers, ranchers, and developers. But vast sections of the magnificent Big Bend are protected as public land, and serious efforts are under way to save, and even expand, remaining natural areas in the Rio Grande Valley.

Backpackers and birders, photographers and rockhounds, botanists and beachcombers will all be endlessly rewarded as they travel across the Lone Star State. Although one hesitates to encourage Texans' tendency to claim the biggest and best of everything, the truth must be told: In natural America, Texas ranks at the very top.

THE PINEY WOODS AND THE GULF COAST

The coastline between the Sabine River and the Rio Grande offers abundant rewards for the naturalist. Despite intrusions of industry, agriculture, and tourism, wild places endure here; important parks and preserves are strung like pearls along the Texas shore. Among them is perhaps the most famous national wildlife refuge in the country: Aransas, the vital winter home of the whooping crane—itself an icon of America's endangered species.

North of the upper Gulf Coast is a rolling landscape of forest and rivers that Texans call the Piney Woods, where towns have names like Lumberton, Woodville, and Pineland. Ecologists dub this region a biological crossroads—with good reason. The great pine forest of the Southeast is at the edge of its range here, and a traveler moving westward soon sees signs of the coming plains. Northern and southern species intermingle in east Texas as well. The best example of this overlap is Big Thicket National Preserve, a protected remnant of one of the continent's most important biosystems where northern, southern, eastern, and western elements coexist in magnificent diversity.

Geologically speaking, the Texas coast is young. It is an accumulation of gravel, sand, and silt carried by rivers from the interior highlands to today's Coastal Plain, where currents of the slowly receding Gulf of Mexico distributed them in layers thousands of feet thick. The weight of

LEFT: *In the marshes of Padre Island National Seashore, layers of fresh water float on a heavier base of salty groundwater. Spreading wetlands such as this provide rich feeding grounds for ducks and wading birds.*

PINEY WOODS & THE GULF COAST: WEST

25 ——— 0 ——— 25 Miles
25 ——— 0 ——— 25 Kilometers

AUSTIN

77

10

36

San Antonio

410

10

37

35

83

239

Tivoli

Port O'Conner

ARANSAS NWR

MATAGORDA ISLAND STATE PARK

WELDER WILDLIFE FOUNDATION

GOOSE ISLAND STATE PARK

Sinton

Rockport

Blackjack Peninsula

TEXAS STATE AQUARIUM

Corpus Christi

77

Kingsville

G U L F   O F   M E X I C O

PADRE ISLAND NATIONAL SEASHORE

Laguna Madre Bay

LAGUNA ATASCOSA NWR

Mansfield Channel

83

Mission

Alamo

Harlingen

106

BENTSEN–RIO GRANDE VALLEY STATE PARK

Rio Grande Valley

281

Brownsville

SANTA ANA NATIONAL WILDLIFE REFUGE

SABAL PALM GROVE SANCTUARY

M E X I C O

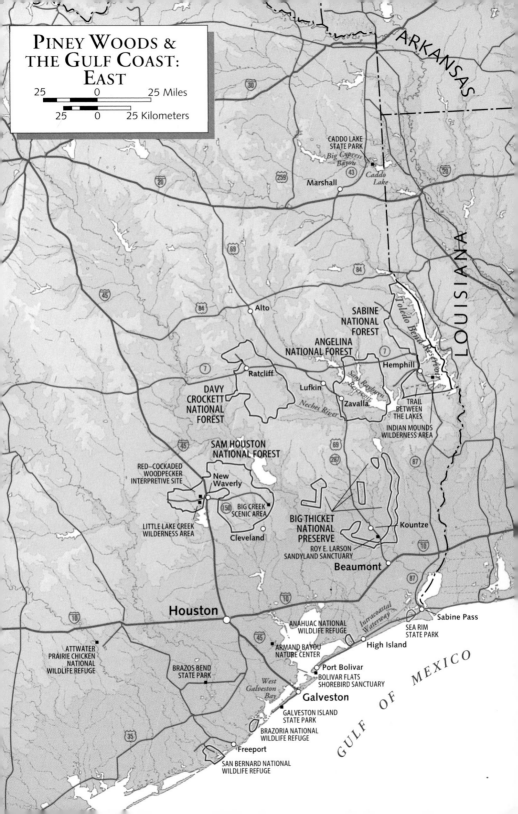

PINEY WOODS & THE GULF COAST: EAST

25   0   25 Miles

25   0   25 Kilometers

ARKANSAS

LOUISIANA

CADDO LAKE
STATE PARK

Big Cypress Bayou

Marshall

Caddo Lake

Toledo Bend Reservoir

Alto

SABINE
NATIONAL
FOREST

ANGELINA
NATIONAL FOREST

Hemphill

Ratcliff

Lufkin

San Rayburn Reservoir

DAVY
CROCKETT
NATIONAL
FOREST

Zavalla

Neches River

TRAIL
BETWEEN
THE LAKES

INDIAN MOUNDS
WILDERNESS AREA

SAM HOUSTON
NATIONAL FOREST

RED–COCKADED
WOODPECKER
INTERPRETIVE SITE

New
Waverly

BIG CREEK
SCENIC AREA

Kountze

LITTLE LAKE CREEK
WILDERNESS AREA

Cleveland

BIG THICKET
NATIONAL
PRESERVE

ROY E. LARSON
SANDYLAND SANCTUARY

Beaumont

Houston

Sabine Pass

ANAHUAC NATIONAL
WILDLIFE REFUGE

Intracoastal Waterway

SEA RIM
STATE PARK

ARMAND BAYOU
NATURE CENTER

High Island

ATTWATER
PRAIRIE CHICKEN
NATIONAL
WILDLIFE REFUGE

Port Bolivar

BOLIVAR FLATS
SHOREBIRD SANCTUARY

BRAZOS BEND
STATE PARK

*West
Galveston Bay*

Galveston

GALVESTON ISLAND
STATE PARK

BRAZORIA NATIONAL
WILDLIFE REFUGE

Freeport

SAN BERNARD NATIONAL
WILDLIFE REFUGE

GULF OF MEXICO

LEFT: *To understand why avid birders flock to south Texas, one need search no further than the beautiful green jay, one of several tropical species that range north only to this part of the United States.*

these alluvial deposits has caused fractures in rock far below, sometimes forcing up domes of salt from older underlying beds. The oil and gas found in such places helped create the Houston skyline—and the well-worn stereotype of the Texas millionaire watching money roll in from pumping wells.

Other riches draw visitors to natural areas: the flashing yellow tail feathers of a green jay; the magnificence of a live oak far older than the United States; the multi-colored glitter of tiny coquina clams on a beach; the beauty of a woodland orchid. Such sights await travelers in eastern Texas and along the state's 370 miles of Gulf Coast, which pass from a moist, temperate land to a drier subtropical habitat that is, in effect, a bit of Mexico transplanted across the border.

This mostly flat terrain offers little "scenery"; marshes, prairies, and scrubland stretch out of sight with no hint of topographic relief. The gentle slope of the Gulf floor near the coast has led to the formation of barrier islands—Galveston, Matagorda, San Jose, Mustang, and Padre are the most significant—that protect half of the state's shoreline. The southernmost, Padre, is the world's longest barrier island; much of it is within a national seashore where visitors can experience the solitude of seemingly endless stretches of beach, dunes, and water. If all Texas's islands and bays are added to the total, the state's coastline grows to more than 600 miles.

Native Americans of the Caddo culture lived in the Piney Woods, farming and creating graceful pottery. Along the coast were small groups

*RIGHT: **Looking vaguely duck-like when it swims across open water, the vividly colored purple gallinule is in fact related to rails and cranes. Its long toes let it walk atop floating vegetation.***

of Indians known as Karan-kawas, hunter-gatherers who harvested fish, turtles, and crustaceans from rivers and bays. Their reputation for fe-rocity postdates persecution by Spanish and French adven-turers. The first of these were members of Pánfilo de Nar-váez's disastrous 1528 expedi-tion from Spain to Florida and points west; survivors spent five years shipwrecked on the coast before continuing overland to Mexico.

Although much has changed since those times, some things remain the same. People still go down to the sea to feast on crabs, oysters, and clams. The Karankawas reputedly covered themselves in fish oil or alligator fat to protect their skin from mosquitoes. Today's visitor may be driven to similar measures when the humming hordes take to the air, but a better idea is to stock ample repellent and wear clothing that screens both biting bugs and burning sun.

The shoreline curves south from the Coastal Bend to the mouth of the Rio Grande, where subtropical brushlands are home to such fasci-nating species as ocelot (a small, secretive cat), hook-billed kite (a snail-eating hawk), and manzanita (a fruiting shrub native to only two counties in the United States). Here too grows the only tree-sized palm native to Texas. The warm climate of the Valley, as Texans call

*OVERLEAF: **Although native pines dominate the Sabine National Forest, its 188,000 acres encompass pockets of diverse habitats. Here early evening light turns grasses silvery in a willow-ringed wetland of the Sabine River.***

21

the area along the lower Rio Grande, makes it one of the country's most productive agricultural centers. Demand for cropland has caused the loss of much original vegetation—which was, in its own right, just as productive. Serious efforts are under way to preserve and restore this threatened habitat so its unique association of plants and animals will always have a home in Texas.

This chapter follows the Texas-Louisiana line south to the Gulf of Mexico, parallels the coastline to the Mexican border, and then turns northwest along the Rio Grande.

THE PINEY WOODS

Those who associate Texas with prairies and arid plains would do well to stop at **Caddo Lake State Park❖,** off Route 43 northeast of Marshall a few miles from the Louisiana line. The high scream of the swamp-loving red-shouldered hawk sounds along Big Cypress Bayou, where trees covered with Spanish moss bring to mind images of the Old South, not the Old West. At 32,000 acres, Caddo Lake, just downstream from the park, was once the South's largest natural lake (a dam now maintains its water level). Although the lake's meandering channels and backwaters are daunting to the inexperienced, canoe rentals at pretty Saw Mill Pond, ringed by cypress and buttonbush, give even casual paddlers a taste of this sometimes eerie environment. Good short hiking trails lead into woods housing an interesting variety of birds, including the fish crow, here near the western limit of its range. Its call is a strangled version of the American crow's familiar *caw;* the two species are practically impossible to distinguish visually.

Fifty miles south of Caddo Lake, 160,000-acre **Sabine National Forest❖** stretches along the west bank of huge Toledo Bend Reservoir, the fifth-largest man-made lake in the United States. Like Texas's three other national forests, Sabine is mostly devoted to the production of pine timber; depending on soil conditions, shortleaf, loblolly, and longleaf pine occur in varying proportions. (A traveler on Piney Woods highways could hardly be blamed for believing that pine trees—stripped of branches and cut to uniform lengths—grow naturally on the back of the ubiquitous log trucks.)

Fragmented by roads and a pipeline, the 11,000-acre **Indian Mounds Wilderness Area❖,** a few miles east of Hemphill off Route

83, nevertheless contains noteworthy attractions, foremost among them some excellent stands of beech and southern magnolia, a forest type that has largely been extirpated elsewhere. Farther south, the 28-mile **Trail Between the Lakes❖** (which, as its name implies, connects Toledo Bend and Sam Rayburn reservoirs) is a well-marked back-packing route providing easy access to day-hiking sections. A first-time visitor should hike the short interpretative loop near the Lakeview Recreation Area (south from Hemphill on Route 87 and east on Route 2928), at the trail's eastern terminus, where a brochure iden-tifies some of the most important trees and shrubs. The McLemore Hills, a few miles westward, are good for walking; a primitive camp-site favored by local hikers is near Lick Branch.

One of the most appealing and rewarding short trails in Texas is in the 154,000-acre **Angelina National Forest❖.** The five-mile **Sawmill Hiking Trail** (Route 69 south from Zavalla and Forest Road 314 east) runs between the Boykin Springs and Bouton Lake campgrounds, paralleling the Neches River for part of its length and winding under good-sized pines, sweet gums, and water and swamp chestnut oaks. River birches and willows line the Neches, and even in winter the spiny evergreen leaves of American holly brighten the woods.

Forest Road 314 also provides access to the **Upland Island Wilder-ness Area,** a few miles north, the largest wilderness (more than 13,000 acres) in the state's four national forests and home to impressive stands of trees. The road traverses a slightly elevated area of longleaf pine with a grassy understory; here sections both north and south of the road are worth exploring to see not only large pines in a parklike setting but also oaks and other hardwoods in the stream bottoms. Another good access point into Upland Island is on its eastern boundary at the inter-section of Forest Roads 303 and 302, where an abandoned road leads westward to Big Creek.

About 50 miles northwest, Route 69 passes the town of Alto (Span-ish for "high"), the high point on a portion of the old San Antonio Road, a "highway" built by Spain in the late seventeenth century to connect its missions. One of those missions was established nearby to convert the Nabedache Indians, whom the Spanish called Tejas, the Indians' word for friends. "Tejas" eventually became "Texas," giving a name to a region, a republic, and in 1845 a state.

LEFT: *Gray-barked beeches, whose triangular nuts are a valuable food for resident wildlife, grow among pines in the Davy Crockett National Forest.*
RIGHT: *The endangered red-cockaded woodpecker (this fellow has a red leg band) survive only in old-growth longleaf pine woods. The male's scarlet nape patch, or "cockade," is almost never seen.*

West of Lufkin via Routes 103 and 7, the view at the Neches Overlook in the **Davy Crockett National Forest❖** might qualify as scenic only in the context of flat east Texas, but it does provide a panorama of the Neches River bottoms and rolling ridgelines in the distance. The 20-mile **Four C National Recreation Trail** (named for the Central Coal and Coke Company, which once logged the area) begins at the Ratcliff Lake Recreation Area, where campers will find all the usual Forest Service amenities, and ends at the Neches Overlook. Along the way it bisects part of the 3,639-acre **Big Slough Wilderness Area,** a mostly swampy tract where hardwoods dominate two-thirds of the forest. Although sections of Big Slough are difficult of access, the Four C Trail and a few abandoned logging roads allow hikers to enjoy a diverse woodland of oak, hickory, sycamore, and other deciduous trees mixed with shortleaf and, in wetter spots, loblolly pine.

The endangered red-cockaded woodpecker lives in all four of Texas's national forests; within the Davy Crockett, for instance, colonies can be found on Route 227 northwest of Ratcliff and on Route 7 east of town. The healthiest population lives about 50 miles south in the **Sam Houston National Forest❖,** which is home to more than 130 colonies. Because these birds need mature pines with an open understory to survive, current forestry practices, including earlier cutting of trees and suppression of fire, have reduced their numbers drastically. The Forest Service is now managing certain areas to benefit the species, and at the **Red-cockaded Woodpecker Interpretive Site❖,** on Route 1375 about five miles west of New Waverly, birds can be seen returning to roost trees just before dusk. Their white face patch and harsh *sreeep* call help separate them from red-bellied, hairy, and downy woodpeckers. Dripping pine sap gives red-cockadeds' roost trees a distinctive "candle-

27

stick" appearance and may help protect the woodpeckers from snakes and other predators.

The **Big Creek Scenic Area❖**, about 25 miles east of New Waverly off Route 150, is surely one of east Texas's most beautiful places. From a

trailhead off Forest Road 217, well-constructed loops lead through a mixed bottomland forest of pine, beech, southern magnolia, willow oak, American holly, and eastern hop hornbeam. Another common tree here, American hornbeam, is often called musclewood because its small, irregularly shaped trunk resembles flexed muscles beneath smooth gray bark. The Double Lake Recreation Area—a fine campground offering swimming, lakeside campsites, and a mountain-bike trail—is 4.8 miles north of the Big Creek trailhead. For those with more ambition (and time), the **Lone Star Hiking Trail** traverses 140 miles of the Sam Houston NF and adjacent private land, from Cleveland in the east to the 3,810-acre **Little Lake Creek Wilderness Area❖** in the west.

ABOVE: *After trapping an insect with its sticky leaf hairs, the sundew, a deadly beauty, uses enzymes to digest the victim.*

RIGHT: *In Big Thicket National Preserve north of Beaumont, the sprightly green of emerging spring leaves contrasts with Wolf Creek below, stained coffee-dark by decaying vegetation.*

The traveler with limited time in east Texas could do worse than to head for **Big Thicket National Preserve❖**, a National Park Service area stretching north of Beaumont and containing a diversity of plant and animal life as great as its history is controversial. In their efforts to create a park here, conservationists persevered for decades in the face of bitter opposition from the timber industry and other interests. Today 13 scattered tracts protect only about 86,000 acres of the former 3.5-million-acre ecosystem. Nevertheless, the Big Thicket is a nearly bottomless treasure chest for the naturalist, harboring 85 species of trees, 26 ferns and fern allies, and 20 orchids.

At the preserve's visitor center, north of the small town of Kountze on Route 69, the Kirby Nature Trail leads through several of the Big Thicket's varied plant communities. In the distinctive "baygall" habitat, named for sweet bay magnolia and gallberry holly, tannin turns acid surface water as dark as coffee; the attractive shrub called swamp cyrilla, or titi, grows around the edges. Bald cypress and water tupelo inhabit low sloughs, while beech, southern magnolia, and loblolly pine reach magnificent size on the slopes above.

The short Sundew Trail at the nearby Hickory Creek Savannah Unit, excellent for wildflowers (May is the peak month), loops through a fine example of a longleaf pine savanna. Sundews, which ensnare insects with their sticky leaves, are just one of four carnivorous plants found in the Big Thicket; another, the beautiful pitcher plant, attracts insects with nectar glands, then traps and digests them to supplement its diet in mineral-poor soil. Pitcher plants are easy to spot along the Pitcher Plant Trail in the Turkey Creek Unit and elsewhere in the preserve.

The Nature Conservancy's **Roy E. Larsen Sandyland Sanctuary❖** (off Route 327 a few miles southeast of Kountze) protects another 5,600 acres of Big Thicket habitat, including an easily accessible upland sandhill-longleaf pine community. It was named for a vice-chairman of Time, Inc., a conservationist who was one of the land donors. Baygalls and other wetlands create habitats for an impressive array of wildflowers. Canoeists can enjoy an eight-mile float trip through the preserve along Village Creek, and the Sandylands Nature Trail is open every day (access from Route 327).

THE UPPER COAST

About ten miles west of the town of Sabine Pass on Route 87, 15,000-acre **Sea Rim State Park❖** spans the distance between the Gulf of Mexico and the Intracoastal Waterway, providing access to both beach and tidal marsh. Herons, egrets, ibis, and seaside sparrows are often visible from the short Gambusia Nature Trail, a boardwalk through a salt marsh; rail, although not rare, are harder to find. Across Route 87, the park's large Marshlands Unit maintains boat trails through a grassy expanse where least bitterns nest and waterfowl are abundant in winter. Muskrat, mink, otters, raccoon, and nutrias (plump rodents introduced

With its long recurved bill, an American avocet (above) is able to quickly canvas a mudflat for food. The roseate spoonbill (left) swings its spatula-shaped bill in great side-to-side sweeps to feed.

from South America) live here, constantly on the lookout lest they become a meal for one of the plentiful alligators. Visitors can take a canoe into the Marshlands Unit or tour the area by airboat.

The little town of **High Island❖,** 25 miles west of Sea Rim off Route 87, is legendary among birders. Not truly an island, it's an isolated patch of woodland (locally called an oak motte) on a slightly elevated site (a subterranean salt dome) that acts as a magnet for songbirds completing their spring migratory flight across the Gulf of Mexico. Every birder hopes to be at High Island in April or May for the unforgettable but difficult-to-predict phenomenon of a "fallout," when north winds cause tired birds to rain from the sky and trees may be alive with warblers, vireos, orioles, and tanagers. The Houston Audubon Society owns two small sanctuaries featuring good trails for birding.

Northwest of High Island off Route 1985, **Anahuac National Wildlife Refuge❖,** another terrific birding spot, is full of ducks and geese (sometimes as many as 50,000 snow geese) in winter. It may be even more famous as one of the last places where the red wolf roamed freely. Partly because of interbreeding with coyotes, the critically endangered canid has been extirpated in the wild; today a captive breeding program is aimed at its eventual reintroduction into parts of its historical range. Although they can no longer expect to see wolves, visitors can enjoy birds such as least bitterns, white and white-faced ibis, mottled ducks, stunning purple gallinules, and a variety of terns and shorebirds. Alligators sun themselves beside ditches, and a

31

ABOVE: *Salt marshes such as this one on West Galveston Bay serve as nurseries for a variety of sea life. Without the marshes, the Gulf Coast environment—and restaurant fare—would be sadly impoverished.*

fat water moccasin, or cottonmouth, can often be spotted crossing a road. Although elusive, all six North American species of rail are found seasonally at Anahuac. The yellow and black rail are especially difficult to glimpse, but sharp-eyed watchers may see a clapper rail in the grass at the edge of an opening.

The next stop westward on the upper Texas coast bird-watching trail is **Bolivar Flats Shorebird Sanctuary❖,** an expanse of beach, marsh, and mudflat on the outskirts of the town of Port Bolivar, just south of Route 87 east of Galveston. Here astounding numbers of waders, gulls, terns, and shorebirds gather during spring and fall migration. Bizarrely colorful roseate spoonbills are not uncommon; white pelicans laze about offshore; flocks of avocets, with their strange upturned bills, feed in shallow water. The number of species that might appear on the flats on a good day in April or September is far too great to list, but birders can be assured that a spotting telescope will provide them with several hours' entertainment.

Accompanied by wheeling flocks of laughing gulls, a short ferry ride leads to Galveston; about ten miles farther west on Route 3005 is **Galveston Island State Park❖,** which covers the width of the island from the Gulf to West Galveston Bay. Four ecological zones—salt marsh, coastal

ABOVE: *Resurrection ferns festoon the long limb of an oak along Armand Bayou near Houston; the fronds shrivel and turn brown in periods of dry weather but spring back to life again when the rains return.*

prairie, sand dunes with interspersed maritime wetlands, and beach—are accessible on four miles of nature trails in the 2,000-acre park.

Back on the mainland, Interstate 45 runs north to the sprawling city of Houston. On its southeastern edge within sight of oil refineries, chemical plants, and the space centers, the **Armand Bayou Nature Center❖** (6.5 miles northeast on Bay Area Boulevard) is a 2,500-acre oasis of woods, wetlands, and perhaps most important, one of the last remaining tracts of coastal tallgrass prairie. Much marsh habitat along the bayou has been lost because of land subsidence resulting from groundwater pumping, but restoration projects are under way. White-tailed deer are common, and swamp rabbits, larger and browner than eastern cottontails, sometimes swim across ponds or streams, always alert for bobcat. Like High Island, Armand Bayou is an important rest stop for migratory birds heading north to their breeding grounds.

Farther down the coast, just southwest of Freeport via Routes 36, 2611, and 2918, 27,414-acre **San Bernard National Wildlife Refuge❖** is, like Anahuac, a vital wintering ground for geese, especially snows. Also like Anahuac, the refuge comprises flat coastal prairie and salt marsh; maximum elevation here is nine feet above the adjoining Gulf. Birds—including nearly all the regular coastal waders and shorebirds—

LEFT: *The letters DDT nearly spelled the end for the brown pelican; birthrates plummeted when few embryos survived because of thin, brittle eggshells. A ban on the pesticide enacted in the early 1970s has significantly aided the recovery of this large coastal bird.*
RIGHT: *Among Texas's wildest places, Matagorda Island offers sunrise solitude, along with alligators, abundant shorebirds, and 39 miles of beach.*

are the most common wildlife species, but nutrias and a few alligators may be seen from the auto-tour road. Nearby **Brazoria National Wildlife Refuge❖** (northeast of Freeport) contains almost 40,000 acres of very similar habitat, but it is open to the public only one weekend a month.

One of Texas's best areas for wildlife observation lies 25 miles inland from San Bernard via Routes 36 and 1462. The nearly 5,000 acres of **Brazos Bend State Park❖** encompass lakes, marshes, and three miles of Brazos River banks. The abundant alligators are responsible for the ban on swimming and for the park's full-page listing of "alligator etiquette" safety rules, including "If you love your pet, keep it on a leash" and "When an alligator stands its ground, opens its mouth, and hisses, you have come too close." Trails and observation platforms allow viewing not just of gators but of birds such as yellow-crowned night herons, roseate spoonbills, black-bellied whistling ducks, and in spring and fall, numerous migrant songbirds. The short, easy trail around Pilant Lake is a good introduction to Brazos Bend.

About 30 miles farther inland, Routes 36 and 3013 lead to **Attwater Prairie Chicken National Wildlife Refuge❖,** near Eagle Lake, an 8,000-acre home for a small population of the endangered Attwater's race of the greater prairie chicken. The refuge once offered a blind from which the "dance," or courtship display, of male prairie chickens could be observed in spring; but the critical state of the population has led managers to close areas where these grouselike birds are found. The refuge is still worth a visit, though, for its populations of wading birds, ducks, and hawks. The crested caracara, the striking black-and-white falconlike bird depicted on the Mexican flag, is found here at the northern extreme of its range.

ABOVE: *Shaped by the wind, live oaks on the Aransas National Wildlife Refuge testify to the harsh conditions at this place where land meets sea.*

RIGHT: *The whooping crane was rare even when Audubon painted this bird with young alligators in the early 1800s. The surviving wild flock (fewer than 150 birds) winters at Aransas.*

THE LOWER COAST: MATAGORDA TO LAGUNA ATASCOSA

For those who arrive well prepared, **Matagorda Island State Park** promises one of the best wild experiences on the Texas coast. The state park is located within Matagorda Island National Wildlife Refuge, but visitors must call the park or Aransas National Wildlife Refuge for details. Accessible only on weekends and holidays by ferry from the mainland town of Port O'Connor (or by private boat at any time), the island contains miles of beaches, tall dunes, and extensive tidal flats supporting such halophytic (salt-tolerant) plants as salt grass, glasswort, saltwort, and cordgrass. Blue and stone crabs live along the bay shore, where oysters form reefs farther out. (Many people, of course, find these species of at least as much culinary as biological interest.) Bottlenose dolphins are often seen from shore or from the ferry; brown pelicans, making a comeback in Texas, nest on nearby spoil islands (formed by dredging for irrigation channels). The threatened Texas horned lizard ("horned toad") sometimes appears on roadsides and near the runways of an abandoned World War II air base.

Matagorda Island, the only publicly owned Texas barrier island, remains almost completely undeveloped. Visitors must bring their own

OVERLEAF: *Varied habitats at Aransas—grasslands, oak woods, ponds, shore, and freshwater marshes such as this one—support an equally great diversity of life. The refuge bird list totals nearly 400 species.*

food and water, and there are no telephones. Camping, fishing, hiking, bicycling, and beachcombing are favorite activities; limited hunting is allowed in the wildlife management area of the island. Because access to emergency aid is limited, visitors should be especially careful around the park's alligators and western diamondback rattlesnakes.

The whooping crane might well symbolize the struggle to save our continent's endangered species—and the place synonymous with this extraordinary five-foot-tall bird is **Aransas National Wildlife Refuge❖,** a 54,829-acre tract on the Blackjack Peninsula south of Tivoli via Routes 35, 239, and 2040. After dropping to a low of 16 birds in 1941 (plus a handful in captivity), the whoopers' wild population has slowly increased to around 150—encouraging, but still precarious.

Undiscovered until 1954, the cranes' nesting grounds in Alberta, Canada's Wood Buffalo National Park are remote and inaccessible; but tens of thousands of people, from serious birders to the mildly curious, have made the pilgrimage to their winter home on the Texas coast from November through March. Ironically, whoopers are seldom seen from within Aransas, although its observation tower may occasionally provide a glimpse of a distant family group of cranes. A better approach is one of the commercial boat tours from nearby Rockport. Captains are experienced at providing adequate views without disturbing the cranes, and the tours always sight other interesting species as well, from loons and ducks to black skimmers and roseate spoonbills. (Boat operators can also point out great egrets, sandhill cranes, snow geese, and white pelicans, which eager visitors often happily misidentify as whoopers.)

Nevertheless, visiting Aransas is not unproductive. A drive around the refuge's 15-mile tour loop, and walks along its trails (bring mosquito repellent), will likely provide excellent views of alligators, white-tailed deer, wild turkeys, and a variety of hawks and wading birds (early morning and late afternoon are best). Lucky visitors may see the small wild pigs called javelinas, or peccaries, not to be confused with the much larger feral hogs that roam Aransas. The entertaining armadillos— "little armored ones," which always bear their young in identical quadruplets—waddle through the brush and with their poor eyesight, often allow close views if approached quietly from downwind.

After contemplating the tenuous existence of the whooping cranes, making a stop at **Goose Island State Park❖**, off Route 35 at the southern tip of Aransas, is comforting. There visitors can admire the Big Tree, a coastal live oak that foresters believe was growing when William the Conqueror defeated King Harold at the Battle of Hastings in 1066. Although there is some disagreement about whether this tree is the national co-champion of its species, its girth and massive arching branches are inarguably impressive.

Welder Wildlife Foundation❖ (about 30 miles west of Rockport, a few miles northeast of Sinton on Route 77) was established "to further the education of the people of Texas and elsewhere in wildlife conservation," and specifically, to find ways in which ranching can coexist with enlightened wildlife management. To share its findings, the foundation holds occasional workshops and often hosts school groups for educational programs. Recent research projects have covered subjects from meadowlark parental care to bobcat ecology. Offered only on Thursday afternoons, tours take visitors through a variety of habitats to see waterfowl, hawks, coyotes, deer, and occasionally javelinas.

Among the places where land meets sea in America, **Padre Island National Seashore❖** occupies a special rank as the longest barrier island in the world. The National Park Service protects more than 65 miles of beaches, dunes, grassland, and tidal flats on this part of the world's longest chain of barrier islands, inviting visitors to enjoy swimming, beachcombing, surf fishing, and camping. Because it is also where desert meets sea, Padre receives less rain than islands farther north and is relatively sparsely vegetated. Most striking of Padre's plants are the picturesque sea oats that wave in the wind atop the dunes—and play an important role in preventing erosion.

The dearth of rain and of major rivers pumping in freshwater contributes to the high salinity of shallow Laguna Madre, separating Padre and the mainland. Although two or three times as salty as the Gulf of Mexico, it teems with life, from wintering waterfowl to crabs, and is a vital "nursery" in the life cycle of crustaceans and fish. Offshore from Padre is the only known saltwater colony of white pelicans in the United States; other islands, both natural and spoil (created by dredging), host breeding gulls, terns, skimmers, herons, egrets, ibis, and other birds.

Padre's dunes and beaches (composed of sand and the crushed shells of countless sea creatures) once gave it the name La Isla Blanca,

LEFT: *At Padre Island National Seashore, sea oats and yellow-flowered beach primroses are more than just picturesque: their strong roots stabilize dunes and prevent beach erosion.*
RIGHT: *The piglike collared peccary, or javelina, is fairly common across much of south Texas. Prickly-pear cactus is a favorite food.*

the White Island. Today passenger cars can drive along the beach for five miles south of the visitor center, reached via Routes 358 and P22 from Corpus Christi. For the 55 additional miles to the Mansfield Channel, four-wheel-drive is needed, and travelers are urged to read cautionary warnings and talk to a ranger about the danger of getting stranded miles from help.

Driving and hiking in the dunes are banned to protect the fragile plant communities that keep these formations from blowing away. Dune and grassland life is accessible and well interpreted, though, along the Grasslands Nature Trail, just south of the park entrance. Fortunate hikers sometimes glimpse a Padre Island kangaroo rat, a tiny long-tailed mammal found only on Padre and Mustang islands.

Raptor fans should note that Padre is an excellent place to see peregrine falcons in migration. As many as 2,000 of these big, powerful predators—making a slow recovery after their precipitous population decline in recent decades—pass through in September and October, and 5 or more may be seen nearly any day in spring or fall. The beautiful white-tailed hawk is also commonly found in grasslands here, especially in winter, when the guttural call of sandhill cranes rings out over the dunes.

From 1978 to 1988, Padre Island was the site of an experimental program to establish a breeding colony of Kemp's ridley sea turtles. The most endangered sea turtle in the world (only about 400 breeding females are thought to survive), the Kemp's ridley is known to nest only on one beach in Mexico. Scientists do not know the age at which the young turtles "imprinted" to Padre may return to nest (or even whether they will), but patrols watch the beaches from spring through summer. Although the chance of seeing a Kemp's ridley (or a loggerhead or green, the other sea turtles most likely to appear) on the beach is virtual-

ly zero, interested visitors are invited to talk to park staff about helping with patrols or to attend a naturalist's presentation about the turtles. For those who manage a trip all the way to beach milepost 60, green sea turtles are found regularly in and around the Mansfield Channel.

Although Padre Island offers a great deal to see, much more of the Gulf of Mexico's ecosystem is underwater, hidden to most observers. An intriguing look at that underwater world awaits visitors at the excellent **Texas State Aquarium❖,** off Highway 181 just north of the Harbor Bridge in Corpus Christi. After entering through a waterfall, visitors get close-up views of inhabitants of Gulf life zones from estuaries (where live birds chatter and stingrays glide through sandy pools) through the near-shore area to coral reefs, bright with colorful angelfish and butterfly fish.

Everyone's favorite exhibit is the huge Islands of Steel tank, which re-creates the artificial reef of an oil-drilling platform. Nurse sharks, massive groupers, sea turtles, barracuda, and other sea creatures circle the sham platform legs in an infinitely varying ballet, oblivious to the delighted faces peering at them. In real life, the community around a drilling site begins when barnacles, hydroids, sponges, oysters, and other unspectacular life-forms attach themselves to the metal legs, forming the basis for the web of interacting elements culminating in the large predators.

Elsewhere in the aquarium, river otters play, and at the Discovery Pool visitors can touch some of the sea's smaller inhabitants, including hermit crabs and lightning whelks (the official Texas state shell). Entertainment values are high at the aquarium, but education is its primary purpose, and attentive visitors leave with a better understanding of the Gulf's vast, yet vulnerable, environment.

Continuing down Route 77 south of Kingsville, travelers pass for many long miles through the legendary King Ranch, at 825,000 acres one of the largest private ranches in the country. The King operation is still run by descendants of Captain Richard King, who bought the original 75,000 acres in 1853. Here ranchers developed the famous Santa Gertrudis breed of cattle by crossing Brahman and shorthorn varieties.

Above: *The green sea turtle is occasionally seen along the Texas coast. Like all sea turtles it faces a shaky future due to human interference.*

Left: *Mesquite, acacia, and salt cedar trees line tidal channels at Laguna Atascosa National Wildlife Refuge.*

Lying 27 miles east of Harlingen via Route 106, **Laguna Atascosa National Wildlife Refuge❖** covers 45,000 acres of scrubland, coastal prairie, and Laguna Madre bay front. Snow and Canada geese and an assortment of ducks (teal, mottled duck, pintail, shoveler, gadwall, wigeon, canvasback, redhead, and ruddy duck) are common in winter, and wildlife watchers here are always alert for rarer sightings. The seldom attained prize is a look at an ocelot, a small, secretive cat whose streaking and spotting make it resemble a miniature jaguar. Because of its nocturnal habits, *el tigre chiquito* is hard to find, but a fleeting view of one is always a thrilling possibility at the refuge.

Released aplomado falcons—medium-sized raptors extirpated as breeders in the United States and being reintroduced at Laguna Atascosa—may appear any time of year. More common are lovely, graceful white-tailed kites—seen hovering and diving for field mice, lizards, and large insects—and Harris's hawks, brown with chestnut shoulders and a white upper-tail band. Crested caracaras, long-legged hawks with conspicuous white patches on their wings and tails, regularly search for carrion.

In late winter along Bayside Drive, a 15-mile auto-tour route that begins near the refuge visitor center, yuccas raise voluminous clusters of white flowers amid the prickly pear cactus and mesquite. The Paisano Trail is a good walk for birding, but remember that western diamondback rattlesnakes find Laguna Atascosa excellent habitat too. Visitors need not remain car-bound if they exercise a bit of caution.

THE LOWER RIO GRANDE VALLEY

The natural environment of the lower Rio Grande Valley has suffered a great deal from human activities. Orange groves and vegetable fields have supplanted native brushland, and the Rio Grande, which once regularly overflowed its banks to renew surrounding land, is now confined to a narrow channel. The Lower Rio Grande Valley National Wildlife Refuge, a Fish and Wildlife Service project not yet open to the public, will create along the river a wildlife corridor where contiguous tracts preserve (or when necessary reestablish) native habitat.

In the meantime, a few places that welcome visitors can provide a true natural valley experience. One of the most attractive is a private reserve, the National Audubon Society's **Sabal Palm Grove Sanctuary❖,** southeast of Brownsville via Route 1419. Sabals are the only palm trees native to Texas, and the small woodland here is one of the last remnants of its kind. In the hard winter of 1983–84, the relatively hardy sabals survived, while many plantings of exotic palms succumbed. Since then, sabals have gained favor in south Texas landscaping—but they look their best amid the tropical vegetation of the sanctuary.

Trails here are excellent places to see typical Rio Grande Valley plants, including granjeño (spiny hackberry), lime prickly-ash, anaqua, manzanita (Barbados cherry), Texas ebony (not a true ebony, but a legume), huisache, retama, and David's milkberry, a tropical shrub whose range barely reaches into south Texas and Florida. Buff-bellied hummingbirds frequent the sanctuary's flowers and feeders, and least grebes—tiny, with brilliant golden-yellow eyes—perform their spring courtship rituals in the *resaca,* an oxbow lake where the Rio Grande

ABOVE: *The Sabal Palm Grove Sanctuary in Brownsville protects one of the last native palm woodlands in Texas; these trees were once so common that an early name for the Rio Grande was* **Rio de las Palmas.**

once flowed. Ocelots and their even smaller feline relatives, jaguarundis, make Sabal Palm their home, but the presence of these secretive predators is hard to confirm.

Most of the same plants—minus the sabal palms—can be found 50 miles upstream at 2,000-acre **Santa Ana National Wildlife Refuge❖,** about 6 miles south of Alamo off Route 281. Here the name of the game is birds: Like the Everglades, Big Bend National Park (see Chapter 3), and the Chiricahua Mountains of Arizona, Santa Ana is a fabled "hot spot" that every serious birder visits sooner or later—and usually revisits often.

The list of notable species might begin with plain chachalacas, brown pheasantlike fowl that welcome every dawn with an amazingly loud chorus of calls. "*Cha-cha-LAHK,*" the birds scream, one rousing another until the air seems to vibrate with their cries. Other targets for traveling birders are black-bellied whistling ducks, white-winged doves, groove-billed anis, pauraques, green and ringed kingfishers, great kiskadees (another species named for its loud call), Couch's kingbirds, green jays, long-billed thrashers, altamira orioles, and olive sparrows. Rarities occasionally seen here include masked ducks, hook-billed kites, gray hawks, red-billed pigeons, clay-colored robins, and tropical parulas.

An open-air bus takes visitors around the refuge's seven-mile tour route in the busy winter season, when snowbirds from the cold North

ABOVE: *The lovely little ocelot is a rare and ultra-secretive resident of Texas brush country. This nocturnal hunter preys on rodents, birds, frogs, and small reptiles.*

RIGHT: *Few Texas habitats are as critically endangered, or as endlessly fascinating, as a subtropical thorn forest, here by the Rio Grande.*

arrive in the Valley in their motor homes and trailers. But Santa Ana is seen best from its trails; the most productive are around Willow and Pintail lakes, near the entrance (where there is a short handicapped-accessible loop). Busy watching for birds, many people near these wet areas may be surprised to look down and find a marine toad at their feet. These huge amphibians, also known as giant toads, can reach seven inches in length (not counting the legs) and are perfectly capable of causing heart palpitations in those not prepared for the sight. Their skin secretions are poisonous to any animal that tries to make them a meal.

About 15 miles farther upstream, just outside Mission via Routes 835 and 2062, **Bentsen–Rio Grande Valley State Park❖** is small (just 588 acres) but full of possibilities. The two-mile Rio Grande Hiking Trail passes through dry thorn-scrub vegetation to lower riparian woodland along the river, home to cedar elms and willows. Beautiful deep-purple indigo snakes—which can grow to eight feet or more and eat the young of other snakes, including rattlers—might be seen here. Hook-billed kites, elusive hawks that feed on land snails, sometimes soar over the treetops as the morning sun warms the air.

Birders visiting Bentsen regularly make the rounds of the trailer loop, where campers place feeders that sometimes attract blue buntings and other rarities; chachalacas, orioles, and green jays are abundant. And a careful watch in dry, sandy areas might turn up a Texas tortoise, which crawls through the scrub on stumplike legs seeking prickly pear cactus to munch.

CHAPTER TWO

PRAIRIES AND PLAINS

W"here the West begins" is a slogan as old as America, and still an inviting one for easterners dreaming of deer and antelope playing under uncloudy skies. Although places from Wichita to Winnipeg claim to be the gateway to wide-open spaces, in reality the western frontier is gradual and mostly intangible—more symbolic than real.

In west Texas, however, the Caprock Escarpment parallels Interstate 27 from the Panhandle toward Big Spring, dividing the midwestern Rolling Plains and the western High Plains as explicitly as a line drawn on paper. "Here," says the Caprock, with finality born of geologic certitude, "is where the West begins."

At Palo Duro Canyon and Caprock Canyons, two fine state parks on the edge of the escarpment southeast of Amarillo, geology has created scenes not only instructive but also spectacularly beautiful. Red shale and sandstone dating to the Permian period, more than 250 million years ago, are topped with Tertiary caliche, a hard limestone that protects the softer rock below. This layer is the "caprock" of the escarpment; at its edge, erosion has sculpted canyons hundreds of feet deep, full of bluffs, ledges, spires, buttes, and the small, picturesque rock formations called hoodoos. The canyons are moister than the surrounding plains, their streams and trees oases for people as well as wildlife.

LEFT: *Yuccas lift fruit pods above clusters of narrow, razor-sharp leaves at Muleshoe National Wildife Refuge; in the distance the ever-present west Texas wind kicks up clouds of dust in a dry playa lake.*

The edge of the High Plains is the most dramatic transition in this chapter, but not the only one. Moving westward from near Paris in the state's northeastern corner, a traveler crosses Post Oak Savanna, Blackland Prairie, Eastern Cross Timbers, Grand Prairie, Western Cross Timbers, and Rolling Plains (also known as Lower or Osage Plains) before reaching the Caprock Escarpment. Not always obvious today, the borders of these regions were blurry even before European settlement: Prairies contained scattered trees, and blackjack and post oak woodlands were punctuated by patches of grassland. In general, the prairies and cross timbers are relatively narrow strips running north-south, grasslands on alkaline clay soil, forests on sandy soil.

Much of north-central Texas has undergone massive changes since pioneer days. The heavy, black limestone-derived soil of the Blackland Prairie, made wonderfully fertile by organic materials, has been almost entirely converted from tallgrass vegetation to agricultural and grazing land; by most estimates, only a few thousand of its 12 million acres remain in a natural condition. The burgeoning Dallas–Fort Worth metroplex buries more land daily under freeways, malls, and subdivisions; overgrazing and fire suppression have widely obliterated native flora. Nonetheless, pockets of natural habitat remain, including a few prized patches of prairie, dotted with wildflowers from spring into fall.

Underlain by gently undulating "redbeds" of sandstone and shale, the Rolling Plains stretch from near Wichita Falls and Abilene westward to the Caprock Escarpment. Once mixed- and short-grass prairie, this region is now mostly crop and cattle land of limited natural-history interest. The most productive areas to explore are the rugged "breaks," where stream erosion has created canyons filled with scrub oaks, junipers, elms, and other trees. This is a land of transition: from red-bellied woodpeckers and blue jays to golden-fronted woodpeckers and scrub jays, from tree-loving squirrels to ground-dwelling prairie dogs, from East to West.

Beyond the escarpment are the High Plains, formed of sand, gravel, and clay washed down from the Rocky Mountains less than 12 million years ago and so evenly distributed that they create a terrain of sometimes amazing flatness. (Levelland is the name of one town near Lubbock.) Spanish explorers called this region the Llano Estacado—

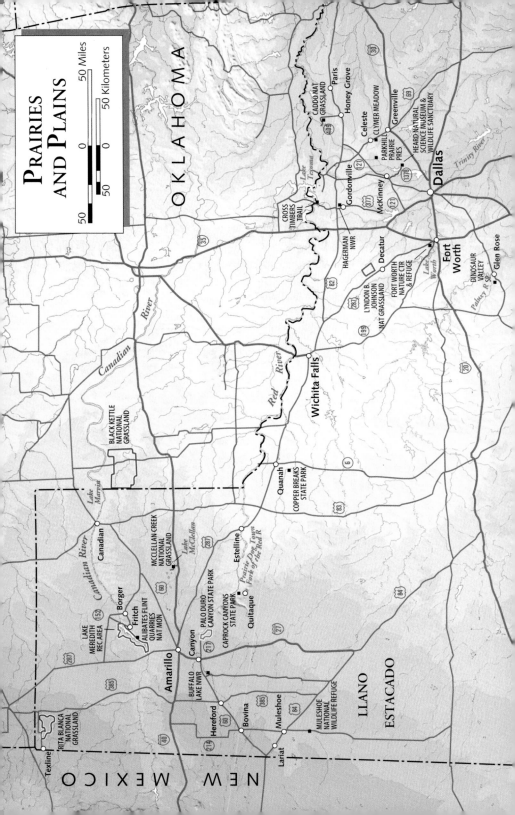

PRAIRIES AND PLAINS

50 Miles
50 Kilometers

50   0

0

50

OKLAHOMA

Paris
CADDO NAT GRASSLAND
Honey Grove
CLYMER MEADOW
Celeste
Greenville
HEARD NATURAL SCIENCE MUSEUM & WILDLIFE SANCTUARY
PARKHILL PRAIRIE PRES
Gordonville
McKinney
Dallas
Trinity River
CROSS TIMBERS TRAIL
HAGERMAN NWR
Lake Texoma
Decatur
Fort Worth
Lake Worth
FORT WORTH NATURE CTR & REFUGE
LYNDON B. JOHNSON NAT GRASSLAND
DINOSAUR VALLEY S.P.
Glen Rose
Paluxy R. S.P.

River
Canadian

Red River

Wichita Falls

BLACK KETTLE NATIONAL GRASSLAND

Quanah
COPPER BREAKS STATE PARK

Lake Marvin
Canadian River
Canadian

MCCLELLAN CREEK NATIONAL GRASSLAND
Lake McClellan
Esteline
Prairie Dog Town Fork of the Red R.

Börger
Fritch
ALIBATES FLINT QUARRIES NAT MON
LAKE MEREDITH REC AREA
PALO DURO CANYON STATE PARK
CAPROCK CANYONS STATE PARK
Quitaque

Amarillo
Canyon

BUFFALO LAKE NWR

Hereford
Bovina
Muleshoe
MULESHOE NATIONAL WILDLIFE REFUGE

LLANO ESTACADO

RITA BLANCA NATIONAL GRASSLAND
Texline
Lariat

NEW MEXICO

the Staked Plains—probably because the land was so confusingly flat and featureless that trails had to be marked with stakes (or piles of buffalo bones). Another possible derivation is that the lack of trees forced travelers to drive stakes to tether their horses at night. One nineteenth-century visitor in no mood for evocative descriptions called the landscape a "vast, dreary, and monotonous waste."

The Llano Estacado and the escarpment canyons were home to several groups of Plains Indians, including the fierce Comanche, whose resistance to encroaching settlement was finally overcome in an 1874 army raid at Palo Duro Canyon. The excellent grazing provided by plains grasslands later led to the establishment of truly Texas-sized ranches, including the XIT, which stretched north-to-south for 200 miles and covered three million acres, and the JA Ranch, founded by the legendary Charles Goodnight. The XIT took in all or part of ten counties, but despite fanciful claims, its name did not mean Ten in Texas.

Beginning near the Red River in north-central Texas, this chapter visits several natural areas surrounding Dallas and Fort Worth before continuing west to the High Plains and the northwestern corner of the Panhandle.

Prairies and Savanna

Although travelers in northeastern Texas may associate the name **Caddo National Grassland**❖ with the natural tallgrass prairies that once occurred here, this Forest Service area west of Paris is former farmland, once severely damaged by erosion but now partly reclaimed for livestock grazing and recreational activities. Much of the "grassland" is forested with post and blackjack oak, eastern redcedar, hickory, elm, and other species typical of the Post Oak Savanna ecological region.

Two fishing lakes north of Honey Grove, about 20 miles west of Paris, are the area's most popular features; the surrounding woods can be productive for songbirds during spring migration. The lakes are accessible via FM Route 409, also known as Bois d'Arc Springs Road—

RIGHT: *Birds found in Texas include (clockwise from top left) ladder-backed woodpeckers, which forage beetle larvae in desert scrub; western kingbirds with their distinctive white outer tail feathers; and ash-throated flycatchers with their distinctive call. Showy red-bellied woodpeckers reach the western limit of their range in Central Texas.*

the name of a tree associated with this part of the country. Tough, re-
silient limbs of bois d'arc (French for "bow wood") provided Native
Americans with bows, and the tree's spherical rough-skinned fruit is
the origin of the common names Osage orange and horse apple.

True blackland tallgrass prairie is as rare in Texas these days as
covered wagons on the Dallas Central Expressway, or nearly so, it
seems. Of 12 million acres of this habitat, fewer than 5,000 acres survives in scattered remnants, the rest fallen victim to its own fertility.

Deposited on the ocean floor when this area was inundated more
than 60 million years ago, the calcareous bodies of countless sea creatures created a rich, limy soil perfect for modern-day agriculture. Prairie
grasses, with their complex root systems, can survive fire, drought, and
hay harvesting, but not plowing; as cotton and other crops proliferated,
the native grasslands were pushed toward extinction.

Happily, a few patches of this fascinating ecosystem still exist, accessible for scientific study, school field trips, and sightseeing. Two of
the best are within a few miles of each other just west of the small
town of Celeste, about ten miles northwest of Greenville. **Clymer
Meadow**❖ is a 540-acre Nature Conservancy preserve (ask for permis-
sion before visiting); **Parkhill Prairie Preserve**❖, west on FM 1562
and south on FM 36, encompasses 436 acres and is part of an open-
space plan for Collin County.

Big bluestem, little bluestem, Indiangrass, switchgrass, and eastern
gama grass are the dominant grass species on the prairies, which
spread across rolling terrain dotted with oak, elm, hackberry, and locust. At various times of year the land is bright with wildflowers, which
may include Indian paintbrush, prairie parsley, prairie coneflowers,
blazing star, Mexican hat, blue sage, sunflowers, and asters. Dickcissels
(small, yellow-breasted buntings) and scissor-tailed flycatchers, both
open-country birds, are abundant from spring through fall.

Ample parking and designated nature trails make Parkhill Prairie a
more convenient place to visit than Clymer. Only part of the preserve is
virgin prairie, and restoration work includes planting a once-plowed

---

LEFT: *At Clymer Meadow, a Nature Conservancy preserve near Greenville, pink Indian paintbrush enlivens a field of white-flowered larkspur and wild carrot. Such prairie scenes are now rare in north Texas.*

tract with seeds of native grassland species. At Clymer Meadow, the Nature Conservancy is conducting important research into controlling erosion and preventing encroachment by nonnative plants, especially tall fescue, a fast-spreading European grass. Because native species are adapted to resist the fires that once regularly occurred here, prescribed burning is an important tool in managing prairies. The results of this research will help determine whether blackland prairie will survive for the scientists and schoolchildren of the next century to explore and enjoy.

The **Heard Natural Science Museum and Wildlife Sanctuary❖**, northeast of Dallas just south of McKinney via Routes 121 and 1378, would be a fine resource anywhere; its location in the second-fastest-growing county in America makes it especially valuable. Within its 274 acres are prairie (managed to restore native vegetation), scrubby upland woods, and bottomland forest, including large sycamores and bur oaks. A one-mile canoe trail passes the woodland alongside Wilson Creek, and foot trails lead to a marshy wetland that attracts waterfowl in winter and herons and egrets in summer.

Besides exhibits on fossils (including the very large skull of a mosasaur, an ancient swimming reptile), rocks and minerals, and local natural history, the Heard Museum houses displays of live animals, including several hawks and owls used in educational programs. Today the largest raptor rehabilitation center in the state, the museum was established by the amazing Miss Bessie Heard, a daughter of one of the pioneer families in this area. She organized birdhouse-building contests as long ago as 1916, planted trees, helped found the McKinney library and the local Red Cross chapter, and remained a notable presence in the community until her death in 1988 at the age of 101.

NORTH AND WEST OF DALLAS

Farther north, about eight miles west of Denison off Route 996, **Hagerman National Wildlife Refuge❖** occupies an arm of Lake Texoma extending south from the main channel of the Red River. Its fields and open water provide wintering habitat for thousands of geese and ducks, and to supplement the natural food in its extensive marshes and shallow ponds, the refuge plants wheat, corn, and milo.

Hagerman is an excellent place for wildlife observation in winter, and in summer herons and egrets—easily seen along the two-mile

ABOVE: *Leafy elms, cedars, and sycamores overhang Rucker's Creek near Fort Worth. The trees are remnants of the Cross Timbers, north-south belts of dense forest that once ran unbroken from Texas into Oklahoma.*

auto-tour route—congregate in large numbers. Muddy flats attract shorebirds, especially in late summer and fall. The Crow Hill Interpretive Trail traverses a patch of natural prairie.

Breakwaters (actually roadbeds leading to some of the many oil wells on the refuge) create protected bays along the tour route where ducks congregate, sometimes offering close views to those who approach quietly. (A car, of course, makes an excellent blind.) Bald eagles perch on waterside trees in winter, lazily watching for dead fish or crippled waterfowl, while northern harriers, less averse to hard work, quarter the fields for rodents. Red-shouldered, red-tailed, Swainson's, and broad-winged hawks all nest here, as do graceful Mississippi kites. Birders should note that generally rare Ross's geese, smaller versions of snow geese, are sometimes found here in relatively high numbers.

Because lengthy hiking trails are literally few and far between in north-central Texas, the Army Corps of Engineers's **Cross Timbers**

LEFT: *The dark silhouettes of oaks, elms, and backberries dot a wintry bluestem prairie in the Lyndon B. Johnson National Grassland.*
RIGHT: *Cautious and seldom seen, bobcat are common in Texas scrub country. Their tracks are often the best clue to their presence.*

Trail❖, which follows the south shore of Lake Texoma for 14 miles, is worthy of mention. The trail runs between the Juniper Point and Rock Creek Camp recreation areas (off Route 377 north of Gordonville), alternating stretches along the rocky shoreline (providing the scenery here) with intervals in the woods.

The trail is named for the Eastern and Western Cross Timbers, two strips of woodland running north from central Texas into Oklahoma. The Cross Timbers—mostly post and blackjack oak, mixed with elm, locust, hackberry, and pecan—separate the Blackland Prairie and the Rolling Plains and enclose the Grand Prairie. These were the last extensive forests that pioneers saw as they traveled west, at least until they reached the Rockies. Sometimes parklike, the Cross Timbers in other places were difficult to transect, forming what one writer has called an "immense natural hedge." Unlike neighboring limy blackland clay, the sandy Cretaceous-period formation underlying the woodlands is conducive to tree growth; but lack of rainfall, shallow rock, and poor soil keep forests here on the stunted side.

Today the **Lyndon B. Johnson National Grassland❖,** about 50 miles northwest of Dallas near Decatur, provides an approximation of the Cross Timbers in presettlement days: Tracts of mostly scrubby trees surround grassy openings, creating attractive patterns of contrasting greens in spring and early summer. Although deer, bobcat, wild turkeys, bobwhite quail, and Mississippi kites inhabit the area, visitors usually focus on the terrain, where Texas assumes a decidedly western feel.

The **Fort Worth Nature Center and Refuge❖** benefits from its position in this transition zone. Located just off Route 199 northwest of the city, the refuge comprises Western Cross Timbers, prairie, and eastern-style bottomland woods along the Trinity River and the shore of Lake Worth. More than 25 miles of hiking trails crisscross the refuge, which at

61

3,500 acres is one of the largest urban natural areas in the country.

Prothonotary warblers, red-shouldered hawks, and wood ducks nest along the Riverbottom Trail, where beavers come ashore at night to gnaw tree trunks and gray foxes quietly stalk rabbits and small rodents. Refuge marshes (one is easily accessible on a boardwalk trail) attract waterfowl and waders. A small herd of bison graze in an enclosed area off the entrance road, and white-tailed deer may appear anywhere.

Prairie covered a larger part of this landscape when wild bison roamed here, but fire suppression and overgrazing allowed invasion by mesquite and other trees. In some areas, refuge workers are removing brush, returning the habitat to a more natural state, and reestablishing wildflowers and grasses that once grew more abundantly.

The change from prairie to encroaching scrub over the past century pales when contrasted with the difference in the environment of 100 million years ago. Along the refuge's Caprock Trail, fossil oyster shells offer tangible evidence of an era when this part of Texas was near the shoreline of a shallow sea. The shells that built ancient oyster beds, along with the remains of an incomprehensibly large number of similar animals, eventually formed the limestone-derived alkaline soil beneath modern north-central Texas grasslands.

In those Cretaceous times, creatures very different from ocean-dwelling invertebrates also lived here. The evocative, even eerie, traces they left are still visible today, half an hour southwest of Fort Worth. One day, after a storm had washed a fresh layer of limy mud over tidal flats at the edge of the sea, a dinosaur now known as *Pleurocoelus* made its ponderous way along the shore. Counting its long neck and tail, it was close to 50 feet in length, supporting 25 tons on its elephantine legs. Although *Pleurocoelus* was a plant eater, the animal following closely behind most definitely was not. *Acrocanthosaurus* was a fierce 30-foot-long carnivore weighing up to seven tons; walking upright and displaying a mouth full of flesh-tearing teeth, it looked something like the famous *Tyrannosaurus rex.*

As the mud dried, the dinosaurs' tracks hardened and later filled with silt and clay. The mud became limestone, the fill material soft shale. We'll never know whether the predator brought down its prey that day, but the footprints the dinosaurs left pique the imagination. They're visible at **Dinosaur Valley State Park❖** off Route 205 near Glen Rose, where the

Paluxy River has eroded the shale to expose the limestone below.

Prints are visible at several points along the riverbed: huge tub-shaped marks of *Pleurocoelus;* three-toed prints of *Acrocanthosaurus,* like those of a giant bird; and other footprints thought to have been made by a dinosaur named *Iguanodon.* Viewing is best during periods of low water, when visitors can walk along the river for a close look at the tracks. A realistic cast of the prints is always visible at the park office, which houses a fine exhibit on dinosaurs, Cretaceous geology, and the history of "dinosaur hunting" in the area. (Some of the best tracks found here were excavated about 1940 and taken to the American Museum of Natural History in New York and the Texas Memorial Museum in Austin.)

Dinosaur tracks are not the only sights at the 1,500-acre park. Two of Texas's rarest and most avidly sought birds, black-capped vireos and golden-cheeked warblers, nest here; they're best spotted in spring and early summer along the trails east of the river. Dinosaur Valley's bird life is a mixture of eastern and western species: great crested flycatchers, black-and-white warblers, and chuck-will's-widows breed near black-chinned hummingbirds, ladder-backed woodpeckers, and rufous-crowned sparrows. An early-morning hike in the park may find a white-tailed deer crossing the Paluxy, its dainty steps a world away from the heavy tread of the creatures that once walked here alongside a primeval sea.

PLAINS AND CANYONS

Breaks is the name early explorers gave the rugged canyons and ravines they encountered as they headed west across the great American grasslands. These "broken" places in the otherwise flat or gently rolling plains are not to be confused with *brakes:* thickets of a single kind of plant such as canebrakes.

Although the name sounds harsh (and in many places the land is just that), breaks are almost always associated with runoff areas or watercourses, where a stream has eroded the soft sandstone that underlies much of the plains. Not only are breaks better watered than the surrounding land, their steep sides create environments protected from the wind, helping plants retain moisture. The forbiddingly named breaks often shelter the only trees within a wide area, and many times served

as temporary or permanent homes for wildlife, Native Americans, travelers, and settlers. So distinctive is the breaks habitat that ecologists recognize it as a separate natural division.

Copper Breaks State Park✣, off Route 6 about 13 miles south of Quanah and about 90 miles west of Wichita Falls, is a good example of broken plains terrain. Although not as expansive or scenic as parks farther west—it might be considered the little brother of Caprock Canyons and Palo Duro Canyon—it's worthy of exploration for eastern visitors who are going no farther.

Scrubby juniper and mesquite, cholla cactus, catclaw acacia, yucca, and prickly pear cactus grow at Copper Breaks (the abundance of the first two indicates past overgrazing), and roadrunners trot along rocky ledges, looking for a lizard lunch. In places such as the Bull Canyon hiking trail, outcrops of sandstone and gypsum are often quite attractive.

For those with limited time, the half-mile Juniper Ridge nature trail provides a good introduction to the area. It's adjacent to man-made Lake Copper Breaks, which juxtaposes arid-country flora and fauna with such water-loving species as cattails, red-winged blackbirds, and bullfrogs.

Eighty miles west (via Routes 287 and 86), a few miles north of the small town of Quitaque (via Route 1065), **Caprock Canyons State Park✣** is one of Texas's great, if little-known, natural places. Its nearly 14,000 acres straddle the Caprock Escarpment, which separates the short-grass High Plains from the mixed-grass Rolling Plains, several hundred feet lower in elevation. The caprock (so called because it caps the escarp-

ABOVE: *The genus name* **Geococcyx** *("ground cuckoo") truly fits the greater roadrunner, a lizard-loving cuckoo that much prefers earthbound travel to flying.*

LEFT: *Cottonwoods, their limbs ghostly white in winter, line a creek bed in Caprock Canyons State Park; junipers, green all year, grow atop a nearby ledge.*

OVERLEAF: *Few natural borders are as dramatic as the Caprock Escarpment, where red sandstone bluffs, topped by harder caliche, mark the meeting of* **Rolling Plains and High Plains.**

65

LEFT: *A large, light gray bird with a distinctive red-skinned crown, long legs, and arching neck, the sandhill crane frequents open marshy wetlands.*
RIGHT: *Tens of thousands of cranes winter at Muleshoe National Wildlife Refuge; at dawn and dusk their croaking calls echo across the plains.*

ment) is hard limestonelike caliche, which helps protect the softer red sandstone and shale underneath. Despite its resistant cap, the escarpment is not immune to erosion; geologic evidence shows that 10,000 years ago it stood nearly three-quarters of a mile farther east.

Water was the architect of this Caprock Escarpment retreat. Within the park, various tributaries of the Little Red River have cut through the sandstone, shaping rugged canyons, narrow ridgelines, and rock formations both monumental and delicate—all the features of Texas breaks (or "badlands") terrain. From lookout points just beyond the park entrance, the panorama can be truly entrancing, especially early and late in the day: Rocks seem to glow in shades of pink, red, and orange, dotted with green hues of grass, shrubs, and small trees.

Although the views through a car window are quite impressive, to see the park well visitors should walk at least a short distance on one of the hiking trails; the path that runs westward from the South Prong camping area is a good choice. In addition to standard sites for tents and trailers, the park allows primitive camping at two places in the backcountry. Horseback riders and mountains bikers have their own trails, and the Caprock Canyons Trailway, a "rail-to-trail" conversion currently under development, will run 64 miles from up on the High Plains east to Estelline.

This far west, mule deer—marked by their huge mulelike ears and black-tipped tails—have begun to appear with the whitetails of the east. Porcupines are sometimes seen ambling along roads and trails at night. The park's strangest animal is the aoudad sheep, controversially introduced into the region from North Africa as a game species for hunters.

Sighting a golden eagle is not guaranteed at the imposing Eagle's Point rock formation, but a number of these magnificent raptors live

in the park. A glimpse of a golden eagle is always a thrill, although visitors should take care to distinguish them from turkey vultures, red-tailed hawks, Swainson's hawks, and ferruginous hawks, which all occur here and, depending on distance and light, can look similar.

WEST INTO THE PANHANDLE

Up on the Llano Estacado (as the southern part of the High Plains is called), heading west from Caprock Canyons, the dramatic scenery of the park can quickly begin to seem like a dream. If the Staked Plain is not the flattest, most topographically featureless landscape on the planet, it will undoubtedly make the play-offs. The High Plains were formed by alluvial material—silt, sand, and gravel—washed down from the slopes of the Rockies and distributed evenly (very, very evenly) by thousands of years of wind, rain, and floodwaters.

This flat terrain contains its share of natural-history sites, including **Muleshoe National Wildlife Refuge❖,** off Route 214 about 15 miles from the New Mexico border. The nearby town of Muleshoe is named for one of the large pioneering ranches in the area. For birders, the Muleshoe refuge is synonymous with sandhill cranes. These long-legged four-foot-tall birds—relatives of the famous whooping crane, but many times more abundant—gather here to winter by the thousands, staging one of Texas's greatest wildlife spectacles. Spreading out during the day to feed in surrounding fields and grasslands, the cranes like to

roost in shallow water at night; the best times to see them at the refuge
are early morning and late afternoon.

The names of Hereford, Lariat, and Bovina, towns north of Muleshoe,
commemorate the ranching heritage of the plains. **Buffalo Lake
National Wildlife Refuge❖,** 15 miles southwest of Canyon off Route
60, recalls a time when enormous herds of bison roamed the grasslands
of mid-America. The refuge is centered on a gash cut into the flat plains
by Tierra Blanca Creek; at one time a lake partially filled this canyon,
but its dam was found to be unsafe, and the lake was drained in 1978.
Reduced rainfall and dropping water tables have since dried Tierra
Blanca Creek, leaving no water source to refill the lake.

Buffalo Lake is still a rewarding stop because the geology of the Llano
Estacado is on display in cliff faces, where a layer of whitish caliche tops
red stone walls. Native Americans may have driven bison over these cliffs,
killing and butchering injured animals on the canyon floor. Thousands of
trees planted here in the late thirties have created an oasis for wildlife,
from mule deer and coyotes to bobcat and badgers.

The half-mile Cottonwood Canyon Birding Trail is a pleasant walk
along a canyon wall, where orchard orioles, yellow-billed cuckoos,

Named for their comically huge ears, mule deer (left) are a common sight along roadsides in western parks and refuges. Its facial markings might well be thought of as war paint: The badger (above) fights fiercely when cornered. True to its name, the burrowing owl (right) nests underground; it often lives in deserted prairie-dog tunnels.

western kingbirds, and blue grosbeaks are among the breeding land birds. Both bobwhite and scaled quail nest here; the former, with its distinctive *bob-white* call, is more common than the scaled quail, sometimes called the western blue quail or cottontop. The old lake still holds water in winter, attracting waterfowl, occasionally in high numbers, as well as a few bald eagles.

Perhaps the most intriguing part of the refuge is the prairie-dog town east of Route 168, where a thriving colony of the little rodents is visible from a short nature trail. No doubt the prairie dogs are completely serious about their enterprises as they scamper around the burrow openings, but a two-legged observer finds it hard not to smile at their hyperactive movements and expressions—especially when, in a moment of excitement, they all rear up on their hind legs and chirp to each other.

Burrowing owls—long-legged diurnal birds that live underground— are often seen near the prairie-dog colony, and visitors would be wise to keep an eye on the ground hereabouts. A snake crossing the path might be a big, aggressive—but harmless—bull snake; on the other hand, it might have a rattle on the end of its tail.

Just beyond the prairie dogs is a 175-acre tract of short-grass prairie designated the **High Plains Natural Area.** Sideoats grama, buffalo grass, and blue grama grow here as they did before cattle and the plow changed the ecological balance of this land. Little of the modern world is visible from the trail's end; hearing a western meadowlark's fluting song on the wind, visitors can easily imagine that a herd of bison is on the move, raising a cloud of dust just over the horizon.

The first European explorers and settlers traveled to the Caprock Escarpment from the east, watching it slowly loom up as they drew nearer. These days, nearly everyone who visits **Palo Duro Canyon State Park❖** drives east along Route 217 from Canyon, an approach that gives the escarpment's appearance a fine dramatic impact. "Where is this great scenic wonder?" the visitor asks, looking across an expanse of nothing. Finally, a crack opens in the flat earth just south of the road and widens to an astonishing spectacle.

Although the Palo Duro Canyon walls display 250 million years of geology, here scientific appreciation takes second place to visual impact. Of the many landscapes across the country that have been compared to the Grand Canyon, this one merits the metaphor. From the scenic overlook at the park visitor center, the panorama extends below: a convoluted maze of mesas and canyons carved by the Prairie Dog Town Fork of the Red River as it sliced the edge of the Llano Estacado to a depth of nearly 800 feet.

Geologists report that the river began its erosive action less than a million years ago and did most of its sculpting in the last 100,000 years; the canyon, which continues to lengthen, reached its present form about 10,000 years ago, when nomadic hunters were pursuing mammoths and other prey with stone lances. Camels, rhinoceroses, and primitive horses are among the long-vanished creatures that once roamed the Palo Duro area. Restored skeletons and fossils are on display in the Panhandle-Plains Historical Museum in Canyon.

The Lighthouse Trail, a 5.5-mile out-and-back walk of only moderate difficulty, is an excellent way to get a better look at this ruggedly scenic area. Signs along the way explain the deposition of the sedimentary rock that forms most of the canyon walls and the much later erosion that shaped them.

In fact, to say that 250 million years of geology are visible here is incorrect; although strata that old are exposed, at least 160 million years of rock are missing, eroded by natural forces before the caliche caprock was deposited in the Tertiary period. Interbedded with the red shale and sandstone here and there, horizontal layers of white gypsum—evidence of periods when ancient seas dried up—look like quartz but are softer. Small eroded formations called hoodoos appear atop the canyon walls, and the Lighthouse, a 75-foot rock pillar rising like a skinny wedding cake, rewards hikers at the end of the trail.

An early-morning walker may encounter a small flock of wild turkeys feeding among the mesquite and juniper or a group of mule deer along the river. Far less likely are sightings of such secretive animals as bobcat and ringtails, catlike mammals resembling small raccoon.

The birds of Palo Duro are an interesting mixture of eastern, western, desert, and woodland species. One of the best is among the most common; at times in spring and summer, painted buntings seem to sing from the tops of trees and shrubs everywhere in the park. Many consider this brilliant, even gaudy, bird the most beautiful species in America. Certainly its colors are more than a match for the variegated canyon walls that provide a backdrop for its bright, bubbly song.

THE NORTHERN PANHANDLE

Opportunities for hiking and nature study are limited in the northern Texas Panhandle because nearly all the land is private farms and ranches where trespassing is seriously discouraged. Nevertheless, a few tracts that the federal government controls are worth a look.

McClellan Creek National Grassland❖, 50 miles east of Amarillo, just north of Interstate 40 off Route 2477, is a 1,400-acre recreation area centered on Lake McClellan. Once a fairly expansive body of water, the lake has suffered seriously in recent years from siltation, but restoration work is under way. The large trees around the shoreline attract songbirds and good numbers of nesting Mississippi kites, small hawks that cruise the summer skies in search of their insect prey with the grace and agility of oversized swallows.

Farther off the main roads, but usually more interesting, is **Lake**

OVERLEAF: *A small mesquite grows along an eroded valley wall in Palo Duro Canyon State Park. Water and wind have sculpted the shale and sandstone of the Caprock Escarpment here into a geological fantasyland.*

Marvin (via Route 2266 north of Canadian), part of the **Black Kettle National Grassland❖,** most of which is in Oklahoma (see Chapter 4). The small lake, 12 miles east of Canadian off Routes 60 and 83, lies just north of the Canadian River. Waterfowl, wild turkeys, beavers, white-tailed deer, songbirds, and raptors (including occasional wintering bald eagles) inhabit the area or visit at various times of year. Considering its often meager flow, the Canadian River supports a surprisingly broad sweep of vegetation in its floodplain. Nature trails around Lake Marvin allow exploration of the drier sandhills environment as well as riparian areas.

The Canadian River has eroded its own breaks terrain in the High Plains, a swath 30 or more miles wide across the Panhandle, bordered by colorful canyons and cliffs. **Lake Meredith National Recreation Area❖,** administered by the National Park Service, stretches nearly 30 miles along the river's path west of Borger (take Route 136 west from Borger and Route 687 north). Varying in size because it supplies water for several cities, Lake Meredith averages about 16,500 acres. In the summer it is immensely popular for fishing, waterskiing, camping, and picnicking; the rest of the year wildlife observation from access sites ringing the lake can be excellent.

Bald eagles are relatively common in winter, sometimes accompanied by a few golden eagles. (Distinguishing a golden from a young bald, which lacks the adult's white head and tail, takes a bit of practice.) Loons, grebes, and ducks of 20 or more species stop over in migration, and many winter on the open water or in shallow coves. Cottonwoods and other trees in places such as Blue Creek, Plum Creek, and McBride Canyon offer refuge to a wide variety of smaller birds and nearly always repay careful searching.

Bordering Lake Meredith off Route 136 south of Fritch is **Alibates Flint Quarries National Monument❖,** where up to 12,000 years ago Stone Age peoples were mining the raw materials for spear points, arrowheads, and tools. Flint from this area was widely traded and greatly prized, and as a result has appeared in archaeological sites far from these quarries. The vaguely Spanish-looking name Alibates, by the way, is derived from Allie Bates, a rancher who once owned this land.

Rita Blanca National Grassland❖ covers about 77,000 acres in the extreme northwestern corner of the Texas Panhandle and nearly 16,000 more across the border in Oklahoma. This federal area, comprising scattered blocks surrounded by private ranchland, was acquired by the government after the Dust Bowl years of the 1930s. Short-grass prairie that should never have been plowed, it rewarded early farmers with a few years of good wheat crops but began to erode badly when drought came. Topsoil blew away in huge black clouds, and much of the region became a barren desert. Reclaimed now as grassland, it is under permit to ranchers for cattle grazing and administered by the Forest Service.

Prairie dogs, burrowing owls, long-billed curlews, and mountain plover are among the interesting species found here, along with a fine selection of raptors, especially in fall and winter. The beautiful ferruginous hawk, a High Plains specialty that has declined in numbers in recent years, makes an occasional appearance. The **Thompson Grove Recreation Area,** off Route 296 east of Texline, is a good place to begin investigating the area.

For many people, the most interesting Rita Blanca inhabitants are the pronghorn, often called antelope although they are instead an exclusively North American species classified in their own family. Both sexes have short curved horns; animals move in small groups, grazing and watching alertly for nearby activity. Travelers should heed warnings about driving in pronghorn country; legendary for their speed, the animals can dart in front of a fast-moving car in the blink of an eye, with unfortunate results for all involved.

ABOVE: *Once erroneously called "ringtail cat," the ringtail is actually a raccoon relative; sharp claws make it a superb climber.*
BELOW: *Highly gregarious black-tailed prairie dogs maintain family social bonds with a variety of physical gestures, including "kissing" and mutual grooming.*

THE TEXAS HILL COUNTRY
AND TRANS-PECOS MOUNTAINS

The Gulf Coast beaches of Texas are beautiful, and the High Plains are awesome in their immensity; but the Lone Star State's most striking landscapes await travelers in the variegated, often rugged terrain stretching between Austin and El Paso. Clear springs, rocky streams shaded by bald cypresses, expansive cave systems, stark desert habitats of cactus and creosote bush, highland forests, deep canyons, mountains born of fire within the earth—all these reward exploration within central Texas and the arid lands west of the Pecos River.

The uplifted limestone region known as the Edwards Plateau is separated from the Gulf Coastal Plain by the Balcones Fault Zone, a J-shaped escarpment running east and north from near Del Rio toward Waco. West of this line are the rolling uplands Texans affectionately call the Hill Country, where rivers and savannalike oak-juniper woods have attracted settlers since the days of the Paleo-Indian hunter-gatherers. Artificial lakes, dude ranches, golf resorts, and retirement communities continue to lure new residents and tourists as burgeoning San Antonio and Austin expand into the hills. Accompanying this growth, though, is a worrisome depletion of the underlying Edwards Aquifer, a huge underground lake vital to Hill Country ecology as well as to its cities, towns, and ranches.

Farther west, rainfall diminishes, vegetation is sparser, and the

LEFT: *Besides separating the United States from Mexico (left), the Rio Grande River also forms the southern border of Big Bend National Park. The eroded limestone cliffs of Mariscal Mountain rise in the distance.*

human population thins out. In Pecos, Brewster, and Presidio counties, visitors can drive for miles on highways and ranch roads without seeing another soul—until finally a pickup truck approaches, the driver inevitably raising a finger from the steering wheel in a friendly greeting.

The Trans-Pecos, also known as the Basin and Range or Mountains and Basins region, comprises many separate mountainous areas, including the Guadalupe, Davis, Franklin, and Chisos ranges. The surrounding Chihuahuan Desert, though hot and dry, is not without its own beauty—especially when a spring rain triggers an explosion of vividly colored wildflowers.

A fascinating array of plants and animals—many rare or highly restricted to Texas ranges—inhabit these diverse lands. The endangered golden-cheeked warbler has become a well-known (and controversial) symbol of the effort to protect Hill Country habitat. The Guadalupe bass is endemic to the region's rivers; San Marcos and Comal springs (both dependent on the Edwards Aquifer) are home to rare fish, such as the fountain darter, and amphibians, including the San Marcos salamander. At the other end of the population scale, millions of Mexican free-tailed bats summer in caves throughout the area, pouring from their roosts at dusk in astonishing, seemingly endless flights.

Mountain lions and black bears roam the high country of Big Bend and Guadalupe Mountains national parks, two of America's finest natural areas. Woodlands of Douglas fir and ponderosa pine are reminiscent of more northerly latitudes, creating environments unique in Texas. Lucifer hummingbirds, Colima warblers, golden eagles, alligator juniper, aspen, and elk are among the notable flora and fauna found in one or both of the parks. Although Big Bend and Guadalupe have much in common, their underlying geologies are very different.

The entire expanse covered in this chapter is a wonderland for geologists, from billion-year-old Enchanted Rock near Fredericksburg to sand dunes, salt flats, and lava flows farther west. The Llano Uplift, also known as the Central Mineral Region, just north of the Edwards Plateau, contains the most ancient rocks in Texas—up to three billion years old. Here a huge mass of magma rose through the earth's crust but never broke the surface; it later cooled into the granite that is quarried today near Marble Falls. Mason County is famous among rock collectors, who search its hills for a variety of specimens includ-

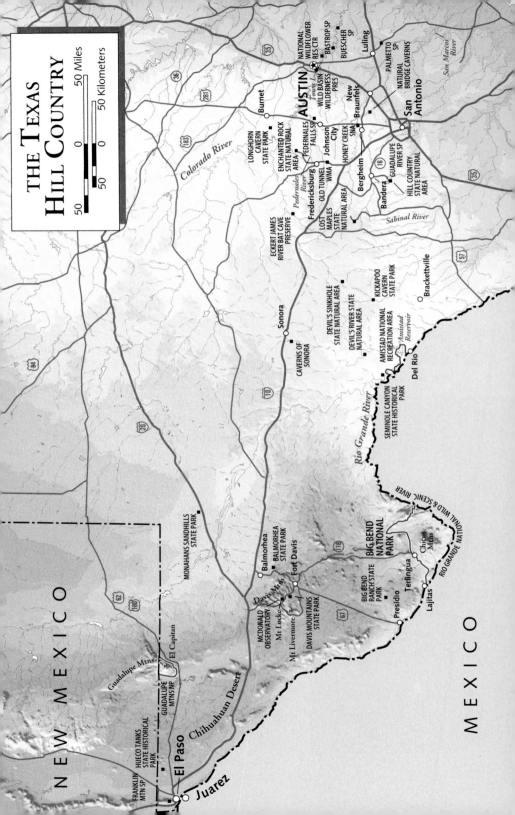

THE TEXAS HILL COUNTRY

50 Miles

50 Kilometers

NEW MEXICO

MEXICO

Juarez

El Paso

FRANKLIN MTN SP

HUECO TANKS STATE HISTORICAL PARK

GUADALUPE MTNS NP

Guadalupe Mtns

El Capitan

Chihuahuan Desert

MONAHANS SANDHILLS STATE PARK

Balmorhea

BALMORHEA STATE PARK

Fort Davis

Davis Mtns

McDONALD OBSERVATORY

Mt Locke

Mt Livermore

DAVIS MOUNTAINS STATE PARK

BIG BEND RANCH STATE PARK

Presidio

BIG BEND NATIONAL PARK

Terlingua

Lajitas

Chisos Mtns

RIO GRANDE NATIONAL WILD & SCENIC RIVER

Rio Grande River

Seminole Canyon State Historical Park

Del Rio

Amistad Reservoir

AMISTAD NATIONAL RECREATION AREA

DEVIL'S RIVER STATE NATURAL AREA

DEVIL'S SINKHOLE STATE NATURAL AREA

KICKAPOO CAVERN STATE PARK

Brackettville

CAVERNS OF SONORA

Sonora

LONGHORN CAVERN STATE PARK

Burnet

Colorado River

ECKERT JAMES RIVER BAT CAVE PRESERVE

Fredericksburg

Pedernales River

LOST MAPLES STATE NATURAL AREA

OLD TUNNEL WMA

ENCHANTED ROCK STATE NATURAL AREA

PEDERNALES FALLS SP

Johnson City

HONEY CREEK SNA

Bergheim

Bandera

GUADALUPE RIVER SP

HILL COUNTRY STATE NATURAL AREA

Sabinal River

AUSTIN

NATIONAL WILDFLOWER RES CTR

WILD BASIN WILDERNESS PRES

Town L.

New Braunfels

San Antonio

NATURAL BRIDGE CAVERNS

PALMETTO SP

BASTROP SP

BUESCHER SP

Luling

San Marcos River

ABOVE: *Noisy, inquisitive scrub jays are familiar residents throughout much of western Texas.*
BELOW: *Golden-fronted woodpeckers usually nest in trees, but a fencepost can serve just as well.*

ing blue topaz, the Texas state gem.

Although not all the sites in this chapter provide payoffs as tangible as a gemstone, all offer real rewards—from spotting the spectacular hunting dive of a peregrine falcon to experiencing the splendor of a field of bluebonnets. The route begins east of Austin and winds through the Hill Country before heading west to the Rio Grande and Big Bend. After passing through the Davis and Guadalupe mountains, it finishes near El Paso, in the westernmost corner of Texas.

HILL COUNTRY AND ENVIRONS

Off Route 183 just south of Interstate 10 near Luling, the 265-acre **Palmetto State Park❖** encompasses biological features that belie its small size. The swampy woodland here has preserved an unusually diverse community of plants, some of them relict species from a cooler, wetter climatic period.

Dwarf palmetto—which grows in the understory beneath oak, elm, sugarberry, pecan, and sycamore—gives the park its name and imparts a tropical feel enhanced by abundant Spanish moss and the related ball moss. The latter grows in round clumps rather than in trailing strands like Spanish moss. Anaqua, a tree more common in south Texas, is found here near the northern limit of its range; its sandpaperlike leaves help identify it.

The park was once known for its "mud volcanoes," boggy places where water percolated to the surface. Changes in the water table, partly caused by agricultural use, have rendered the "mud boils" extinct; but artesian wells help maintain swamp flora such as buttonbush and

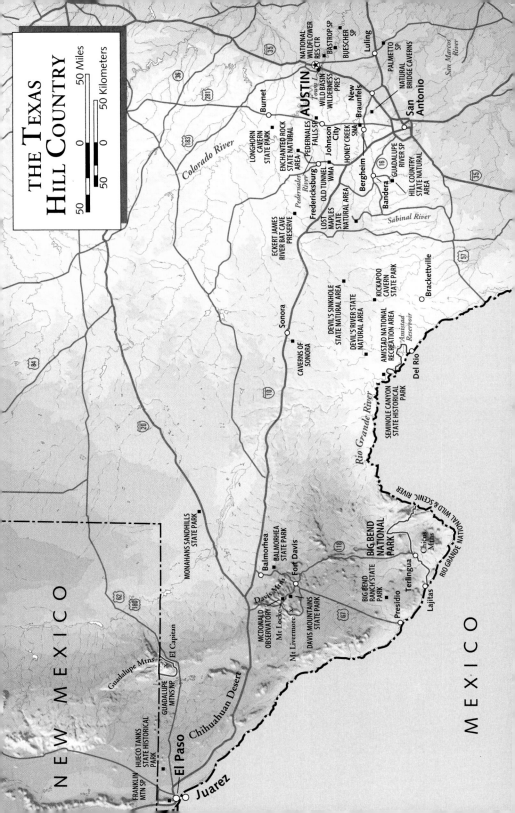

THE TEXAS HILL COUNTRY

50 Miles

50 Kilometers

NEW MEXICO

MEXICO

AUSTIN

San Antonio

El Paso

Juarez

Colorado River

Pedernales River

Sabinal River

San Marcos River

Rio Grande River

RIO GRANDE NATIONAL WILD & SCENIC RIVER

Chihuahuan Desert

NATIONAL WILDFLOWER RES'CTR
BASTROP SP
BUESCHER SP
Luling
PALMETTO SP
NATURAL BRIDGE CAVERNS
Burnet
LONGHORN STATE PARK
ENCHANTED ROCK STATE NATURAL AREA
PEDERNALES FALLS SP
WILD BASIN WILDERNESS PRES
New Braunfels
Fredericksburg
OLD TUNNEL WMA
Johnson City
HONEY CREEK SNA
Bergheim
GUADALUPE RIVER SP
ECKERT JAMES RIVER BAT CAVE PRESERVE
LOST MAPLES STATE NATURAL AREA
Bandera
HILL COUNTRY STATE NATURAL AREA
Sonora
CAVERNS OF SONORA
DEVIL'S SINKHOLE STATE NATURAL AREA
DEVIL'S RIVER STATE NATURAL AREA
KICKAPOO CAVERN STATE PARK
Brackettville
AMISTAD NATIONAL RECREATION AREA
Amistad Reservoir
Del Rio
SEMINOLE CANYON STATE HISTORICAL PARK
MONAHANS SANDHILLS STATE PARK
Balmorhea
BALMORHEA STATE PARK
Fort Davis
Davis Mtns
MCDONALD OBSERVATORY
Mt Locke
Mt Livermore
DAVIS MOUNTAINS STATE PARK
BIG BEND NATIONAL PARK
Chisos Mtns
BIG BEND RANCH STATE PARK
Terlingua
Presidio
Lajitas
FRANKLIN MTN SP
HUECO TANKS STATE HISTORICAL PARK
GUADALUPE MTNS NP
Guadalupe Mtns
El Capitan
Town L.
NATIONAL WILDFLOWER RES'CTR

35
36
281
183
281
16
57
35
10
84
20
62
180
118
67

ABOVE: *Noisy, inquisitive scrub jays are familiar residents throughout much of western Texas.*
BELOW: *Golden-fronted woodpeckers usually nest in trees, but a fencepost can serve just as well.*

ing blue topaz, the Texas state gem.

Although not all the sites in this chapter provide payoffs as tangible as a gemstone, all offer real rewards—from spotting the spectacular hunting dive of a peregrine falcon to experiencing the splendor of a field of bluebonnets. The route begins east of Austin and winds through the Hill Country before heading west to the Rio Grande and Big Bend. After passing through the Davis and Guadalupe mountains, it finishes near El Paso, in the westernmost corner of Texas.

HILL COUNTRY AND ENVIRONS

Off Route 183 just south of Interstate 10 near Luling, the 265-acre **Palmetto State Park**❖ encompasses biological features that belie its small size. The swampy woodland here has preserved an unusually diverse community of plants, some of them relict species from a cooler, wetter climatic period.

Dwarf palmetto—which grows in the understory beneath oak, elm, sugarberry, pecan, and sycamore—gives the park its name and imparts a tropical feel enhanced by abundant Spanish moss and the related ball moss. The latter grows in round clumps rather than in trailing strands like Spanish moss. Anaqua, a tree more common in south Texas, is found here near the northern limit of its range; its sandpaperlike leaves help identify it.

The park was once known for its "mud volcanoes," boggy places where water percolated to the surface. Changes in the water table, partly caused by agricultural use, have rendered the "mud boils" extinct; but artesian wells help maintain swamp flora such as buttonbush and black willow, as does occasional flooding of the San Marcos River.

A very different environment occurs 40 miles to the northeast, at **Bastrop State Park❖,** home to a forest long known as the Lost Pines of Texas. This stand of loblolly pines, covering altogether about 70 square miles, is separated from the extensive Piney Woods of eastern Texas by more than 100 miles of post oak savannas. Sandy soil encourages the growth of pines and provides habitat for the endangered Houston toad, an amphibian endemic to only seven counties in southeastern Texas. The toad is more often heard than seen; its high trill lasts several seconds.

Another frequent sound within the park is the musical chipping trill of the pine warbler, which, as its name implies, nests almost exclusively in pines. This small yellow bird sings not only in the spring breeding season, but on sunny days throughout the year. Also a distinctive part of the Lost Pines, the raucous "laughing" call of the pileated woodpecker reveals the presence of this big black-and-white bird with a flaming red crest.

The 8.5-mile Lost Pines hiking trail loops through the woods east of the main body of the park; primitive camping is allowed, but because of the easily eroded sandy soil, mountain bikes are prohibited. Those who wish to see more of the area by car or bicycle can follow Park Road 1, which runs 13 miles southeast to **Buescher State Park❖,** winding constantly up, down, and around hills along the way.

After its founding in 1982 by Lady Bird Johnson, the **National Wildflower Research Center❖** occupied a site in the flat farmland east of Austin. In 1995, it moved to a new facility located on 42 acres southwest of the city, in true Hill Country habitat. Reach the center via I-35 to Slaughter Lane west to South Loop 1. A dramatic walkway leads to a courtyard surrounded by an exhibit gallery, auditorium, and Children's Little House; the architecture is a blend of Spanish, ranch-style, and German, reflecting regional influences. Beyond are a wildflower meadow, 23 terraced demonstration gardens, and oak woodlands.

The setting may be new, but the center's mission remains the same:

OVERLEAF: *The state's best-known, best-loved, and official wildflower, the bluebonnet carpets a springtime meadow in Texas Hill Country. The true Texas bluebonnet grows only in the eastern part of the state.*

to promote the protection of native flora and to educate the public—private citizens as well as landscape designers—about the ecological and economic importance of native grasses, wildflowers, shrubs, and trees. As an example, one outdoor exhibit compares fertilizer, pesticide, and water use on a typical high-maintenance ornamental lawn and on lawns of native plants. Gardening and landscaping aside, a visit to the center is an enlightening experience for anyone interested in wildflowers and other plants of central Texas.

As a university site boasting an active environmental community, Texas's capital city of Austin offers several natural attractions for visitors. One of the best is **Wild Basin Wilderness Preserve❖,** a 227-acre tract of woods, grassland, and streams on the west side of town off Route 360. Trails winding through much of the area provide opportunities to see varied wildflowers and birds, including the scrub jay, the black-crested form of the tufted titmouse, and the beautiful painted bunting. Texas mountain laurel, Spanish oak, live oak, yaupon holly, and cedar elm are among the preserve's trees. Also found here is the Texas madrona, a rare tree locally that was once called "naked Indian" because of its smooth reddish bark.

One of Texas's greatest wildlife spectacles takes place—partly, at least—on the doorstep of downtown Austin. Each spring, hundreds of thousands of Mexican free-tailed bats return to roost under the **Congress Avenue Bridge** over Town Lake (actually a dammed section of the Colorado River). Emerging in dense columns at dusk to feed on insects, the little mammals can easily be seen from an observation area on the southeast side of the bridge or from commercial bat-watching cruises. Females have their pups beginning in June; when the population peaks a few weeks later, the colony may total 1.5 million animals.

Several Hill Country caves also house large bat colonies. **Eckert James River Bat Cave Preserve❖,** a Nature Conservancy preserve in Mason County, hosts six million bats. **Old Tunnel Wildlife Man-**

RIGHT: *The fearsome-looking leaves of agave (top left) were an important source of fiber for Native Americans. Small pods of prickly-pear cactus (top right), known as* napolitos, *are eaten by wildlife and humans. An "indicator" species of the Chihuahuan Desert, lechuguilla (bottom right) is found nowhere else in the world. After blooming, the red flowers of strawberry cactus (bottom left) produce large, deliciously sweet fruit.*

agement Area❖ south of Fredericksburg, **Kickapoo Cavern State Park**❖ near Brackettville, and nearby **Devils Sinkhole State Natural Area**❖ are all excellent bat-viewing sites. Kickapoo and Devil's Sinkhole are also home to cave swallows that nest inside. To minimize disturbance to the breeding bat colonies, visitation is limited to guided tours at all sites.

Two of America's rarest birds, the black-capped vireo and the golden-cheeked warbler, live in the Texas Hill Country, and the latter breeds only here. Their preservation is a goal of the new, and as yet undeveloped, **Balcones Canyonlands National Wildlife Refuge**❖ in the rolling country northwest of Austin on County Road 1431 at Lago Vista. As Austin expands and bedroom communities mushroom, the warbler has become a symbol of the conflict between growth and conservation and a powerful political issue, as environmentalists debate developers, ranchers, and others who fear government control of large tracts of land. The battle has heated and cooled repeatedly in recent years and will probably continue for many more.

Nevertheless, progress is being made in protecting some of the habitat that the golden-cheek needs to survive. The female warbler uses strips of bark from the Ashe juniper, locally called cedar, to build her nest, and the birds feed heavily on insects living in oaks. Much oak-juniper woodland has been cleared already; in the heart of the warbler's range, at least 40 per cent of its habitat is gone.

One place the golden-cheek can reliably be found during its breeding season, late March into summer (it spends the winter in Central America), is **Pedernales Falls State Park**❖, about 38 miles west of Austin via Route 290 and Ranch Road 3232 and some 10 miles east of Johnson City via Route 281 to Ranch Road 2766. Males are often heard singing their buzzy song near the park's Hill Country Nature Trail and along the river. Besides the warbler, the hilly, heavily wooded park is home to white-tailed deer, black-tailed jackrabbits, wild turkeys, bobwhite quail, and such "western" birds as black-chinned hummingbirds, golden-fronted woodpeckers, ash-throated flycatchers, scrub jays, and rufous-crowned sparrows.

The falls on the Pedernales River are an attractive series of low cascades over layers of limestone dating back 300 million years. The tilted strata here were pushed from their original horizontal position by

ABOVE: *The charm and beauty of Texas Hill Country streams have long attracted settlers, vacationers, and artists.* Bluff of the North Fork of the Guadalupe River *was painted by Julian Onderdonk in April 1913.*

the Llano Uplift, the geologic event that created extensive granite intrusions just to the north. Nearby Enchanted Rock provides a closer look at the uplift.

Thirty-five miles south, off Route 46 near Bergheim, **Guadalupe River State Park❖** is, like Pedernales Falls, an intriguing blend of east and west. Inca doves, ladder-backed woodpeckers, and canyon wrens give the birdlife a western flair, yet bald cypress trees grow along the edge of the river, and eastern phoebes nest on the tall limestone bluffs. Identified by its broken lateral stripe and rows of spots on its belly, the Guadalupe bass, a Hill Country endemic and the official state fish of Texas, lives in the river that gave it its name. The cool, crystalline waters of the Guadalupe are immensely popular with swimmers, canoeists, and inner-tubers, both in the park and outside its boundaries. The stretch of the river upstream from New Braunfels is always crowded on summer weekends.

The adjacent **Honey Creek State Natural Area** comprises much the same habitat as the state park, but visitation is limited to guided tours (check at the park office for details). Here, land managers are trying to restore the live oak–grassland ecosystem that existed before European settlement, and native grasses such as Indiangrass, little

ABOVE: *Weathering has created large cracks in the smooth pink granite of Enchanted Rock, near Fredericksburg; accumulated soil supports a succession of plants, from grasses to trees such as these live oaks.*

bluestem, and switchgrass are making a comeback where they were displaced by trees and shrubs.

No traveler should leave the Hill Country without visiting **Enchanted Rock State Natural Area❖,** about 15 miles north of the distinctly Germanic town of Fredericksburg via Route 965. This huge dome of pink granite is only a tiny part of an unimaginably large mass of igneous rock—a batholith—that rose from deep within the earth hundreds of millions of years ago, pushing up a section of what is now central Texas as it neared the surface. Here, younger, softer rock overlying the Llano Uplift has been worn away, exposing the resistant granite underneath.

Although the geology of Enchanted Rock—and its sheer, stark beauty—are reason enough to visit, its biological aspects are noteworthy as well. A short, not-too-strenuous climb to the top of the rock leads past islands of vegetation in various stages of succession on the seemingly barren granite surface. Plant life in Enchanted Rock's "vernal pools" begins with algae; as soil and organic matter accumulate, quillworts, sedges, grasses, wildflowers, and even small trees follow. These ephemeral pools also host tiny invertebrates called fairy shrimp, which survive dry periods as eggs, hatching when rains return. Basin bellflower and rock quillwort, both of which grow here, are endemic to the Llano region.

The word *natural* truly means something in the name **Hill Country State Natural Area❖**. This 5,400-acre tract, a former ranch about 10 miles southwest of Bandera off Route 1077, is little developed; only primitive camping is allowed, so night sounds run to coyote wails and chuck-will's-widow whistles, not generators and televisions. The area is especially popular with horseback riders, who share an extensive trail system with hikers. Wildlife includes the shy nocturnal ringtail, sometimes called ringtailed cat, although this raccoon cousin is feline only in its grace and quickness. Both the golden-cheeked warbler and black-capped vireo breed here and can usually be found in spring and early summer.

Only 30 miles farther west via Routes 470 and 187, **Lost Maples State Natural Area❖** is yet another Hill Country jewel: off the main travel routes, but well worth a detour. It's named for a population of bigtooth maple, a relative of sugar maple, found here at the eastern limit of its range. Surviving in the shelter of the deeply eroded Sabinal River canyon, where they are protected from heat and wind and nourished by deep river-bottom soil, the trees are thought to be relicts of a Pleistocene-epoch ice age. Fall foliage color is not a common phenomenon in south Texas, so the park is often very crowded in November, when these famous maples turn vivid red-orange.

Lost Maples is a virtual zoo of rare or restricted-range flora and fauna. Texas madrona, witch-hazel, sycamore-leaf snowbell, American smoke tree, and Canada moonseed are among the special plants; golden-cheeked warblers and black-capped vireos nest in the oak woods, and tiny green kingfishers are sometimes seen perched low over the river. Texas salamanders, Texas cliff frogs, and barking frogs (which inflate their bodies to tremendous size when frightened) are three unusual amphibians found in the area. The rare Guadalupe bass can be sighted occasionally in the clear rivers, although a glimpse of the common longear sunfish is more likely.

Like many other limestone areas, the Edwards Plateau is abundantly underlain by caves where water moving slowly through cracks in the rocks for millennia eroded extensive passageways along fault lines through the permeable rock. **Natural Bridge Caverns❖** west of New Braunfels and **Longhorn Cavern State Park❖** southwest of Burnet are two of the better commercial cave operations; another is **Caverns of**

Sonora❖, south of Interstate 10, eight miles west of the town of Sonora. (In a car-window geology lesson, layers of sedimentary lime-stone laid down millions of years ago are easily visible at road cuts along this stretch of the highway.)

The walls of the Caverns of Sonora are crowded with small, intri-cate formations (properly called speleothems), some rare or unknown in other caves. A "butterfly," created by two fishtail helictites, is the cave's most famous feature. (A helictite is formed when water flows sideways or upward through a thin tube by capillary action.) Some of the rooms are amazingly complex displays of stalagmites, stalactites, "soda straws," "popcorn," and similar shapes. For the sheer number of speleothems per square foot, few if any caves can match this one.

Amistad National Recreation Area❖, northwest of Del Rio, centers on 67,000-acre Amistad Reservoir, created by a dam on the Rio Grande. Although waterskiing, fishing, and related pursuits are the main attrac-tion here, the presence of so much water in an arid part of the world creates favorable conditions for wildlife as well. Ducks winter on the lake, and the ringed kingfisher, a south Texas specialty noticeably larger than the familiar belted kingfisher, is present all year. Two other birds commonly seen are the Chihuahuan raven and the Harris's hawk, one of America's most beautiful raptors. Snakes, lizards, jackrabbits, and white-tailed deer are abundant, and with a little luck visitors may en-counter a group of the small wild pigs called javelinas, or collared pec-caries. In addition to nature trails at Diablo East and the Pecos area, sev-eral other access sites ring the eastern end of the reservoir.

The area around Amistad is best known for Paleo-Indian rock art dating back as far as 6000 B.C. Fine examples can be seen at **Seminole Canyon State Historical Park❖** (home of Fate Bell Shelter, famous for ancient pictographs), **Devils River State Natural Area❖,** and **Panther Cave❖,** accessible only by boat from Amistad Reservoir. Also an excellent spot for wildlife observation, Devils River is noted for its reptile population. The Devils River pupfish is an en-demic and endangered local resident.

RIGHT: *Organic material streaks steep limestone cliffs above the Pecos River in Amistad National Recreation Area. Nearby caves and bluff shelters contain an extensive collection of Paleo-Indian rock art.*

ABOVE: *The Christmas Mountains rise beyond Sotol Vista in Big Bend National Park. Native peoples harvested the starchy "heart" of sotol (a member of the lily family) for food; they wove the long leaves into mats.*

THE BIG BEND COUNTRY

With absolutely no danger of exaggeration, **Big Bend National Park❖** can be described as one of the earth's great wild places. That it is one of our least-visited national parks is both a pity and a blessing: The travelers who crowd other, more popular parks are missing a land of endless wonder; the people who do visit find an abundance of space and solitude in Big Bend's 800,000 acres of desert and mountains.

Big Bend lies within the Chihuahuan Desert, a biotic region straddling the Rio Grande and encompassing parts of the United States and Mexico. Although the great majority of the park is desert or sparse grassland, a thin strip along the river is well-enough watered to support cottonwoods, willows, mesquite, buttonbush, and reeds—a verdant riparian zone that is an important factor in Big Bend's amazing diversity of plant and animal life. Beavers—hardly a typical desert species—live in riverside burrows, sharing the habitat with leopard frogs and mud turtles. The nature trail at Rio Grande Village, in the southeastern part of the park, is a good place to explore the floodplain.

Rising in the middle of the park are the Chisos Mountains, crowned by 7,825-foot **Emory Peak.** The comparison to a wooded island in a desert sea is as apt as it is inevitable. Mountain slopes and rugged

94

ABOVE: *Sedimentary-clay badlands near the western entrance to Big Bend National Park hide dinosaur fossils within their folds. The great variety of rocks found in the region makes the park a geologist's paradise.*

canyons support oaks (including the endemic Chisos oak), junipers, maples, ashes, and hackberries, and in the park's highest areas, ponderosa pines, Douglas firs, and even a few quaking aspens remain as relicts from a time when the climate was wetter and cooler. A small race of white-tailed deer, the Sierra del Carmen whitetail, is found only in Big Bend mountains and a few nearby Mexican ranges. Deer are among the prey of the park's mountain lions; the big cats are secretive and seen by few visitors, although backcountry hikers are advised to be aware of their presence.

Big Bend ranks with the top birding spots on the continent; more kinds of birds (about 450) have been sighted here than in any other national park. The most avidly sought species is the Colima warbler, a gray-and-buff bird whose United States nesting range is confined to a few high Chisos canyons. The park is also the best place to find the colorful little lucifer hummingbird, which feeds at the blooms of the impressively tall century plant. (A type of agave, the not quite accurately named century plant may live 50 years or more before it flowers once and dies.) Golden eagles, peregrine falcons (several pairs nest in the park), band-tailed pigeons, acorn woodpeckers, gray-breasted jays, crissal thrashers, black-capped vireos, gray vireos, painted redstarts, he-

The ears of the black-tailed jackrabbit (left) help dissipate desert heat. Although mountain lions (above), locally called panthers, occasionally catch jackrabbits, deer are their usual prey.

patic tanagers, varied buntings, painted buntings, black-chinned sparrows, and Scott's orioles are a few of Big Bend's notable species. Two favorite birds among visitors, birders or not, are the roadrunner, a long-tailed cuckoo that—true to its name—runs after lizards and other prey, and the tiny elf owl, hardly bigger than a sparrow. (Contrast the owl with *Quetzalcoatlus,* a fossil pterodactyl discovered at the park in 1971. Believed to have been the largest flying creature that ever lived, this giant had a wingspan of about 50 feet.)

The only people who might match birders in their enthusiasm for Big Bend are geologists. A favorite destination for university geology class trips, the park region combines sedimentary rock, laid down when seas covered the land hundreds of millions of years ago, and igneous rock from a much later period, all tilted and faulted in various episodes of mountain building. The Chisos Mountains are volcanic in origin; in places, ancient lava flows and tuff (soft rock formed from volcanic ash) are exposed on the surface. At Santa Elena Canyon, the Rio Grande and its prehistoric predecessors relentlessly wore through the uplifting limestone Mesa de Anguila to sculpt cliffs 1,500 feet high.

Trails in Big Bend range from easy strolls such as the Window View Trail, in the Chisos Basin, to difficult overnight backpacking trips across the desert. The park's most popular trails begin in the basin and climb into the mountains; the nearly ten-mile loop through Laguna Meadow and Boot Canyon offers excellent scenery and a chance to see Colima warblers from April through summer.

The varied trails allow visitors to experience all Big Bend's natural communities and see a wide variety of fascinating plants. An agave called lechuguilla, an "indicator species" of the Chihuahuan Desert (a

Lucifer hummingbirds (left) are usually seen near agaves on the arid mesas of western Texas. Scott's orioles (above) are common, colorful inhabitants of Big Bend's grasslands.

plant found only in this area), is common in much of the park. Creosote bush, an abundant desert plant, produces a toxin that keeps other plants at a distance, thereby commanding a greater share of the scarce and precious rainfall. Big Bend is well supplied with cacti, which display beautiful flowers following spring rains. Among the most unusual is living rock cactus, a flat, most unplantlike plant endemic to northern Mexico and the Big Bend area.

Another 277,000 acres of Chihuahuan Desert are protected at **Big Bend Ranch State Park❖,** just west of the national park. At the Barton Warnock Environmental Education Center, near Lajitas, exhibits and a botanical garden provide a good introduction to the region. Thirty miles of mostly primitive hiking trails wind through the southern part of the park. A five-mile (one-way) hike leads up a drainage to Rancherías Falls, where water drops 70 feet during seasonal pour-offs; even when the stream isn't flowing, the canyon walls provide a close look at ancient lava flows. A shorter, less strenuous walk descends into Closed Canyon, a deep, dramatically narrow gorge leading to a series of pour-offs above the Rio Grande. An even easier experience is a guided bus tour of Big Bend Ranch (check at the education center for schedule and fees).

Except for animals of the high mountains, most of the faunal elements of the national park are present in the park, including javelinas (peccaries), mule deer, mountain lions, coyotes, ringtails, and such desert birds as scaled quail, lesser nighthawks, verdins, cactus wrens, black-tailed gnatcatchers, pyrrhuloxias, and black-throated sparrows. Western mastiff bats, the largest in the United States, roost on Big Bend cliffs by day, leaving at dusk to forage for insects.

The **Rio Grande National Wild and Scenic River❖,** administered by

97

LEFT: *Too often persecuted over much of its vast range, the golden eagle finds protection—and nesting sites—in Big Bend's wilderness mountains and rocky canyons.* RIGHT: *Dawn gilds the cliffs of Mariscal Canyon on the Cross Canyons Trail. Here the Rio Grande flows north, forming the "big bend" that gave the region its name.*

the national park, covers nearly 200 river miles bordering the park and continuing downstream. Float trips through awe-inspiring Santa Elena, Mariscal, and Boquillas canyons can be made privately (a permit is required) or with an outfitter (companies are based in Terlingua and Lajitas). The latter is the better choice for most visitors; the bottom of an inaccessible 1,200-foot canyon is no place for inexperience or trouble.

Route 170 from Lajitas northwest to Presidio has become known as **El Camino del Rio** ("The River Road")—and as one of the most celebrated scenic drives in America. For nearly 60 miles the route follows the Rio Grande in a sometimes tortuous path through canyons and under tall cliffs, climbing hills and dropping again to skirt the river. At dawn or dusk (the best times to drive), travelers may see mule deer and coyotes near the road and a wide assortment of snakes on it. Jackrabbits, abundant along the highway, would be fun to watch but for their unfortunate habit of waiting until the last possible moment to try to scamper across in front of a passing vehicle. R.I.P.

TRANS-PECOS MOUNTAINS AND BASINS

Like the craggy peaks of the Chisos, the Davis Mountains are volcanic in origin, their mostly rounded summits extending northwest from the historic town of Fort Davis. Igneous material came to the surface through faults here during the late Tertiary period, perhaps 50 million years ago. Resistant to erosion, Davis summits rise steeply above the Chihuahuan Desert, topped by 8,382-foot **Mount Livermore,** the fifth-highest mountain in Texas. (All the higher peaks are in Guadalupe Mountains National Park.)

The Davis range receives slightly more rainfall than the rest of the

Trans-Pecos, enabling it to support desert grasslands and, higher in the mountains, oak-juniper forests. The elevational change and moisture create a wildlife paradise, but nearly the entire region is privately owned and inaccessible. One fortunate exception is **Davis Mountains State Park❖,** four miles west of Fort Davis on Route 118; located on mid-level slopes, the park provides a sampling of both desert and mountain. Scenic Skyline Drive rises to an overlook at nearly 6,000 feet offering rewarding panoramic views.

Grayish rock squirrels can be seen sunning on boulders, and scrub jays often appear as flashes of blue, darting into cover along roads. The wildlife star of the park is probably the Montezuma quail, elsewhere a shy, elusive, and uncommon species that has occasioned many a frustrating, fruitless search over its southwestern range. Here the clown-faced quail have become habituated to people; at times they're practically brazen in their appearances at campsites and feeding stations.

To see more of the mountains, continue westward along Route 118 and then loop back to Fort Davis on Routes 166 and 17. Traversing habitats from highland ponderosa pines to low grassland, this 70-mile route is likely to provide sightings of mule deer and pronghorn (often

Left: A dramatic sky and light dusting of snow highlight ridges and canyons in the foothills of the Davis Mountains. Low clouds obscure the range's highest peaks, including Mount Locke, site of the University of Texas's world-renowned McDonald Observatory.

called antelope, although this exclusively American species is not a true antelope).

Those whose interests extend beyond our planet should drive up Mount Locke to the **McDonald Observatory❖** (about 15 miles west of Fort Davis off Route 118), operated by the University of Texas. Located here in the Davis Mountains because of the clear air and distance from light-polluting cities, the observatory offers programs, guided tours, and thrice-weekly "star parties." The 107-inch telescope, housed in a gleaming white dome, is available for public viewing once a month. The nine-meter Hobby-Eberly Telescope, scheduled for completion in mid-1997, will be the second largest telescope in the world.

From beyond the stratosphere to below the surface: **Balmorhea State Park❖,** near the town of the same name about 25 miles north of Fort Davis, at first glance seems to contain just an unusually large (62,000-square-foot) and deep (30-foot) swimming pool. There, in fact, sits the world's largest spring-fed pond; San Solomon Springs pumps 25 million gallons of water a day into the pool, which then empties into irrigation canals. (Irrigation here dates to the days of the Apache, who used spring water to nurture their crops.) Several species of fish inhabit the clear pool, including the Comanche Springs pupfish and Pecos mosquito fish, both endangered. The rare fish are sometimes seen by divers and snorkelers, but such common species as sunfish and Mexican tetras stage a more conspicuous show.

Snakes, lizards, roadrunners, and mule deer roam the dunes at

---

Overleaf: Afternoon clouds build up around the western escarpment of El Capitan in Guadalupe Mountains National Park. Part of a Permian reef formation, the Guadalupes now harbor aspen, elk, and black bears.

Monahans Sandhills State Park❖, just north of Interstate 20 between Odessa and Monahans. The dunes roam too, changing height and shape with the wind, which is a near-constant presence in this west Texas landscape. (Noticing a hinged metal service-station sign swinging almost horizontally in a gale, a visitor to Monahans once asked the attendant if the wind blew that way all the time. "Oh, no," the man said, "sometimes it blows really hard.")

Sand that forms the 70-foot dunes in the park was blown here from riverbeds in New Mexico in a dry climatic period after the last ice age; altogether, the dune field stretches 200 miles to the northwest. Much of the region is covered with vegetation, including the peculiar Havard oak. Also called shin oak, this tree is easily seen in the park; full grown, it may be only 3 feet tall, although its roots can reach down 90 feet to find water.

Even in a state liberally endowed with natural areas, **Guadalupe Mountains National Park❖** (about 90 miles east of El Paso off Route 180/62) stands out. It stands out literally because 8,749-foot **Guadalupe Peak** is the highest point in Texas (nearby summits rank numbers two through four); it stands out figuratively because it supports great breadth of habitat and diversity of flora and fauna.

Looking up at the sheer face of **El Capitan,** the massive pinnacle that has been a landmark since Mescalero Apache hunted here and the Butterfield stage passed by, a traveler may find it hard to imagine that the Guadalupe Mountains were once under the ocean. But El Capitan and the rest of the range are actually exposed portions of the world's largest known fossil reef, built by sponges, bryozoans, and other equally humble sea creatures 250 million years ago. Carlsbad Caverns, just over the state line in New Mexico, are part of this same limestone reef.

Today's national park encompasses Chihuahuan Desert, where cholla cactus, agave, and sotol grow, and mountain peaks covered in ponderosa pine, Douglas fir, aspen, and alligator juniper (named for its blocky, scalelike bark). In between, **McKittrick Canyon,** a place of near-legendary beauty, is home to oaks, Texas walnut, bigtooth maple, and velvet ash, deciduous trees that create a breathtaking fall-foliage display. The rare Texas madrona grows here too; it was once called "naked Indian" for its smooth reddish bark, which cracks and peels in older trees. (In Mexico, similar trees are called "gringos" because their bark

ABOVE: *The "tanks" at Hueco Tanks State Historical Park collect water from seasonal rains. Tiny freshwater shrimp here spend most of the year in dormancy, coming to life only when sufficient moisture is present.*

comes off in papery strips like the skin of a sunburned paleface.)

Ecologically, the Guadalupe Mountains are like a bit of the Rockies reaching into Texas. Elk (introduced here in the 1920s after the native animals were extirpated), black bears, mountain lions, porcupines, red squirrels, and Texas's only chipmunks live here, as do bald eagles, peregrine falcons, and such mountain birds as band-tailed pigeons, white-throated swifts, pygmy nuthatches, mountain chickadees, Clark's nutcrackers, and Steller's jays.

Although the Guadalupes are magnificent even from a distance, little of their true richness can be experienced from a car. Only backpackers and hikers can enjoy places such as the Bowl, a forested canyon in the park's expansive wilderness area, and the upper reaches of McKittrick Canyon, with its towering rock cliffs. The Permian Reef Geology Trail is a fairly strenuous nine-mile-round-trip hike that showcases the limestone reef and its abundant fossils.

Trails at Frijole Ranch and the McKittrick Canyon Visitor Center are good for those with only a short time in the park; those with several days for exploration will find unlimited possibilities. Backcountry hikers should take ample water (at least a gallon a day per person) and be careful of late-summer thunderstorms. Visitors who want to say that they have stood on the highest mountain in Texas can make the 4.2-mile hike from the Pine Springs campground to the top of Guadalupe Peak; the trail gains 3,000 feet in elevation, and suitably splendid views reward those who hike it.

At **Hueco Tanks State Historical Park❖,** about 20 miles east of El Paso off Route 180/62, natural rock basins (*hueco* is Spanish for hole or hollow) have provided water for humans since the days of Paleo-Indians, perhaps as long as 10,000 years ago. Pictographs testify to the site's popularity as a gathering place for Native Americans. These days, rock climbers enjoy the challenge of scaling convoluted walls of syenite on the park's low, bare hills, which rise like isolated islands in the desert. Although many kinds of typical west-Texas wildlife appear here, the most interesting fauna are probably the tiny freshwater shrimp that live in the basins; their population fluctuates widely depending on rainfall and temperature.

Dominating the view for miles around, the Franklin Mountains loom starkly over the cities of El Paso and Juárez, Mexico. This rugged range—pushed into its angular profile, like so much of western North America, by folding and faulting—is home to **Franklin Mountains State Park❖,** one of Texas's newest and largest parks. Little developed and sparsely vegetated, Franklin Mountains is a wilderness area especially appealing to hikers who appreciate the solitude of primitive cross-country routes; travelers on Route 375, the Transmountain Road, enjoy fine views and a sampling of this uncompromising terrain. Wildlife is most common around springs, but anyone glancing skyward at the right moment might glimpse a red-tailed hawk, a prairie falcon, or perhaps even a golden eagle—persecuted for decades, yet still a majestic presence in the skies and an enduring symbol of the West.

RIGHT: *Prickly pear cactus and mesquite grow on the steep slopes of the Franklin Mountains near El Paso. Some of the most ancient rock in Texas—more than a billion years old—is exposed in this rugged range.*

OKLAHOMA

OKLAHOMA:
SOUTHERN SWAMPS
TO WESTERN MOUNTAINS

Few other states encompass as much natural diversity as Oklahoma. Its range of habitats, and their inhabitants, may surprise people whose impression of the state is based on old photographs of the famed 1889–95 land rushes, all of which seem to show horseback riders and covered wagons raising clouds of dust as they race across featureless prairies. Add a scattering of twentieth-century oil wells, and one popular portrait of the Sooner State is complete—although, as visitors soon learn, it's also inaccurate.

Like Texas, Oklahoma is a place of transition; the imaginary line that divides eastern from western North America bisects it. Bald cypresses grow in the bottomlands of the southeastern corner, less than 300 feet above sea level. In the extreme west, at the tip of the long, narrow Panhandle, pinyon and ponderosa pines occur at elevations approaching 5,000 feet. Kentucky warblers, pileated woodpeckers, and flying squirrels live in the forests of the east; canyon wrens, ladder-backed woodpeckers, and rock squirrels reside in the drier open spaces of the west. Grasslands are home to prairie dogs, prairie chickens, and relict herds of the bison that once roamed the plains in immense numbers.

A traveler crossing Oklahoma from east to west could hardly fail to mark the physical change from the rugged Ouachita Mountains and the ancient rounded Ozarks—both heavily forested—through the

---

PRECEDING PAGES: *Big sky, broad prairie: Verdant spring grass coats the rolling landscape at the Tallgrass Prairie Preserve near Pawhuska.*
LEFT: *Junipers dot eroded sandstone at Black Mesa; these high bluffs in western Oklahoma shelter numerous species native to the Rockies.*

111

scrubby oak Cross Timbers, strips of woodland running from Texas to Oklahoma, to the grassland of the High Plains. Less obvious is another, tremendously important, contrast: the decreasing amount of precipitation. Not only is rainfall much sparser in the western half of the state, but near-constant wind sweeping across the plains saps moisture from plant life, making habitats even drier than annual precipitation levels indicate. In some western places, almost no trees grow away from watercourses.

Those interested in geology find Oklahoma an absorbing textbook. The parallel ridges of the Ouachita Mountains, in the southeast, were formed when the massive pressure of continental movement caused folding and faulting of sandstone and other sedimentary rock. The Ozarks, to the north, are a high plateau deeply dissected by the erosive force of rivers. The Arbuckle Mountains of south-central Oklahoma may be the most variegated chapter in the state's geology text: limestone, sandstone, shale, conglomerates, and granite have all written their parts in these very old, heavily eroded highlands. In the southwest, the Wichita Mountains are mainly granite, worn and broken into a rugged jumble of rocks, most easily explored at Wichita Mountains National Wildlife Refuge near Lawton and Quartz Mountain State Park farther west.

The Gypsum Hills, west of the rolling shale and sandstone Redbed Plains of central Oklahoma, constitute a distinctive physical region. Composed of gypsum interbedded to varying degrees with other materials, they range from low hills to bluffs to sparsely vegetated badlands. The gypsum is evidence of an ancient ocean, which left the mineral behind as it dried out.

Buttes of the Glass Mountains, east of Woodward in north-central Oklahoma, sparkle with selenite, a crystalline variety of gypsum. (A visiting British geologist's pronunciation of *Glass* gave rise to the alternative name *Gloss*, as the mountains are still occasionally called.) At Salt Plains National Wildlife Refuge, visitors can dig for selenite crystals, found just beneath the surface of a huge, flat expanse of salt—a dry "sea" that is probably the state's most arrestingly odd landscape. Alabaster Caverns State Park is one of the country's largest gypsum caves, offering an inside view of the "Gyp Hills."

The Nature Conservancy's Tallgrass Prairie Preserve, where grassland

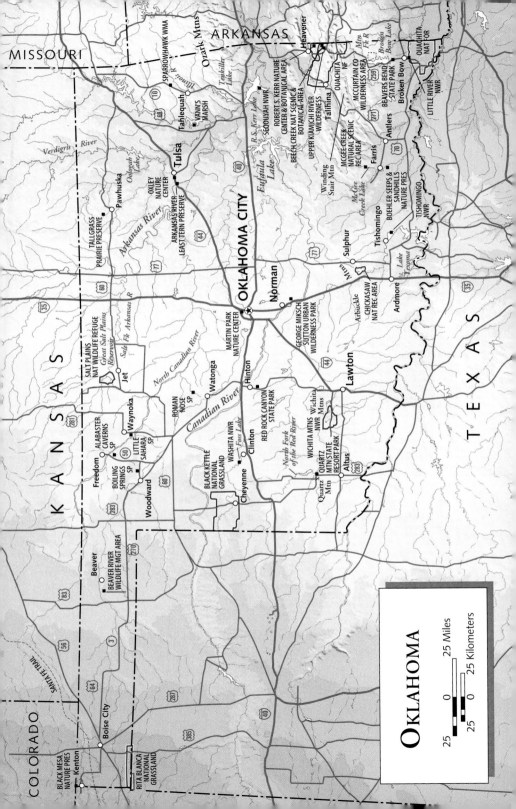

rolls to the horizon like ocean waves, is protecting and restoring a remnant of a seriously endangered ecosystem that once stretched nearly unbroken across much of America's midsection. In the drier Panhandle, mixed-grass and short-grass prairie cover the mostly flat High Plains, formed from sand and gravel washed down from the Rocky Mountains in the Pleistocene epoch—relatively recently in geologic terms.

On the far western border of the Panhandle, Black Mesa rises from

the plains to a height of 4,973 feet. Created by an ancient lava outflow, the mesa habitat is unique in Oklahoma, providing a home for many species rare in the state. In its flora and fauna it is in essence a part of the Rocky Mountains, meeting the prairie far east of the main range.

Salamanders and sand dunes, pelicans and prairie dogs, eastern beech and western juniper, ancient forests and wide-open spaces—the mosaic of the Oklahoma landscape contains more than its share of contrasts. Much of this diversity is protected within a fine collection of parks, preserves, and refuges, accessible to anyone with the ambition to explore.

ABOVE: *Gypsum crystals in red clay near Waynoka form a juxtaposition symbolic of western Oklahoma's geology.*

This chapter begins in the Ozark Mountains of the northeast and travels south and west, paralleling the Red River valley before curving back eastward. The route then crosses northern Oklahoma and ends in the High Plains of the Panhandle.

NORTHEAST OKLAHOMA: THE OZARKS

In Eastern Oklahoma, several expansive reservoirs—among them Kerr Lake on the Arkansas River, Eufaula Lake on the Canadian, and Oologah Lake on the Verdigris—attract thousands of anglers, water-skiers, and campers. For those who prefer their streams natural and un-dammed, recreational choices are more limited. The brightest spot on their map is the **Illinois River,** Oklahoma's most popular scenic stream.

For 70 miles, from just west of the Arkansas line to the backwaters of Tenkiller Lake east of Muskogee, the Illinois flows freely through the Ozark Mountains, inviting canoeists, tubers, and swimmers to enjoy its waters. Anglers too find the river appealing, not least because it remains clear enough to support a population of smallmouth bass.

The Illinois is not a white-water stream to challenge expert paddlers; most of the time its rapids reach only class II: easy enough for beginners to practice their skills and still enjoy occasional fast-running rocky sections. Usually the flow is adequate for floating throughout the year, thanks in part to tributaries such as Flint Creek. The 32 miles from the Chewey bridge to the Route 62 bridge near Tahlequah can be crowded on summer weekends; many longtime Illinois-lovers prefer to canoe in spring and fall—and even winter—to enjoy a more solitary experience.

ABOVE: *Ferns, phlox, fire pinks, and young maples near Tulsa are a microcosm of the moist eastern Ozark woodlands.*

Along the Illinois, bluffs as high as 400 feet offset sections where development and roads crowd the banks. At **Sparrowhawk Wildlife Management Area❖**, off Route 10 northeast of Tahlequah, a hiking trail along the bluffs provides fine views of the river below. Information on floating the Illinois, as well as a list of canoe outfitters, is available from the Oklahoma Scenic Rivers Commission in Tahlequah.

Just a short drive north from the Muskogee Turnpike on Route 69 between Muskogee and Wagoner, **Vann's Marsh❖** is a small but interesting wildlife area. Prairie dogs (introduced here in 1987) go about their "town" business in a field just east of old Route 69; binoculars are helpful in observing their alternately playful and serious-looking activities. A substantial number of nonmigratory "giant" Canada geese breed on a nearby lake, products of an effort to establish these birds along the Arkansas River and some of its tributaries. A mile-long nature trail circles a marsh where herons and egrets feed in summer;

LEFT: *Common across the western plains, Swainson's hawks gather in large flocks each fall for their long migration to South America.*
RIGHT: *Young willows create a dense thicket along the marshy edge of Robert S. Kerr Lake at Sequoyah National Wildlife Refuge near Vian.*

red-winged blackbirds and scissor-tailed fly-catchers perch on trees and telephone wires. Calling stridently from mudflats, killdeer, common and colorful plover, demonstrate why their scientific name is *vociferus.*

The **Oxley Nature Center**❖ in Tulsa's Mohawk Park comprises 800 acres of varied habitats, including rare bottomland forest, woodland, lake, creek, marsh, and old field. One of eight trails winding through the area, the North Woods Loop traverses a mostly undeveloped forest tract often full of migrant songbirds in spring and fall. Herons and egrets are frequently seen around the center's wetlands, and bald eagles sometimes roost in lakeside trees during winter.

The nature center also operates **Redbud Valley Nature Preserve**❖ a few miles to the east. Within this 220-acre natural area are plants of both the eastern Ozark Mountains (including sugar maples) and grasslands to the west. North-facing limestone bluffs are home to columbine, Dutchman's-breeches, and a variety of ferns.

The graceful least tern—as its name implies, it's America's smallest tern, only about the size of a cardinal—once nested on river sandbars throughout much of the country. Dams and navigation projects have destroyed much of its habitat; what remains is often disturbed by off-road vehicles and thoughtless boaters and picnickers. At the **Arkansas River Least Tern Preserve**❖, in the heart of downtown Tulsa, the little birds are strictly protected during their spring and summer nesting period. (Least terns winter from Mexico to northern South America.) They're easily seen from spots within Tulsa's River Parks and from a pedestrian bridge at 31st Street.

Sequoyah National Wildlife Refuge❖, just south of Interstate 40 at Vian, is one of Oklahoma's premier birding spots. Its 20,800 acres on the west end of Robert S. Kerr Lake include open water, bottomland forest, and ponds. The refuge is known for its wintering population of bald eagles; dozens of the big raptors may be present on an average

ABOVE: *Built by folding and faulting, the Ouachita Mountains on the Arkansas-Oklahoma border form parallel east-west ridges. The heavily forested Ouachitas rank among the wildest landscapes of the region.*

midwinter day, along with tens of thousands of geese, dabbling ducks, and other waterfowl. White pelicans are commonly found on refuge waters for much of the year; their numbers peak during fall migration.

Most of Sequoyah's birds are typical of eastern woodland and agricultural areas: Tufted titmice and Carolina wrens flit through the woods, common yellowthroats skulk in shrubby areas, and northern orioles sing from cottonwoods near the refuge office. Western and midwestern species present as transients or breeders include Swainson's hawks, roadrunners, western kingbirds, Harris's sparrows, yellow-headed blackbirds, and great-tailed grackles. A six-mile tour road makes wildlife viewing accessible to all visitors, and the Horton's Slough Nature Trail, near the entrance, leads to an oxbow wetland and an observation tower.

SOUTHEAST OKLAHOMA: THE OUACHITAS

Established in 1907, 1.6-million-acre **Ouachita National Forest❖** is the oldest and largest national forest in the southern United States. Although most of the forest is in Arkansas, Oklahoma's 290,000-acre segment includes several areas of recreational and natural-history interest.

118

The Ouachita Mountains were formed by folding and faulting of rock under pressure caused by tectonic movement; their long, low ridges, running east and west, are in effect gigantic wrinkles on the earth's surface. The easiest way to experience a bit of the mountains is to drive the 54-mile **Talimena Scenic Byway,** which winds from Mena, Arkansas, to Talihina, Oklahoma. For most of its length, the roadway follows ridgetops, offering motorists a succession of splendid views of hills densely covered in pine and hardwoods. Curving endlessly up, down, and around on the road, visitors easily understand why a high point at the west end of the drive is called Winding Stair Mountain. A visitor information station on Route 271, seven miles northeast of Talihina, stocks interpretive literature—notably a mile-by-mile guidebook—that can make a trip on the scenic byway more enjoyable.

Three short trails at the **Robert S. Kerr Nature Center and Botanical Area**❖—on the Talimena Scenic Byway 13 miles west of the Arkansas state line—provide signposted information on geology, plants, and wildlife and give travelers with limited time an opportunity to see a bit of the Ouachita woodland.

The more adventurous will enjoy hiking in the **Beech Creek National Scenic and Botanical Area**❖ just eight miles south of the drive as the crow flies, but several miles longer by way of Routes 259 and 63 and bumpy Forest Road 6026. The 7,500-acre scenic area encompasses and protects the watershed of Beech Creek, which enjoys very high water quality. Fine stands of mature beech grow in the stream bottoms; American holly is found here at the periphery of its range. Black walnut and Ozark chinquapin grow on moister north-facing slopes. Individuals of the latter species inevitably become infected with the deadly chestnut blight, but they continue to send up new sprouts. The Rich Mountain salamander, a Ouachita endemic species, appears just north of the Beech Creek area. Cerulean warblers, birds of mature eastern forests that have declined alarmingly in recent years, have been known to nest here.

The 192-mile **Ouachita National Recreation Trail** runs from Talimena State Park to near Little Rock, Arkansas; its 57 westernmost miles are in Oklahoma, paralleling the Talimena Scenic Byway. Short segments are accessible at several points, including Winding Stair Campground. The Ouachita Trail is a good way to explore the 9,371-

119

LEFT: *On a hillside at Beavers Bend Resort Park, gray green lichens subtly complement short-lived purplish spiderwort flowers, which wither and liquefy in the midday heat.*

acre **Upper Kiamichi River Wilderness❖,** a rugged, heavily wooded tract just south of the scenic drive. More than a third of the 12,151-acre **Black Fork Mountain Wilderness❖** is on the Oklahoma side of the state line, but Black Fork Mountain's stunted oak forests and mysterious "rock glaciers" are more easily accessed by way of an old road off Route 270 in Arkansas (see Chapter 5).

Two historical crime notes: An old moonshiners' trail once followed the state line in this area, giving whiskey-runners the chance to elude Arkansas officers by stepping over the line to the west, Oklahoma officials by turning eastward. Twenty miles west, the picnic area called Horse Thief Spring is not at all fancifully named; horse thieves were so active in this area around the turn of the century that outraged citizens in Heavener formed an Anti-Horse-Thief Association, which remained vigilant until World War I.

The **McCurtain County Wilderness Area❖,** 22 miles north of Broken Bow off Route 259, is remarkable in several respects. Although most wilderness areas are federally designated, this 14,087-acre tract within the Ouachita Mountains was set aside as a game preserve by the Oklahoma legislature in 1918 and has been little disturbed since. The area contains the last remaining mature shortleaf pine–oak forest in the country, as well as a population of rare and endangered red-cockaded woodpeckers.

Once a sacred precept in places such as this, fire suppression was believed essential to maintain a protected area's "naturalness." Today, ecologists taking a longer-term view have realized that recurring fires were a key element of the great southern pine woods. Fire suppresses hardwoods, encourages young pines, and creates the open, parklike conditions that the red-cockaded woodpecker needs to survive. The sweet-singing Bachman's sparrow also thrives in such pine-grassland habitat. In the future, controlled burning designed to re-create a truly natural woodland will be part of the management plan in the wilderness area. In the Ouachita National Forest, the same philosophy is being applied to selected tracts.

Visitors can see part of this important area by walking a nature trail eight miles east of Route 259. Along with shortleaf pine, trees include sugar and red maple, sweet gum, dogwood, and various oak and hickory species. The major portion of the wilderness, a rugged tract east of Broken Bow Lake, is accessible only with a permit from the area manager, who can be contacted through the Chamber of Commerce in Broken Bow.

On the Mountain Fork River just south of Broken Bow Lake, off Route 259, **Beavers Bend Resort Park❖** is noteworthy for the diversity of its flora: It contains the greatest number of tree species found in any Oklahoma state park. Bald cypresses (certainly a surprise to those who think of the Sooner State as plains and arid badlands) grow along the river, where barred owls hoot and pileated woodpeckers utter their loud laughing cries as they fly from tree to tree.

Beavers Bend lies in a beautiful setting: Steep-sided ravines lead down to the waters of the Mountain Fork, and tall bluffs tower over the river in several places. The park nature center offers a variety of programs and can provide information about hiking trails in the area. The David L. Boren Trail stretches 24 miles north to Hochatown State Park. For those with less time or energy, an excellent choice is the Cedar Bluff Trail, which leads to a fine vantage point for watching the sunset.

Preservation of bottomland hardwoods was the goal behind the creation of **Little River National Wildlife Refuge❖,** just south of Broken Bow. One of the newer areas in the federal refuge system, Little River provides important wintering habitat for ducks such as mallard, American wigeon, and gadwalls. The 15,000-acre refuge also hosts breeding birds including wood ducks, red-shouldered hawks, red-headed woodpeckers, fish crows, wood thrushes, northern parulas, American redstarts, Swainson's warblers, and Louisiana wa-

terthrushes. On sunny days, map and red-eared turtles bask on logs, and alligators and mud snakes are both found here near the northwestern edge of their ranges. A disjunct population of bird-voiced tree frogs occurs on the refuge, west of their main range. In the spring and summer mating season these little singers, less than two inches long, give a penetrating series of whistles.

SOUTH-CENTRAL OKLAHOMA

McGee Creek Natural Scenic Recreation Area❖, west of Antlers off Route 3/7, is one of southern Oklahoma's finest wild places. Its 8,900 acres, part of **McGee Creek State Park,** are mostly shortleaf pine–oak woodland crisscrossed by pretty streams and rugged canyons. A network of trails allows access for hikers, mountain bikers, and horseback riders, but permits are required, and the number of visitors is limited to preserve the wilderness experience. Stays of up to four days are allowed for backpackers. The natural area borders a "quiet water zone" on McGee Creek and the upper waters of McGee Creek Lake, where gasoline-powered boats are banned to help maintain the peace and quiet that visitors here seek. A one-mile nature trail at the end-of-the-road overlook parking area offers a good brief introduction to this rocky terrain. Ferndale Bog, a special site within the scenic area noted

Swampy places such as this one at Tishomingo National Wildlife Refuge (far left) provide habitat for green herons and prothonotary warblers. Yellow-headed blackbirds (left) are uncommon visitors; painted buntings (above) are abundant nesters.

for its botanical diversity, is an upland bog more typical of places farther north and east.

Diverse flora is also the attraction at the Nature Conservancy's **Boehler Seeps and Sandhills Nature Preserve❖,** south of the small town of Farris on Route 109A (Crystal Road). At no other known site in Oklahoma do bluejack oak sandhills and acid hillside seep natural communities occur together. Here, bluejack oak, a scrubby tree that prefers dry soil, grows near small-headed pipewort, a tiny, extremely rare wildflower that requires moist conditions. Some pipeworts are commonly known as hatpins for their buttonlike flower heads atop bare stalks; this species is similar in appearance but grows only two to four inches tall. Twenty-six plants rare in Oklahoma are found at Boehler Seeps. While enjoying the wildflowers and other flora, remember that pygmy rattlesnakes, copperheads, and cottonmouths also find this habitat attractive.

Tishomingo National Wildlife Refuge❖, just outside the town of the same name via Refuge Road, is one of south-central Oklahoma's best wildlife-viewing areas. Like many federal refuges, it's primarily managed for waterfowl, though numerous other species benefit from the protected habitat as well. Bald eagles perch in trees along the shoreline of Lake Texoma in winter, and migrant gulls and white peli-

123

cans sometimes assemble by the thousands. Woods, fields, and willow-lined sloughs attract a variety of wildlife; prothonotary warblers sing *"sweet-sweet-sweet"* in swampy places, and white-tailed deer bound across fields where grain is raised for wintering geese and ducks. Indigo buntings, found in scrubby areas, are sometimes confused with eastern bluebirds: Buntings lack the chestnut throats and chests of bluebirds, which are members of the thrush family.

Two of America's most beautiful birds, the scissor-tailed flycatcher and the painted bunting, are common breeders at Tishomingo. Large flocks of the former species, Oklahoma's state bird, often gather in fall before flying south to winter in Mexico and Central America. A field full of these gray-and-pink birds, trailing their long, fluttering tails, is an entrancing sight.

"Mountains are earth's undecaying monuments," the novelist Nathaniel Hawthorne wrote. Within the time frame of human history, he was right. That geologic forces operate under different rules is attested by the Arbuckle Mountains, thought to have once been comparable to today's Rockies. Over the eons the Arbuckles have been worn down to much less monumental size, evidence of the unrelenting power of erosion.

Chickasaw National Recreation Area❖ is in the northeastern foothills of the Arbuckles, which rise north of Ardmore. Some of the mountains' variegated geology is apparent at Bromide Hill, south of the town of Sulphur, where sandstone, shale, and conglomerates are exposed in deposits up to 270 million years old. Nearby is a more animated attraction: a small herd of bison, visible from a trail just west of Route 177. Although much of the recreation area surrounds a lake appealing mostly to boaters and water-skiers, the northern Travertine District contains fine nature trails winding alongside pretty Travertine Creek, which along its path leaps over several small waterfalls, including one grandly called Little Niagara.

Trails through the oak-hickory woods east of the nature center (built over the creek) are the quietest and most likely to offer wildlife

RIGHT: *Travertine Creek, in the Chickasaw National Recreation Area, flows through a spring forest of oak, hickory, pecan, and sycamore.*
OVERLEAF: *The rugged ridges of the Wichita Mountains are part of the exposed and eroded crown of a vast underground mass of granite.*

sightings. The main trail here leads to Antelope and Buffalo springs, two freshwater springs. A few of the many mineral springs whose purported medicinal qualities made Sulphur a turn-of-the-century spa to rival Hot Springs, Arkansas, 220 miles to the east, are still flowing. Six trains a day once brought guests to bathhouses and fancy resort hotels in Sulphur, but little trace of that bygone era of "taking the waters" remains today.

SOUTHWEST OKLAHOMA: WICHITA MOUNTAINS

No matter how many times one has seen bison depicted in movies or books, the presence of a 2,000-pound male, standing six feet high at his massive shoulder hump, on the roadway at a distance of a few yards is an awesome experience. It is, literally, enough to stop traffic—at least anything short of a well-armored tank. Such encounters are common occurrences at **Wichita Mountains National Wildlife Refuge❖,** northwest of Lawton off Route 49 west, one of the country's first and most famous refuges. The herd of bison (less accurately called buffalo) here dates back to restocking efforts shortly after the turn of the century, when the millions of animals that once roamed the plains had been so reduced in number that extinction was a real possibility. Today, not only bison but elk (also reintroduced after the native subspecies was wiped out by hunting) and Texas longhorn cattle live and prosper among the weather-worn granite outcrops of the Wichita Mountains.

Although big mammals get most of the attention, the refuge is much more than a drive-through zoo. Hiking trails offer access to rugged mountains, scrub-oak woodland, and grassland. Backcountry camping is allowed, with a permit, in the 5,000-acre **Charons Garden Wilderness Area❖.**

In the Wichita Mountains, eastern travelers truly begin to feel the transition to the West: eastern bluebirds breed here, but a few mountain bluebirds winter; Carolina wrens of the East nest in wooded and brushy places, while the West's canyon wrens sing their haunting, descending song from granite slopes. Rufous-crowned sparrows, a southwestern specialty, also nest in the refuge's rocky hills.

At the refuge's prairie-dog town, patient visitors may glimpse life within the little mammals' "pigmy republic," as the writer Washington Irving called it. Irving toured what was then Indian Territory in the

ABOVE: *Wichita Mountains National Wildlife Refuge is home not only to bison but to herds of elk and Texas longhorn cattle. Today's thriving bison herd dates to 1907, when 15 animals were reintroduced into the refuge.*

early nineteenth century, writing in his journal that prairie dogs were "of a sprightly mercurial nature; quick, sensitive, and somewhat petulant." Their yelps, sounding like those of "very young puppies," caused them to be named dogs by early explorers, although they are squirrel-like rodents, not canines.

Quartz Mountain State Resort Park❖, 17 miles north of Altus off Route 6, ranks among Oklahoma's most scenic areas. The park borders a 6,700-acre lake created by a dam on the North Fork of the Red River; abundant water in a generally arid region fosters a great diversity of plant and animal life. Located in an outlying range of the Wichita Mountains, the park surrounds hills of ancient reddish granite that rise starkly and steeply from the plains, from a distance appearing higher than they really are. Rugged slopes are dotted with oak woods amid jumbles of massive boulders. Although live oaks are generally evergreen (hence their name), the ones found here (among the northernmost in the state) sometimes drop their leaves in hard winters. Cottonwoods and willows grow in wet areas, and western mesquite and eastern pecan (near the edge of its range) are found here as well. Both the Oklahoma state tree, the redbud, and the state wildflower, the Indian blanket or gaillardia, grow in the park.

The New Horizon Trail up Quartz Mountain is worth walking not only for the chance to see songbirds and other wildlife, but for the fine vistas along the way. Hikers may find a collared lizard (the state reptile) sunning itself on a rock. How this greenish, big-headed, aggressive reptile got the folk name "mountain boomer" is a mystery be-

129

cause it makes no sound. When in a hurry it sometimes rises up and runs on its hind legs like a tiny tyrannosaur.

CENTRAL OKLAHOMA: GRASSLANDS AND GYPSUM HILLS

The U.S. Forest Service's **Black Kettle National Grassland❖**, near Cheyenne off Route 283, may be of more historical than natural-history interest. Named for a Cheyenne chief killed in a controversial 1868 raid by Colonel George Armstrong Custer, the grassland comprises scattered tracts of former dust-bowl lands, left denuded by agricultural practices in the 1930s. Contouring, reseeding, and installing dams, fences, wells, and windmills helped reclaim abused prairie, and today these revegetated grasslands at the edge of the High Plains are primarily used for cattle grazing and as wildlife habitat. A drive through the area may turn up white-tailed deer, wild turkeys, black-tailed jackrabbits, and in summer Mississippi kites, graceful hawks that feed mostly on insects.

Varied habitats host a wide range of species at **Washita National Wildlife Refuge❖**, at the northern end of Foss Lake northwest of Clinton off Route 33. Grasslands, croplands, woods, mudflats, shallow marshes, and open water are all found here, although access points are more limited than at many other refuges. From observation areas along the lakeshore, large rafts of wintering ducks can sometimes be seen, including dabblers such as mallard, gadwalls, pintail, green-winged teal, and wigeon, and divers such as ring-necked ducks, common goldeneyes, buffleheads, and both hooded and common mergansers. Geese (mostly Canadas, though white-fronted and snow appear as well) graze in fields, and in spring and fall sandhill cranes fill the air with their bugling cries.

Badgers, coyotes, and bobcat hunt small prey throughout the refuge, but they're seen mostly by chance. Spotted and striped skunks are common, as is their deadly enemy, the great horned owl. This powerful nocturnal predator seems not to mind skunks' chemical defense spray and feeds on them so often that nearly every fresh owl specimen—a

LEFT: *Steep-sided Red Rock Canyon was used as a shelter and winter camp by Plains Indians. Modern campers can pitch their tents beneath high bluffs of soft red sandstone laid down some 200 million years ago.*

131

LEFT: *Male greater prairie chickens inflate their colorful neck sacs, give a hooting call, and "dance" to attract females in the spring mating season.*
RIGHT: *Prairies have evolved to survive frequent fires. Here native grasses with deep root systems sprout under charred trees at the Tallgrass Prairie Preserve.*

car-killed bird by the roadside, for instance—has at least a faint skunky aroma clinging to its feathers.

Red Rock Canyon State Park❖, near Hinton off Route 281, is a prairie oasis. A spring-fed stream flows between steep canyon walls of soft sandstone, creating within the arid surroundings a wetter, cooler microclimate where moisture-loving sugar maples grow 200 miles west of their main range. Crowded with picnic sites and camping areas, the small park (310 acres) could hardly be called wild, but it's worth a visit for its striking beauty.

A few miles north of Watonga, via Route 8A off Route 8, **Roman Nose State Park❖** is set in a wooded canyon between gypsum hills, a terrain sometimes called the gypsum breaks. Whitish gypsum, visible in outcrops atop the hills, was deposited as an inland sea evaporated more than 200 million years ago. In debating whether oceanic evaporation alone can explain the thick layers of the material found in the region, geologists speculate about possible causes of an unusual concentration of gypsum-forming minerals in the seawater.

Human activity here long predates today's picnickers, campers, and golfers. Cheyenne and Arapaho made winter encampments in this protected spot, escaping the bitterly cold winds of the plains farther north. (The park's name honors Henry Roman Nose, a chief of the Southern Cheyenne at the turn of the century.)

A nature trail near the park lodge passes through bottomland woods of cottonwood, American elm, pecan, redbud, hackberry, and chinquapin and bur oaks. Cardinals, red-eyed vireos, great crested flycatchers, and northern orioles breed here; rufous-crowned sparrows and Bewick's wrens are found in rocky areas with scrubbier vegetation. A pair of small lakes at the north end of the park add to the variety of resident flora and fauna by providing riparian habitat.

Two fine natural areas preserve a bit of wildlife within the sprawl-

ing Oklahoma City metropolis. The **Martin Park Nature Center**❖ in the northwestern part of the city has a series of hiking trails through woodlands, as well as a colony of black-tailed prairie dogs easily studied from an observation platform. Eighteen miles south of Oklahoma City in Norman, the **George Miksch Sutton Urban Wilderness Park**❖, named for the renowned ornithologist and artist who taught at the university in this town, includes mixed forest, grassland, marshes, and ponds especially good for birding.

NORTHERN OKLAHOMA: TALLGRASS PRAIRIE AND HIGH PLAINS

When European settlers came to America, a belt of tallgrass prairie covered 142 million acres across the middle of the continent, from the Gulf of Mexico into what is now Canada. Its uniform aspect was deceiving; in fact it was a complex and highly productive ecosystem maintained by the interplay of natural forces. One force was grazing by bison, which roamed the prairies in such numbers that Native American tribes built whole lifestyles around them, and early explorers could hardly find words to describe the spectacle of a herd on the move. Fire, too, played a part as it regularly roared across the land, suppressing woody vegetation but not harming prairie grasses, which store their vital living parts safely underground, ready to send up green sprouts with the next spring.

The expanding United States destroyed the great bison herds, partly because killing the animals provided food and "sport" and partly because eliminating them was a way to destroy the Plains Indians too. Settlers turned the prairie into wheat fields and cornfields and pastures and fought fires whenever they could. Increasingly, tallgrass prairie came to exist only in scattered patches too small to be anything more than reminders of what had been lost—nonworking parts of a once-great machine. Many believe that of all the country's major ecosystems, tallgrass prairie is the most endangered.

Because such remnants are so rare, the Nature Conservancy's **Tallgrass Prairie Preserve❖**—36,000 acres in northeastern Oklahoma north of Pawhuska acquired in 1989—is truly one of America's most important natural areas. Once again, bison will graze an expansive tract of rolling prairie; 300 animals were reintroduced here in 1993, and preserve managers hope to increase the herd to 2,000. Once again, fire will regularly blacken the earth, returning nutrients to the soil and encouraging the dominant prairie grasses: big bluestem, little bluestem, switchgrass, and Indiangrass. After a wet spring, big bluestem can grow well above head high at its maximum height in late summer. The muted colors of the grasses are brightened by a rainbow of wildflowers: blazing star, gentians, wild indigo, coneflowers, milkweeds, prairie clovers, sunflowers, wild hyacinths, and many more.

A host of creatures less conspicuous than the ponderous bison live on these grasslands. With its shovel-like front legs, the bizarre-looking prairie mole cricket digs a burrow in the earth, using the hole as a resonator to amplify its "song" and attract females more effectively. Birds from red-tailed hawks to diminutive dickcissels, finches that resemble miniature meadowlarks, breed on the preserve, and both grasshopper and lark sparrows perch on fence wires in summer. Hard to see for much of the year, greater prairie chickens dance and "boom" in springtime mating rituals at regular display sites called leks; their stomping movements inspired some Native American dances. Visitors to the preserve may encounter white-tailed deer, badgers, coyotes, or ornate box turtles.

ABOVE LEFT: *The aptly named rainbow grasshopper (here on an acacia) is a common resident of the western plains.*

ABOVE RIGHT: *Scrubby woods and old fields are prime habitat for the indigo bunting; males often sing from conspicuous spots.*

LEFT: *The prehistoric-looking armadillo has poor vision but an excellent sense of smell. Females give birth to quadruplets, all of the same sex.*

BELOW: *Often seen basking on floating logs, the red-eared turtle frequents quiet streams and favors muddy shores.*

A trip along the preserve drive is one way to see the tallgrass prairie. Another is to walk the nature trail near headquarters. One- and two-mile loops pass through woodland and prairie and alongside Sand Creek, a perennial stream that is the preserve's main watercourse. At present, bison are most likely to be seen from the road west of the headquarters.

Fresh from the forests of the East, early pioneers crossing the vast grasslands often found the landscape unsettling. Many wrote of the overwhelming solitude they felt at seeing nothing but grass and sky; others frankly loathed what they considered a barren wasteland. Today, the same scenes are likely to evoke very different emotions— but the overriding point is that they are still there. The Tallgrass Prairie Preserve gives us all a chance to experience an American panorama that could easily have disappeared forever.

Contrasted with the thickly vegetated tallgrass prairie, the state's salt plains, in north-central Oklahoma north of Jet, could belong to a different planet: thousands of acres of nearly featureless salt flats that seem on the surface as inhospitable as Mars. A curious phenomenon, in the midst of seemingly endless cropland and pastures, these flats look from a distance like a calm body of water and up close like a gigantic snow-covered parking lot. In some places, the only signs of life

The bizarre landscape of the Great Salt Plains (left) stretches across 11,000 acres of north-central Oklahoma; selenite crystals just below the surface attract rock collectors. This seemingly barren expanse provides important habitat for the diminutive snowy plover (above). The white-faced ibis (right) is more likely found on nearby wetlands at Salt Plains National Wildlife Refuge.

are rock hounds probing below the surface for selenite, a type of gypsum that here forms clusters of crystals with a sandy inclusion creating an unusual hourglass pattern.

But first looks can be deceiving. Native Americans once fought over access to these flats, not only for the salt but for the right to hunt the abundant wildlife attracted to the area. Even though the Salt Fork of the Arkansas River is dammed to create 8,890-acre Great Salt Plains Reservoir, the area is still immensely productive. **Salt Plains National Wildlife Refuge❖,** which encompasses most of the lake and surrounding flats and marshes, is one of Oklahoma's best year-round birding spots. Among the highlights are nesting snowy plover, avocets, and least terns; rare sightings of whooping cranes (transients on spring and fall migration) and abundant migrant sandhill cranes and white pelicans; great numbers of migrant shorebirds; large flocks of Franklin's gulls (small black-headed gulls that nest on prairies far from the sea); wintering bald and golden eagles; and large mixed flocks of wintering ducks and geese.

Those willing to look past the big, showy species may find at various times of year such interesting songbirds as Bewick's, sedge, and marsh wrens; Bell's vireos; painted buntings; clay-colored, lark, grasshopper, and Harris's sparrows; and yellow-headed blackbirds.

137

Both eastern and western meadowlarks are found here; although the two species look almost identical, even a beginning birder can quickly learn to tell them apart by song. Sea purslane is one of a number of halophytic (salt-tolerant) plant species found on the flats.

Although the refuge includes widely varied habitats, access points are limited. The place to start is the 1.25-mile Eagle Roost Nature Trail, near the headquarters (2 miles south of Route 11), which traverses woodland, shrubby areas, and marsh and passes a small platform over-looking a bay that sometimes teems with waders, waterfowl, and shore-birds. A shuffling in the leaves beside the trail may announce an armadillo or a small flock of wild turkeys. White-faced ibis, with long decurved bills, stalk their prey in swampy places. The refuge's 2-mile auto-tour route passes through marshy areas where wood ducks breed. An observation tower here may reward spring and fall visitors with a sighting of a whooping crane; geese and ducks winter in great numbers, and herons and varied songbirds are present in summer.

Nesting snowy plover, least terns, and avocets prefer the salt flats but are sensitive to disturbance; their breeding areas should never be closely approached. Refuge personnel can suggest the best places for wildlife viewing, depending on the time of year. The selenite-digging area is across the refuge from the headquarters, a few miles east of Route 8. Digging is allowed from April through mid-October.

Little Sahara State Park❖, just south of Waynoka off Route 281, lives up to its name: Hundreds of acres of sand dunes up to 75 feet high give the park a decidedly desertlike aspect. The dunes, formed of sand deposited by a river during the Pleistocene and blown north by thousands of years of prevailing winds, are one of Oklahoma's most interesting geologic features. Unfortunately for those who wish to explore the area's natural history, the park—described as one of the country's top three destinations for off-road-vehicle enthusiasts—literally swarms with dune buggies and other ORVs day and night.

The atmosphere is much quieter at **Alabaster Caverns State Park❖,** about 15 miles northwest off Route 50 near Freedom, one of the largest gypsum caves in the world (and the largest open to the

Left: *Relentless erosion has carved countless canyons in the gypsum plains near Alabaster Caverns State Park. Seasonal streams in these low areas supply the moisture needed by cottonwoods and other trees.*

public). The caverns were formed in the late Pleistocene by water slowly eroding cracks in soft gypsum deposits. Visitors walk a little less than three quarters of a mile through passageways glittering with selenite, a crystalline form of gypsum, and in many places the white alabaster walls show the grooving and smoothing effects of flowing water—a process continuing today in some parts of the cave. The erodible nature of gypsum was vividly demonstrated in 1992 when an aboveground natural bridge, once a prominent attraction in the park, collapsed, a victim of rain, wind, and the expansive force of freezing water.

Travelers in western Oklahoma who show signs of sylvan withdrawal because of the scarcity of trees should head for **Boiling Springs State Park❖,** just outside Woodward off Route 34C. Here they find not patchy oak-juniper scrub but real woods: cottonwood, elm, ash, locust, hackberry, oak, and willow in a dense riparian forest along the North Canadian River. Orioles whistle, yellow-billed cuckoos give their strange *"cow-cow-cow"* call, red-bellied woodpeckers hammer, and Mississippi kites soar overhead at this shady refuge, where wild turkeys and white-tailed deer are resident and often seen. The park was named for springs that pass through underlying limestone and surface in river sands, swirling tiny rock particles and resembling boiling steam.

THE PANHANDLE

The route now turns westward into the Panhandle—and into the short-grass High Plains, where the terrain clearly belongs to the true

West. The landscape here is not conventionally scenic, though many views convey a certain majesty. From the top of a rise, the panorama encompasses an impressive sweep of rolling grassland, marked with scrawled lines of trees along streambeds. On a blue-sky day, when puffy clouds are scattered from horizon to horizon, the world can seem an awfully big place.

At **Beaver River Wildlife Management Area❖,** 11 miles west of Beaver, such western species as mule deer and black-billed magpies join the fauna. Although this area is off the beaten track (visitors should check in advance to be sure of access), it can be highly productive for wildlife observation. Pheasants and wild turkeys are found here, and porcupines live in wooded areas along watercourses. At the prairie-dog town, a patient watcher may glimpse a long-legged, fierce-eyed burrowing owl, a diurnal owl that lives in abandoned burrows and is often seen comically bobbing up and down. Of greatest interest to birders is a blind from which the mating dance of the increasingly scarce lesser prairie chicken can be seen; the birds' hollow "booming" calls can be heard from the courtship grounds in spring.

OVERLEAF: *Hard volcanic basalt caps the tableland of Black Mesa in extreme northwestern Oklahoma. Softer underlying sandstone erodes into steep slopes, connecting the mesa with the short-grass prairie below.*

LEFT: *The Western Hemisphere's swiftest land animal, the pronghorn can hit 70 mph in short bursts. Once commonly called "antelope," this plains runner is no kin to true Old World antelope.*
RIGHT: *The adaptable coyote resists human persecution, remaining common in a wide variety of habitats. Its diet ranges from fruit to rabbits to insects.*

Although most of the **Rita Blanca National Grassland❖** is in Texas (see Chapter 2), nearly 16,000 acres of reclaimed dust bowl lands, now used for grazing, are scattered across the Panhandle south of Boise City. Recreational opportunities here are limited, but a drive along the back roads south of Route 56/64 might turn up pronghorn (often wrongly called antelope), swift foxes, long-billed curlews, or mountain plover. The latter two are shorebirds that prefer to nest in these grasslands, far from any ocean shore.

One of the state's most fascinating natural areas is also one of the most remote: **Black Mesa Nature Preserve❖** rises in the extreme northwestern corner of the Panhandle, near the point where Oklahoma, Colorado, and New Mexico meet. Kenton, the closest town, is less than three miles from New Mexico and is the only place in the state where clocks are set on Rocky Mountain time. The flat-topped mesa is topped by what remains of the lava flow from a now-extinct volcano that erupted between 30 and 20 million years ago. Formed of sandstone capped with more erosion-resistant basalt, the plateau extends 45 miles through New Mexico to its source in Colorado; the section in Oklahoma is the easternmost tip of the flow.

Biologically speaking, Black Mesa may also be considered the easternmost extension of the Rocky Mountains. The mesa, its rocky slopes, and nearby areas are home to more than two dozen plants and animals rare in Oklahoma. Pinyon and ponderosa pines and Rocky Mountain juniper grow here; golden eagles, Say's phoebes,

Cassin's kingbirds, pinyon jays, common ravens, and canyon towhees are some of the birds that nest locally.

Some 1,600 acres, encompassing much of the mesa top and parts of its talus slopes, are managed jointly by Black Mesa State Park and the Nature Conservancy. Off-road vehicles and cattle grazing are prohibited, allowing the natural short-grass prairie to recover and protecting other natural features. A four-mile trail—beginning off a road that runs north of Route 325 just east of Kenton—leads to a granite monument atop the mesa marking the highest point in the state, 4,973 feet above sea level. Although straightforward, the way to the top can be a rigorous hike, especially on a hot day.

Along with Black Mesa and its wildlife, this isolated corner of Oklahoma is home to other noted attractions. North of the state park, the famous Old Maid rock, named for its prim and proper profile, is a bit of whimsy in eroded stone. The Cimarron Cutoff, a section of the nineteenth-century Santa Fe Trail, crosses Route 325 between Boise City and Kenton. And a creek bed near the nature preserve entrance reveals evidence of travelers that passed through these parts even earlier: dinosaur tracks that may date back close to 200 million years.

ARKANSAS

ARKANSAS:
HIGHLAND FORESTS AND LOWLAND SWAMPS

The first lesson in Arkansas's natural history is an easy one, re-
quiring only an outline map of the state and a little imagination. Picture a line running from the northeast, where the
Missouri Bootheel notches the corner, to the point where
Texas takes a corresponding bite out of the southwest. One quick diagonal stroke divides and defines the Arkansas landscape: To the north of
the line are mountains; to the south, lowlands. This geologic dichotomy
finds a parallel in Arkansas's social history; at times Arkansas has
seemed two different states, one southern and one midwestern. Nothing in nature, however, is truly as uncomplicated as a straight line.
Arkansas's highlands and flatlands are further divided into six natural
divisions, each encompassing many permutations of terrain and vegetation, from prairies to rocky mountaintops to sluggish backwaters of
the Mississippi River.

The Ozark Mountains of the northwest, one of Arkansas's two
major upland areas, are in geologic terms an "eroded plateau" of
sandstone and limestone, the latter formed from the remains of bil-
lions of sea creatures that lived and died here when the land was covered by water. After tectonic forces uplifted the region perhaps 300
million years ago, rivers wore through the rock, creating today's steep-
sided valleys. Caves are common in the easily eroded limestone;

PRECEDING PAGES: *An angler's favorite, the crystalline Little Missouri River
follows a rocky path between forested Ouachita Mountain ridgelines.*
LEFT: *The bald cypress–ringed wetlands at the Big Lake refuge are ancient
remnants of the Great Swamp that once covered northeastern Arkansas.*

traces of Native Americans, including pictographs and rock carvings, are found throughout the area in their former bluff shelters.

In the rugged Ozarks, transportation and communication remained difficult until well into this century. This isolation preserved a traditional mountaineer way of life often caricatured as hillbilly. In the contemporary world of freeways, air travel, and cable television, it survives mostly as a theme for tourism—an important element in regional commerce.

Hardwood forests of oak, hickory, maple, and beech cover much of the Ozarks. (Thomas Nuttall, the famed naturalist and explorer who traveled across Arkansas in 1819 and later became curator of the Harvard Botanical Garden, described the territory as "a vast and trackless wilderness of trees," and today slightly more than half of Arkansas remains wooded.) Although many once-pristine streams have been lost to dams and reservoirs, several beautiful rivers—notably the Buffalo, America's first national river—still flow freely through some of the wildest lands between the Rockies and the Appalachians.

The Ouachita (WASH-ih-taw) Mountains of west-central Arkansas run east-west—an alignment unusual in North America. The tremendous pressure of continental movements more than 200 million years ago resulted in the folding and faulting of long parallel sandstone ridgelines, which weather to sandy soil where shortleaf pine forests thrive. The Ouachitas host several endemic animal species, including rare fish in upland streams and salamanders on moist mountain slopes.

Well before the first European explorers arrived in the Ouachitas, Native Americans were relaxing in the thermal waters of what is now Hot Springs National Park. The supposed healing power of the springs led to their eventual designation as a federal reservation. This region is also the only place in North America where diamonds are scattered across the earth's surface—the glittering consequence of an ancient volcanic eruption.

The Arkansas River valley forms a natural division that separates the Ozarks and Ouachitas, combining features of both highland regions. Coal, once a major economic resource here, reveals locations of ancient peat beds, created from plants that grew in these lowlands eons ago. Several flat-topped, mesalike mountains rise as much as 1,500 feet above the river valley, their sandstone caps having protected them from millennia of erosion. Magazine Mountain, Arkansas's highest peak, is

celebrated for the diversity of life on its summit and slopes.

The sandy soil of southern Arkansas's rolling Gulf Coastal Plain recalls an era when a much more northerly Gulf of Mexico lapped against beaches here. Again, pine forests (including much loblolly) predominate, intensively exploited by timber companies. White-tailed deer, which thrive in cutover areas, are abundant; the endangered red-cockaded woodpecker, which requires old-growth pines, survives in much-reduced numbers.

Eastern Arkansas's Mississippi Alluvial Plain (or Delta) region is part of the Old South of bald cypress trees and meandering flatland rivers. Pioneers cleared almost all the bottomland-hardwood forest that covered this area to plant cotton and later other row crops. The infamous "Great Swamp of Arkansas," a vast tract of annually flooded wetlands, made travel difficult during settlement times but was a paradise for waterfowl, bears, bobcat, and other wildlife. One 1840s visitor wrote that it was "covered by the most wonderful, luxuriant primeval forest one could imagine in all the earth." Although drainage projects and river channelization have largely displaced this ecosystem, Arkansas's remaining bottomland forests are among the nation's most productive and diverse natural areas. The floodplains of the White and Cache rivers, for instance, may well constitute the world's most important wintering area for mallard ducks.

Contained within the Delta is Crowleys Ridge, a long, narrow upland capped with fine wind-deposited sediment called loess. Botanically, this wooded ridge has more in common with the hills of Tennessee than with the rest of Arkansas, supporting several plant species uncommon elsewhere in the state. Native Americans and European pioneers established settlements on Crowleys Ridge, above the swampy surrounding lowlands.

Although Arkansas is the second-smallest state lying entirely west of the Mississippi River (only Hawai'i is smaller), and although its natural resources have sustained abuse as well as use, its mountains, rivers, and forests still offer rewards to those who take the time to explore them.

LEFT: *Autumn arrives in the Ozarks. The mountains' flat tops testify to their origin as an uplifted and eroded plateau; over millions of years, streams have carved deep valleys into the underlying sedimentary rock.*

Beginning in the Ozark Mountains of north-central Arkansas, the route for this chapter follows a generally counterclockwise path, concluding in the Mississippi River lowlands of the northeast.

THE OZARKS AND THE ARKANSAS RIVER VALLEY

Although beginning an Arkansas tour underground might seem strange, **Blanchard Springs Caverns❖,** in the north-central section of the state 15 miles north of the picturesque village of Mountain View via Route 87 to Route 14W, rewards the subterranean visitor with one of America's most beautiful cave systems. Then, too, it's instructive to see the venerable Ozark Mountains from the inside. Water built them (by means of the myriad sea creatures whose bodies formed their soft limestone bedrock 350 million years ago), water shaped them (rivers cut valleys into the Ozark Plateau), and in places like Blanchard Springs water has hollowed out their core.

Cavities formed by groundwater seepage grew larger over the millennia until water began to flow through a fracture system in the bedrock beneath the hillside here. When the water table dropped, the old stream course remained as a long convoluted cave. Continuing seepage carried minerals (mostly calcium carbonate, the basic material of limestone) into the cave, creating stalactites, stalagmites, flowstones, "soda straws," and other speleothems.

Blanchard Springs Caverns remains a "living" cave whose speleothems are still growing—although at a pace too slow to be described even as glacial. Its rarely seen animal dwellers include cave crickets, blind salamanders, and endangered Indiana and gray

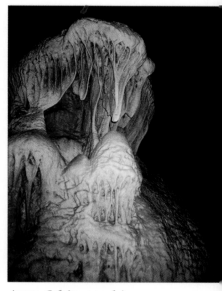

ABOVE: *Calcite, or calcium carbonate, crystals glitter on a flowstone shape called Dragon's Head in Blanchard Springs Caverns.*

LEFT: *The underground river that formed (and still shapes) the caverns pours out of the rocky mountainside at Blanchard Springs.*

OVERLEAF: *Layers of an ancient ocean floor can be clearly seen in the bluffs rising above the Ozark's Buffalo River, one of America's finest canoe streams.*

bats. The caverns are well managed and protected by the U.S. Forest Service, which offers two different tours. The Dripstone Trail, open all year, passes through the older, more ornately decorated part of the caverns. The longer, more strenuous (700 stair steps) Discovery Trail, open only in summer, takes visitors through a deeper, younger cave system, where formations are less abundant but a stream still flows, vividly demonstrating the process of cave creation.

That underground stream gushes from a steep bluff as the eponymous Blanchard Springs, soon joining North Sylamore Creek, a rocky, crystal-clear brook that tempts every warm-weather camper (Forest Service sites are nearby) with a series of fine swimming holes. The Ozarks are blessed with many such rivers, and just west of Blanchard Springs Caverns is the wildest and loveliest of them all.

The first to be so honored, **Buffalo National River❖** received its

LEFT: *Winter hiking along the Buffalo River offers splendid scenery, a spell of solitude, and—perhaps best of all—no ticks, chiggers, or mosquitoes.*
RIGHT: *Once nearly extirpated in Arkansas, the black bear is again a fairly common, although seldom seen, resident.*

designation in 1972 after a long, bitter fight to save it from damming—the fate of too many other once free-flowing Arkansas streams. The National Park Service now administers a protected corridor 135 miles long, encompassing some of the most beautiful riverside terrain anywhere on the continent. The river is easily accessible from Routes 65, 14, 7, and 74.

In spring, experienced canoeists and kayakers ride the surging white water of the upper Buffalo along the 23 miles from Ponca to Pruitt. During the peak season, from mid-March through May, plan to float this section on a weekday if possible, because weekend crowds do nothing to enhance the river experience. A popular trip for boaters is the short hike to the ribbon waterfall at Hemmed-in Hollow; dropping 173 feet, it's the highest between the Appalachians and the Rockies.

From Pruitt downstream to its confluence with the White River, the Buffalo becomes progressively tamer. Even beginning floaters can enjoy a trip down this placid and beautiful stretch, which poses only a few gentle rapids to negotiate. The lower river is floatable even in summertime, when the upper portion is usually too low for boats. Concessioners in Ponca, Jasper, and Silver Hill rent canoes and offer shuttle services for trips of a few hours or several days.

Although shooting rapids in spring high water is exhilarating, a lazy approach to the Buffalo offers many rewards: drifting beneath nearly 500-foot limestone bluffs (perhaps contemplating the millions of years necessary for these horizontal layers to accumulate on the ocean's floor), stopping on a gravel bar for lunch and a swim, or just lying back in the sun and listening to birdsongs. Red-shouldered hawks,

ABOVE: *Panoramas of nearly unbroken woodland abound in northwestern Arkansas, as in this view from the Scenic 7 Byway in the Ozark National Forest. Oaks and hickories predominate in the mostly hardwood forest.*

yellow-billed cuckoos, wood thrushes, northern parulas, prothonotary warblers, and Louisiana waterthrushes are among the breeding species here. Anglers drop lines for smallmouth bass, sought-after fish not nearly as common as they once were in Arkansas. Smallmouth need clear, unpolluted streams to survive, and the pristine Buffalo provides important habitat.

The Park Service offers several developed campgrounds, but overnighting on the Buffalo traditionally means making camp on one of the dozens of gravel bars lining the river. These sites provide a great wilderness experience, but plan an escape route and keep alert—rain upstream can cause the river to rise quickly.

Eventually a system of hiking trails will run nearly the length of Buffalo National River; today, trails at Ponca, Pruitt, Hemmed-in Hollow, Lost Valley, and Buffalo Point reach some of the park's most interesting areas. The latter two lead to Native American bluff shelters. Along the river, abundant wildflowers reward hikers in spring. Ozark witch hazel displays its yellow blooms as early as January; hepatica, bloodroot, green dragon, jack-in-the-pulpit, shooting star, columbine, bellwort, and many others follow, lending color to the Buffalo River country.

Wildflowers are also attractions at **Baker Prairie Natural Area❖,** a 71-acre preserve near Route 65 in Harrison, 15 miles north of the Buffalo River. The adventurer Henry Rowe Schoolcraft, who traversed this area about 1820, wrote: "The prairies . . . are the most extensive, rich, and beautiful, of any which I have ever seen west of the Mississippi River." Although little of the original Osage prairie remains today, Baker Prairie suggests how this tallgrass habitat looked in presettlement times. Royal catchfly and Ozark least trillium are two rare wildflowers found here; both bloom in spring, as does Indian paintbrush, which blankets the area with its orange-red blossoms. Other special species at Baker are grasshopper sparrows, uncommon breeders in Arkansas, and prairie mole crickets, bizarre-looking insects that build burrows specially shaped to amplify their mating calls.

South of Buffalo National River is the vast **Ozark National Forest❖,** sprawling across more than a million acres of rugged mountains, steep valleys, and rocky streams. Many visitors make their first acquaintance with the area by driving the famed **Scenic 7 Byway,** which follows Route 7 south from Harrison and enjoys a long history of publicity as one of the most picturesque roads in America. Overlooks along the highway provide a lesson in Ozarks topography; the flat-topped mountains in the distance graphically demonstrate their ancient origin as an uplifted and eroded plateau.

The Sylamore Scenic Byway (near Blanchard Springs Caverns), the Ozark Highlands Byway (Route 21 north of Clarksville), and the Pig Trail Scenic Byway (an astonishingly convoluted journey along Route 23 north of Ozark) are three other good roads for sightseeing, but no one should visit the Ozark National Forest by car alone. Streams such as the Mulberry River, Big Piney Creek, and Illinois Bayou challenge canoeists with spring and fall white water. A variety of hiking trails, some shorter than a mile, allow the traveler to abandon civilization and, if only temporarily, feel the solitude that's part of the Ozarks' magnetism.

The ultimate northwest Arkansas trek is the **Ozark Highlands Trail,** which begins at Lake Fort Smith State Park near Mountainburg and traverses 160 miles of woods and hills to the Buffalo River east of Jasper. Only well-prepared backpackers should attempt long-distance walks along this often-isolated trail; precautions must include protecting food and gear from black bears, which, although not common, are making a

161

comeback in the Ozarks. Many short sections of the trail make fine day hikes. At **White Rock Mountain,** a Forest Service area north of Ozark offering campsites and rustic cabins at the summit, a spur trail leads down to pretty Shores Lake. Circling the mountaintop, the Rim Trail affords views unmatched in Arkansas.

Near the eastern terminus of the Ozark Highlands Trail, about 20 miles southwest of Marshall, is 11,822-acre **Richland Creek Wilderness,** one of five wilderness areas in the national forest totaling 65,000 acres. A short trail from the adjoining primitive campsite heads upstream to Twin Falls, where the perfection of the swimming hole is rivaled by the wild beauty of the surroundings. Because the forests of the Ozarks (indeed, of nearly every corner of Arkansas) have been cut over through the years, almost no real virgin woods exist. As time passes, though, wilderness areas like Richland Creek will rival the magnificent landscape that existed when the Osage hunted here, before the sound of axes and chain saws broke the silence of the valleys.

Many of the natural attractions of northwestern Arkansas are exemplified south of Fayetteville (reached via Route 71 to 170) at **Devils Den State Park❖** off Route 74 near Winslow, just west of the Ozark National Forest. Named for a cave formed by slippage of huge sandstone blocks, the park nestles in a valley of the Boston Mountains, the most southerly division of the Ozarks. Among its 22 miles of hiking trails is one along Lee Creek, where fossils of ancient sea creatures are abundant in streamside rocks. Another follows a portion of the Butterfield Overland Mail stage line. Devils Den is excellent for birds; several species of warblers breed in the park, and roadrunners, here near the northern limit of their range, are often seen—where else?—along the road.

South of the Arkansas River, just off Route 217 north of Charleston, 564-acre **Cherokee Prairie Natural Area❖** is the largest tract of un-

plowed tallgrass prairie in Arkansas. Here Indiangrass, switchgrass, and big and little bluestem wave in the summer wind; abundant wildflowers include pale-purple coneflowers, purple prairie clover, and the uncommon narrow-leaved puccoon. Lucky visitors may glimpse a beautifully marked ornate box turtle, threatened in Arkansas by loss of its grassland habitat and unscrupulous collectors. Scattered across the tract are many "prairie pimples," low mounds whose origin remains the subject of conflicting theories. Some believe they mark places where soil accumulated beneath scattered shrubs thousands of years ago, when Arkansas had a dry, desertlike climate.

The physical significance of **Magazine Mountain,** south of Paris about 30 miles southeast of Cherokee Prairie, is apparent to all: At 2,753 feet the highest peak in Arkansas, it dominates the surrounding Arkansas River valley. Scientists, however, see perhaps the state's most important home for a variety of rare plants and animals, ranging from an amphipod (a tiny crustacean) found nowhere else in the world to the rare maple-leaved oak. Protected from summer heat by the towering bluffs along Magazine's north face, hay-scented fern and Appalachian woodsia are two ferns found here at the extreme southwestern limit of their ranges, possibly relict species from a time when Arkansas's climate was cooler than at present. Conversely, the rufous-crowned sparrow, a bird of the hot, dry Southwest, lives in very small numbers on Magazine's south side, near the northeastern extreme of its range.

Summer campers at the Forest Service's Cameron Bluff site on Magazine are serenaded each morning by ovenbirds and gorgeous scarlet tanagers, both common on the mountain. A short trail leads to the summit, and another to Cove Lake, 11 miles away. The latter is a pleasant hike through mixed woodland—even more appealing if the hiker has arranged for a ride, rather than a long trudge, back up Magazine.

Holla Bend National Wildlife Refuge❖, on the south bank of the Arkansas River south of Russellville via Route 7 to Route 155, is the winter home of thousands of Canada and snow geese and as many as two dozen bald eagles. The birds, easily seen from the refuge's auto-

LEFT: *Rising in the distance over the Arkansas River valley, Petit Jean Mountain is one of several sites in northwestern Arkansas where Native Americans left rock carvings and paintings in shelters on the bluffs.*

ABOVE: *A male wild turkey puffs up in a spring court-ship display. The wary turkey is a match for all but the most patient hunter.*
LEFT: *Thermal waters at Hot Springs National Park create a moist microclimate where ferns and mosses flourish through the year.*

tour route, include in winter ducks (mostly dabblers such as mallard and American wigeon) and hawks (red-tails, northern harriers, American kestrels, and occasionally rarities such as peregrine falcons). Armadillos, white-tailed deer, coyotes, and bobcat are among the mammals commonly seen. Summer visitors to Holla Bend will find scissor-tailed flycatchers, beautifully colorful painted buntings, and perhaps a hen turkey shepherding a flock of young.

The low, flat mountain looming to the east of Holla Bend is Petit Jean Mountain, like Magazine Mountain a monadnock whose sandstone top has protected it from millennia of erosion. In 1933, the craggy beauty of Petit Jean (named for the romantic legend of a young Frenchwoman who followed her explorer-lover to America) caused it to be designated Arkansas's first state park. At **Petit Jean State Park❖**, a trail leads from the park lodge down to steep-sided Cedar Creek Canyon; at its head scenic Cedar Falls drops into a deep natural rock amphitheater. Indian Rock House is a Native American bluff shelter still showing signs of its early inhabitants.

THE OUACHITA MOUNTAINS

Hot Springs National Park❖ takes many visitors by surprise, probably because of expectations raised by the magic term *national park.*

166

By contemporary standards, Hot Springs should be a national monument or perhaps a national historical site; certainly its past merits the latter designation. According to legend, Native American tribes put aside their differences to share the thermal waters here, and the springs' "healing" powers were so highly valued that in 1832 the springs' site became the first reserve ever designated by the federal government for public use. Today, all but a few of the 47 springs have been covered, their flow channeled to bathhouses and hotels where, despite a decline in "taking the baths," thousands still come to soak.

The journey made by all that hot water (nearly a million gallons a day) is as convoluted as the squeezed-together folds in the surrounding Zig Zag range of the Ouachita Mountains. To begin, rainwater sinks into the ground through fractures in chert and novaculite northeast of the springs. Somewhere deep in the earth it meets heated rock and then flows upward through faults in sandstone to surface—4,000 years later—at a temperature of 143 degrees Fahrenheit.

Pleasant trails crisscross this small park (which wraps around a growing city), passing through stands of shortleaf pine up to 250 years old—some of the best mature pine groves in the Ouachitas. Visible along some of the trails are outcroppings of novaculite, which Native Americans extracted for stone tools; this valuable commodity was an important trade item, and fine-grained "Arkansas whetstone" is still renowned for sharpening knives. In the realm of scientific minutiae, a primitive blue-green alga (*Phormidium treleasei*) that grows in the open springs is found in only a handful of other places in the world.

The oldest and largest national forest in the South, the 1.6 million-acre **Ouachita National Forest**❖ stretches across the mountains west of Hot Springs into Oklahoma. Portions of this wild and rugged land were seriously considered for national-park status in the 1930s, but politics interfered. Today's traveler has a choice of 33 developed recreation areas, 7 wildernesses, 7 scenic areas, 2 scenic byways, a national recreation area (Winding Stair Mountain, discussed in Chapter 4), and an endless number of rocky creeks and secluded hollows to explore. A national

OVERLEAF: *Although geology and a colorful human past are the park's main attractions, Hot Springs offers scenes of beauty and solitude as well. Here, autumn hardwoods line a rocky Ouachita Mountain creek.*

ABOVE: *Flanking a lichen-encrusted log, fire pinks spangle a glade along the Talimena Scenic Byway. The crimson flowers appear in Arkansas's mountains from April to June.*

RIGHT: *Exposed on a high ridge to winter wind and summer sun, white oaks on Rich Mountain struggle to survive in a hostile environment; full grown, they may stand less than 15 feet tall.*

forest map showing the intersecting maze of logging roads is a necessity for travelers leaving the principal routes through the forest—7, 27, 270, and 8—in search of isolation. Along the back roads, especially early in the morning, watch for wild turkeys, common in the Ouachitas.

Challenging the hardiest adventurer is the 192-mile **Ouachita National Recreation Trail,** beginning at Talimena State Park in Oklahoma and continuing almost to Little Rock, in central Arkansas. Most people tackle only short sections at a time. One of the best segments begins at Lake Sylvia near the trail's eastern terminus (about 30 miles west of Little Rock) and heads westward into the 10,105-acre **Flatside Wilderness Area;** a short spur ascends to the top of Flatside Pinnacle, a rocky outcrop affording long-distance views westward over the Ouachitas.

Southeast of Mena, in western Arkansas, the trail bisecting the 14,433-acre **Caney Creek Wilderness Area** makes a fine overnight hike. A little over nine miles one way, it crosses Caney Creek more than a dozen times as it winds through a typical Ouachita Mountain landscape of pine and mixed hardwood, including stands of beech. Valleys such as this one in the Ouachitas are usually broader than similar areas in the Ozarks because mountains were pushed up around them; Ozark

valleys were eroded down into a flattish plateau by rivers.

Just east of Caney Creek off Route 8, **Little Missouri Falls** is one of Arkansas's most beautiful spots; a short trail leads to a viewpoint above this series of rocky drops. Beginning a few miles below the falls, experienced canoeists and kayakers can float 20 miles of the Little Missouri after spring rains. Part of the national Wild and Scenic River system, the Little Missouri boasts rapids up to class IV in the first eight miles. The adjacent **Albert Pike Recreation Area** makes a good base for floaters.

Following Route 88 west of Mena, **Talimena Scenic Byway** winds 54 miles along Ouachita Mountain ridgetops to Talihina, Oklahoma. Talimena may be less well known than other scenic roads and parkways, but its vistas are as grand and all-encompassing as any in the central United States. After passing exposed rock where folded stratifications demonstrate the tectonic forces that built these ridges, the byway crests along 2,681-foot **Rich Mountain,** a rewarding place for nature study. Moist north-facing slopes are forested with white oak, black walnut, basswood, sugar maple, beech, umbrella magnolia, and Ohio buckeye. The Rich Mountain salamander, which lives in wet places under rocks, logs, and leaves, is endemic to the area. Hooded warblers and scarlet tanagers, both among Arkansas's most beautiful birds, nest here.

Paralleling Rich Mountain to the north lies 7,568-acre **Black Fork Mountain Wilderness❖,** centered on 2,403-foot Black Fork Mountain. On the south side of the summit are several "rock glaciers," or accumulated rock boulder falls, of still-debated origin. The woodland atop the mountain contains examples of stunted forest, where full-grown white oaks rise only 10–15 feet tall, pruned to their dwarf stature by cold winds, ice, and summer droughts. A six-mile trail leaves Route 270 and climbs the eastern end of Black Fork, beginning at a connection with the Ouachita National Recreation Trail.

The 5,200-acre **Cossatot River State Park and Natural Area❖,** about 15 miles south of Mena off Route 246, protects an 11-mile segment of one of America's finest mountain streams—a river of legendary difficulty for canoeists and kayakers. With rapids rated up to class V, the Cossatot—which earned its early French name *casse-tête,* or "skull crusher"—is not a river for the inexperienced or unprepared. The Cossatot would be better known if planning a float trip were easier: After spring rains, the river rises and falls "as quickly as a toilet flushing," according to a local boater.

Even those leery of riding its white water find the Cossatot a beautiful place to visit, with a long list of biologically interesting species. The leopard darter, a globally imperiled fish, lives here, as do many plants of state or national concern, including Ouachita leadplant, Waterfall's sedge, southern lady's-slipper orchid, and Ouachita Mountain twist flower. For most people, though, the main attraction of the Cossatot is the sheer rugged beauty of its rocky rapids, clear water, wooded slopes, and glades. To sit beside the river is a special treat after traversing the heavily logged timber-company land surrounding it.

Another kind of treat awaits lucky visitors to **Crater of Diamonds State Park❖,** off Route 301 south of Murfreesboro, which offers nothing special in the way of scenery, but occasionally makes someone rich. The top of an ancient "pipe" of volcanic material is exposed in a rocky 35-acre field here, and for a small fee, all comers can search the pile and keep whatever they find. Since the field was discovered in 1906, more than 70,000 diamonds have been carried away, including a monster of 40 carats and several over 10 carats.

For those whose interest is geologic rather than mercenary, the diamond-bearing material in the volcanic pipe is called lamproite; it was exposed when the sea receded 50 million years ago after having erupted from the earth long before that. The diamonds, of course, are simply carbon squeezed very tightly for a very, very long time.

Those seeking birds rather than gems flock to **Millwood Lake,** about 15 miles north of Texarkana off Route 32, the best place in Arkansas to see a wide variety of species, especially waterfowl. Loons, herons, egrets, ducks, gulls, and terns are common on the lake at different times of year. One or two pairs of bald eagles, scarce breeders in the state but slowly increasing, nest in tall dead trees in the middle of this 29,500-acre reservoir. A number of rarities have been spotted at Millwood, including wanderers from the north (little, Sabine's, and glaucous gulls, black-legged kittiwakes, and northern wheatears) and the south (wood storks, bridled terns, and Inca doves).

EASTERN ARKANSAS AND CROWLEYS RIDGE

Human activities have changed Arkansas's Gulf Coastal Plain and Mississippi Alluvial Plain natural divisions more than they have the Ozark and Ouachita mountains. The lowlands were easier to clear than the rugged highlands (on the treeless Grand Prairie, no clearing was necessary), and the Mississippi, Arkansas, and White rivers—the highways of pioneer times—encouraged settlement by providing reliable transportation. Although visitors can still find places in the mountains that feel far from civilization, these days eastern Arkansas offers few such opportunities. The area's rich natural heritage has not completely disappeared, but it is scarcer—and greatly valued and protected.

Preserving extensive wetlands where the Ouachita and Saline rivers meet in the southeastern corner of the state, **Felsenthal National Wildlife Refuge❖** (easily accessible from Route 82 about 40 miles east of El Dorado) covers 65,000 acres of bottomland hardwoods and marginally higher loblolly pine–hardwood forest. Spanish moss (not a moss at all, but an epiphyte related to pineapple) reaches its northern limit here along Arkansas's southern border; in places its ghostly form gives Felsenthal a tropical feeling.

The Felsenthal lock and dam allow the refuge to flood large areas of forest in winter, providing habitat for ducks, other waterbirds, and a host of Neotropical migrants. Bald eagles gather in winter too, to sup-

plement their fish diet by scavenging sick and wounded ducks. Although seldom seen, alligators glide through Felsenthal's waterways. The refuge also supports a high population of endangered red-cockaded woodpeckers. Several roost trees are located near Route 82; ask staff members about the best way to see the birds without disturbing them.

Warren Prairie Natural Area❖, bordering Route 8 a few miles southeast of the town of Warren, is one of Arkansas's most unusual habitats. Here the saline soil inhibits but does not completely prevent tree growth, creating a savannalike landscape of grassy openings with scattered patches of low trees and shrubs. Dwarf palmettos, Arkansas's only native palms, are common on the prairie. Of greatest interest to botanists are two special plants: Texas sunnybell, whose white flowers grow on a foot-high stalk, and the extremely rare, extremely obscure geocarpon, about the size of a matchstick.

East of Felsenthal and Warren Prairie, the Mississippi Alluvial Plain begins—a narrow strip along the Mississippi River that widens in northeastern Arkansas. Generally, the land is as flat as a parking lot and in places just as interesting for the naturalist. In parts of southeastern Arkansas cotton is still king, and rice, soybeans, and winter wheat dominate elsewhere. Except for poorly drained bottoms along streams, large tracts have been almost completely deforested.

Lake Chicot State Park❖, just east of Lake Village off Route 144, is situated at the northern end of Arkansas's largest natural lake—actually an old oxbow of the Mississippi, which wandered widely before its modern-day containment by dams and levees. *Chicot* is the French word for stump, and there are plenty of them, but most of Chicot's trees are living bald cypresses, decorated in late summer with thousands of waterbirds that gather here after breeding.

Great, cattle, and snowy egrets; green, great blue, and little blue herons; black-crowned and yellow-crowned night herons; and double-crested cormorants are abundantly present, and such state rarities as white ibis, roseate spoonbills, and wood storks sometimes wander in as well. The best way to see the birds is on barge tours offered by the

---

LEFT: *Bottomlands in Felsenthal National Wildlife Refuge are flooded each winter to create waterfowl habitat. Mallard are abundant here, resting and feeding among bald cypresses, oaks, and sweetgums.*

park, which take visitors to parts of the lake inaccessible by land. The park office can also provide information on driving the tall levees paralleling the Mississippi River. These unusual routes often afford looks at wildlife ranging from hawks and turkeys to coyotes and deer. While driving, check the adjoining "borrow" pits (where earth was excavated, or borrowed, to build the levees) for waterfowl. Pied-billed grebes, rare breeding birds in Arkansas, sometimes nest in these wetlands.

Extending for 90 miles along the lower White River, the **White River National Wildlife Refuge**❖ is one of the South's most important natural areas. The refuge comprises 155,000 acres of mostly bottomland hardwood forest, a habitat that is among the most biologically productive—and most threatened—in America. Once ubiquitous in the southern Mississippi River watershed, this kind of land teemed with mammals, reptiles, amphibians, and songbirds and was home to millions of wintering waterfowl. Now 90 percent of this habitat is gone, its rich alluvial soil used to grow food and fiber.

Together with the Cache River drainage in northeastern Arkansas (where a new national wildlife refuge is being developed), White River was named a Wetland of International Importance in 1990, primarily because of its value as waterfowl habitat. As much as 10 percent of the continent's mallard population may winter in this area, along with

ducks of many other species. The wood duck, making a comeback from low numbers earlier this century, and the beautiful hooded merganser both remain in the refuge in summer to nest. Farmland in and around the refuge provides food for tens of thousands of wintering Canada, snow, and white-fronted geese.

Besides waterfowl, White River is home to bald eagles, which failed to breed in Arkansas for more than 25 years because of loss of habitat, persecution, and toxic pesticides; when they returned in the 1980s, their first nests were here. These remote forests also house a population of black bears although they have been extirpated in the rest of the state. And songbirds live here in abundance, among them good numbers of elusive Swainson's warblers, now uncommon everywhere in their southeastern United States range. Mississippi kites, red-shouldered hawks, wild turkeys, and redheaded woodpeckers are often seen along refuge roads.

White River NWR is not always an easy place to visit because much of the area is flooded and inaccessible in winter and spring. (The muddy White River drops layers of rich silt year after year in the renewing force that makes the land so productive.) Visitors entering by boat should make sure they have a good map, local advice, or a guide—or all three—before penetrating the swampy maze of streams and backwaters.

At Jacks Bay, east of the small town of Tichnor, unpaved but generally good roads lead to a typically wooded portion of the refuge and a primitive campground. A more accessible section is Striplin Woods, a state natural area just south of the White River bridge at Saint Charles. Here, in a breathtakingly majestic

ABOVE: *Its daggerlike bill adapted for spearing unsuspecting prey, the great blue, a swamp resident, is North America's largest heron.*

LEFT: *Confined in its course here by Ozark hills, the White River soon transforms into a sluggish bottomland stream.*

BELOW: *Little blue herons in blue adult plumage are easy to identify, but the all-white immatures are often mistaken for other species.*

woodland on the west bank of the river, huge overcup and willow oaks tower overhead. The lack of trails only makes the area more like the hardwood forests that once stretched nearly unbroken across the South. After the spring floods recede, visitors can follow the road bordering Striplin Woods into the White River floodplain for a better look at this habitat (get a map and seek advice at the refuge office in De-Witt before proceeding).

A swamp of a different kind is featured at **Louisiana Purchase Natural Area❖,** a 35-acre tract off Route 49 about 25 miles west of Helena. In contrast to bottomlands, where water levels rise and fall dramatically, this "headwaters" swamp maintains a fairly constant depth most of the year. A short boardwalk leads into woods harboring nests of lovely, shining-gold prothonotary warblers, typical birds of southern wetlands. Bird-voiced tree frogs, which call like a man whistling for a dog, are found here, as are swamp cottonwoods, whose leaves are larger with rounder tips than those of the common eastern cottonwood.

European settlers entering Arkansas early in the nineteenth century found more than a half-million acres of grassland stretching from the lower Arkansas River to near today's town of Carlisle, on Interstate 40. The Grand Prairie, as it came to be known, was a disjunct part of the tallgrass prairies that covered much of the central United States. Compact clay soil discouraged tree growth, as did the complex root systems of prairie vegetation. Fire regularly sweeping across the area burned saplings but did no permanent harm to grasses.

That same water-retaining clay soil was also perfect for growing rice, today a major crop in eastern Arkansas. Of the original half-million acres, where bison once wallowed and prairie chickens danced, only a few tiny tracts of virgin prairie still exist. Two easily accessible remnants are 40-acre **Roth Prairie Natural Area❖,** just south of Stuttgart off Route 165, and 242-acre **Railroad Prairie Natural Area❖,** a narrow strip bordered by Route 70 and an old railroad right-of-way between Carlisle and De Valls Bluff.

On both preserves big bluestem and other grasses grow as high as eight feet, and the spring and summer display of wildflowers is a botanist's delight. The blooming plants here include creamy long-bracted wild indigo, tuberous grass pink, prairie evening primrose, pale purple coneflower, beardtongue, compass plant, Carolina larkspur, prairie

ABOVE: *At Louisiana Purchase Natural Area, a boardwalk leads into the heart of a "headwaters" swamp, where new leaves of bald cypresses and water tupelos float on dark waters and tint the atmosphere a soft green.*

parsley, and liatris. Sand cherry, a small shrub with white flowers, is a northern species found in Arkansas only on the Railroad Prairie.

The rivers of the south-central United States have not always followed their present-day paths. Within the past two million years, the Arkansas, the Mississippi, and even the Ohio have swept back and forth across what is now eastern Arkansas, scraping away soil and leaving newer deposits of silt. At one time, the Arkansas River ran more directly south from the eastern Ouachita Mountains, the Mississippi flowed down the bed of today's White River, and the Ohio traversed part of northeastern Arkansas.

A narrow strip of land, running from Missouri down into eastern Arkansas, was left relatively untouched in the most recent of these meanderings. Later, in a period of drier climate, this slightly higher strip became a barrier for wind-blown dust, and a thick layer of fine, glacially ground sediment, or loess, accumulated atop it. Thus was formed Crowleys Ridge, a "highland" towering all of 250 feet above the flat bottomlands of the Mississippi Alluvial Plain. Even this small difference, though, makes Crowleys Ridge unique among Arkansas's natural divisions.

At the southern end of Crowleys Ridge, between the towns of Marianna and Helena, **Saint Francis National Forest✧** covers 20,946 acres. By far the smallest of Arkansas's national forests, it offers limited recreational facilities compared with the Ozark and the Ouachita. Camping, swimming, and fishing are allowed at two small man-made lakes, and the 21-mile Saint Francis Scenic Byway traverses the length of the forest. During times of low water, visitors can follow a dirt road through bottomland woods to the west bank of the Mississippi River.

The naturalist who wants to investigate Crowleys Ridge should head to **Village Creek State Park✧,** 13 miles north of Forrest City off Route 284. The park's 7,000 acres encompass a long, wide valley showcasing this singular environment, and interpretative displays at the visitor center provide a good introduction to the area.

The easy Arboretum Trail, which begins almost at the visitor center's front door, and the Big Ben Nature Trail, across the road, are fine short walks. The Military Road Trail, which follows a portion of the first official route between Memphis and Little Rock, is a loop of slightly more than two miles through beautiful woodland, passing alongside Village Creek and returning atop a ridgeline.

In places, especially on the Big Ben trail and along the old Military Road, the easily eroded character of the fine loess is obvious. The old road has been worn so far down that a hiker's head is often below the level of the flanking banks; time and the elements have deeply rutted exposed bluffs.

The forests of Crowleys Ridge may remind eastern travelers of the Appalachians. The tulip tree (also called tulip poplar or yellow poplar, although it is a magnolia), an impressively tall eastern tree that grows naturally nowhere else in Arkansas, is easily identified by its blunt-tipped leaves and pretty tulip-shaped yellow flowers. Butternut (or white walnut), sugar maple, cucumber tree (another magnolia), and beech are other noteworthy trees of the lush woodland that thrives in this rich soil. Less obvious is climbing magnolia vine, another species not found elsewhere in the state.

Only a short distance separates the high ground of Village Creek on Crowleys Ridge from the low, wet woods of **Wapanocca National Wildlife Refuge✧,** a former hunting club that now provides a winter

The ring-necked duck (above left) should probably have been named ring-billed: Its neck mark is seldom seen. Many consider the strikingly colored wood duck (above right) the most beautiful waterfowl in North America.

home for waterfowl in the Mississippi Alluvial Plain. Unlike many similar areas, the refuge is easy to visit because it is only about a mile east of Interstate 55 near Turrell. Just over half the ducks here are mallard, and gadwalls, pintail, blue-winged and green-winged teal, wigeon, shovelers, ring-necked ducks, buffleheads, and ruddy ducks are also common. Colorful wood ducks breed in nest boxes. Canadas are the most abundant geese, accompanied by smaller numbers of snows and white-fronts. A six-mile auto-tour route allows observation of these and other typical species of the bottomlands.

Farther north, at the Missouri border near Blytheville off Route 18, **Big Lake National Wildlife Refuge❖** is a remnant of the "Great Swamp of Arkansas," an enormous expanse of wetlands now mostly destroyed by drainage projects and deforestation. In 1915, President Woodrow Wilson issued an executive order preserving a portion of the threatened ecosystem, which today is part of the 11,038-acre refuge.

Although Big Lake attracts astounding numbers of wintering waterfowl—at times more than a million ducks and geese have been present—the refuge is worth a visit any time of year for its seemingly endless stands of bald cypress. In the northern part of the refuge, an official wilderness area protects 2,600 acres of this habitat. Because Big Lake is mostly open water, the main body of the cypress swamp is hard to see without a boat, but even from a distance the sight is impressive—a fleeting image of the spectacle this land must have presented when Arkansas Territory gained statehood in 1836.

CHAPTER SIX

LOUISIANA:
DIVERSE REWARDS FROM ABUNDANT WETLANDS

To think of natural Louisiana without thinking of water is nearly impossible. The engines of almost all the state's ecosystems run on water, from the Mississippi River—tamed by levees and slightly less mighty than it once was—to the Gulf of Mexico to countless swamps, oxbow lakes, and creeks. In few other states is water so vital to commerce, recreation, and transportation. And in the land of jambalaya and blackened redfish, to ignore the culinary bounty that accompanies all this liquidity is close to a sin.

As the pelican flies, Louisiana's coastline is less than 400 miles, but islands, inlets, deltas, and convoluted bay shores multiply that figure many times over. The state's marshlands, straddling the boundary between land and sea, account for 40 percent of the nation's total; so great is their productivity, and that of the adjacent Gulf, that some years Louisiana provides nearly a fifth of the country's seafood catch. Farther inland, fecund swampland (including the Atchafalaya, the country's largest river-basin swamp) produces a harvest of more than a billion crawfish a year, keeping pots boiling in restaurants and kitchens across Cajun country and on down to New Orleans. Alligators, their population resurgent, and wintering waterfowl are among the most obvious of the myriad creatures that depend on Louisiana wetlands, both salt and fresh, for homes.

PRECEDING PAGES: *Pink azaleas and live oaks hung with Spanish moss arch over a canal at Avery Island, where alligators and nutrias abound.*
LEFT: *Louisiana's coast is a place of constant change: River-borne sediments and gulf currents interact to create and destroy solid ground.*

185

Water, in the form of yearly flooding, creates the rich habitat of the magnificent southern bottomland forest. But because the big timber of the bottoms attracts loggers, and the soil makes excellent farmland, these hardwood forests have disappeared at an ever-accelerating rate over the past century. In Louisiana, patches of remaining bottomland hardwoods are preserved in a growing number of national wildlife refuges, many so new that they have few or no provisions for visitors.

All of Louisiana lies within the Gulf Coastal Plain, but its terrain is more varied than that location implies. In the "Florida Parishes," north of Baton Rouge, loess-capped hills boast the state's highest diversity of vegetation. The rolling lands of the northwest, including the pine-covered Kisatchie Hills, often provide significant relief—even a few genuine canyons. Along the southwestern coastline, low ridges of sand and shell called cheniers support trees and shrubs vital to migratory songbirds. Farther east, the unimaginably great weight of accumulated alluvial sediments has forced up domes of salt from deep in the earth, creating islands of high ground in the marshes.

A fascinating aspect of the Louisiana landscape is the natural levees built by the Mississippi and other large rivers. As they flood and recede, these waterways deposit successive layers of silt adjacent to the main channel, so that land near the river is actually higher than the surrounding countryside. Smaller streams flow away from their larger sources—distributaries rather than tributaries. Many of these side channels are called bayous, from the Choctaw word for creek.

Forebodingly, Louisiana is rapidly losing land along parts of its coastline. The Mississippi, which once regularly changed its outlet to the Gulf (it has had at least five different deltas in the past 6,000 years), is kept from wandering by human-built levees; now the river dumps its fine silt—which once built, renewed, and enriched the coast—over the continental shelf far out at sea. Canals through marshes cause erosion and saltwater intrusion, hastening the loss of the solid shore. As the impact of this loss has grown, both state and federal agencies have given it increasing attention—and with reason. Wetlands loss affects not only wildlife, but people who live along the coast, work in the seafood industry, and enjoy the fruits of one of the most complicated and productive ecosystems in the world.

This chapter's journey through Louisiana begins in the swamps of

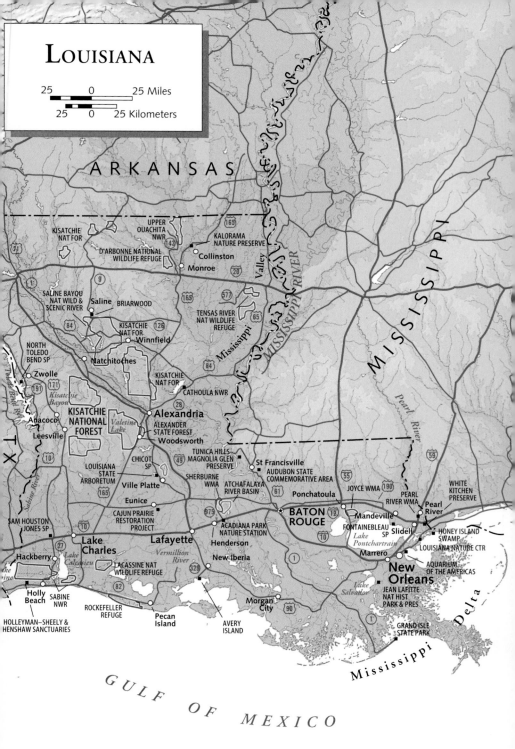

LOUISIANA

25   0   25 Miles

25   0   25 Kilometers

ARKANSAS

MISSISSIPPI

KISATCHIE
NAT FOR

UPPER
OUACHITA
NWR

KALORAMA
NATURE PRESERVE

D'ARBONNE NATIONAL
WILDLIFE REFUGE

Collinston

165

143

Valley

Monroe

20

MISSISSIPPI RIVER

71

SALINE BAYOU
NAT WILD &
SCENIC RIVER

9

Saline   BRIARWOOD

165

577

TENSAS RIVER
NAT WILDLIFE
REFUGE

65

KISATCHIE
NAT FOR

126

84

Winnfield

NORTH
TOLEDO
BEND SP

Natchitoches

Mississippi

84

1

Zwolle

191

171

KISATCHIE
NAT FOR

CATHOULA NWR

Pearl River

MISSISSIPPI

Kisatchie
Bayou

KISATCHIE
NATIONAL
FOREST

Valentine
Lake

Alexandria

28

Anacoco

Leesville

ALEXANDER
STATE FOREST

Woodsworth

10

LOUISIANA
STATE
ARBORETUM

CHICOT
SP

49

TUNICA HILLS
MAGNOLIA GLEN
PRESERVE

St Francisville

AUDUBON STATE
COMMEMORATIVE AREA

55

59

WHITE
KITCHEN
PRESERVE

TX

Sabine River

165

Ville Platte

SHERBURNE
WMA

ATCHAFALAYA
RIVER BASIN

61

Ponchatoula

JOYCE WMA

190

PEARL
RIVER WMA

Eunice

CAJUN PRAIRIE
RESTORATION
PROJECT

975

BATON
ROUGE

12

Mandeville

Pearl
River

SAM HOUSTON
JONES SP

10

Lake
Charles

Lafayette

ACADIANA PARK
NATURE STATION

Henderson

FONTAINEBLEAU
SP

Lake
Pontchartrain

Slidell

HONEY ISLAND
SWAMP

LOUISIANA NATURE CTR

Hackberry

27

Lake
Calcasieu

Vermillion
River

New Iberia

1

Marrero

New
Orleans

AQUARIUM
OF THE AMERICAS

LACASSINE NAT
WILDLIFE REFUGE

325

10

Holly
Beach

SABINE
NWR

82

ROCKEFELLER
REFUGE

Pecan
Island

Morgan
City

90

Lake
Salvador

JEAN LAFITTE
NAT HIST
PARK & PRES

HOLLEYMAN–SHEELY &
HENSHAW SANCTUARIES

AVERY
ISLAND

1

GRAND ISLE
STATE PARK

Mississippi Delta

G U L F   O F   M E X I C O

Mississippi

the southeast and travels westward along the Gulf Coast before heading northeast and then west to explore the prairies, river basins, and pine forests to the north.

SOUTHEAST LOUISIANA: SWAMPS AND MARSHES

The Pearl River, which forms part of the border between Mississippi and Louisiana, is one of the South's great bottomland streams, home to bald eagles and alligators. As it nears the Gulf of Mexico, the Pearl splits into a maze of·channels and backwaters that early explorers called **Honey Island Swamp** for its many "bee trees." Seventy thousand acres of this second-largest swamp in Louisiana (only the Atchafalaya is bigger) are protected in federal, state, and private reserves.

Low-lying, often-inundated terrain makes access to the river floodplain tricky. One option is a mile-long nature trail at **Pearl River Wildlife Management Area❖,** just off Interstate 59 north of the town of Pearl River. As it loops around a small pond, the trail provides a chance to see deer, wild turkeys, forest songbirds, and the typical oaks and hickories of a southern hardwood bottomland. Exploring at a time outside hunting season is advisable.

For a quick peek into the Honey Island habitat, the Nature Conservancy's **White Kitchen Preserve❖** is well worth a visit. A short boardwalk, beginning at a picnic area where Routes 90 and 190 meet east of Slidell, leads through a curtain of Spanish moss into an open marsh full of water lilies, buttonbush, pickerelweed, and two *Sagittaria*-genus water plants called arrowhead and bull-tongue. A bald eagle nest nearby has been in continuous use for several decades. Yellow-crowned night herons and snowy egrets are among several species of waders that search the shallows for fish, frogs, and crustaceans.

The best way for most people to see the Pearl River bottoms is with one of the local commercial boat tours. Dr. Wagner's Honey Island Swamp Tours at Slidell, operated by a biologist with long experience in the region, take visitors on a ride south along duckweed-covered channels through dense tupelo–bald-cypress backwaters to White

---

LEFT: *Before trees leaf out in early spring, tiny green duckweed plants cover the still waters of Honey Island Swamp. This wildlife paradise on the Pearl River is home to black bears, bald eagles, and wading birds.*

Kitchen Preserve. Alligators are common along the way, often allowing a close look. Swamp birds such as wood ducks, swallow-tailed kites, red-shouldered hawks, and prothonotary warblers are sometimes seen, and occasionally a big barred owl—whose "*Who cooks for you, who cooks for you-all?*" call is one of the most evocative sounds of the southern forest—stares down at a passing boat from a tall tree.

Early settlers gave the name *loblolly,* an old English word for a thick stew, to mudholes and other wet places in the woods. Eventually the term was applied to a type of pine abundant throughout the softwood forests of the South. In 1995, a severe infestation of the southern pine beetle destroyed most of these pines at **Fontainebleau State Park❖,** west of the Pearl River off Route 190 near Mandeville. However, water oaks reach impressive size here, and in fall the woods are decorated with the pretty bunched, lavender fruit of French mulberry—which is neither French nor a mulberry and is probably better called by its other common name, American beautyberry. Birding is excellent in the spring, and the park's shoreline along huge Lake Pontchartrain often affords sightings of wintering loons, grebes, ducks, gulls, and other waterbirds.

Hurried travelers seeking a glimpse of a Louisiana swamp should exit Interstate 55 just south of Ponchatoula at **Joyce Wildlife Management Area❖.** A 1,000-foot boardwalk here leads into a tupelo–baldcypress wetland heavily logged early in this century. Immense stumps suggest how the swamp once looked—and will again someday. Willow, red maple, buttonbush, and royal fern grow profusely along the way. Through the warmer months, boardwalkers can enjoy abundant water-spider orchids; these plants send up tall clusters of flowers that with a little imagination resemble small green spiders.

In the Big Easy, "wildlife" might well be taken to mean the rowdy clubs along Bourbon Street. For visitors whose tastes include natural history as well as food and fun, though, New Orleans offers some fine attractions. The splendid **Aquarium of the Americas❖,** on the edge of the French Quarter at the foot of Canal Street, should rank at the top of the list.

Few people have a chance to explore the deep-water environment of the Gulf of Mexico, and getting a glimpse of the murky underworld of Mississippi River swamps is harder still. The Aquarium of the Americas addresses this dilemma with exhibits concentrating on these

ABOVE: *Fan-shaped leaves of palmettos dot the understory along a board-walk trail at the Barataria unit of Jean Lafitte preserve. Usually low-growing, the small palm sometimes develops a trunk up to ten feet tall.*

two important habitats. In the first, sharks, rays, sea turtles, huge groupers, and other Gulf creatures swim through the legs of a model oil rig, demonstrating how these structures act as artificial reefs, hosting their own interdependent saltwater communities. In the Delta exhibit, paddlefish, gar, and catfish swim among indoor cypress knees. For popularity, though, nothing can compete with the aquarium's white alligators, which float in the dark water like eerie swamp ghosts. Displays on Caribbean reefs and the Amazon River are among the aquarium's other features.

Located in Joe W. Brown Memorial Park on the eastern edge of the city off Interstate 10, the **Louisiana Nature Center**❖ occupies former marshland drained early in the century; the highest point on the center's 86 acres is seven feet below sea level. (Indeed, the entire city of New Orleans owes its dry state to a ring of levees around the city and pumps that remove storm water.) Three trails wind through wetlands, woods, and old fields, past oaks and large sugarberries. Wildflowers here include spider lilies, woolly rose mallows, irises, and dozens of

ABOVE: *Once slaughtered for silky plumes, the now protected snowy egret is again common in southern wetlands.*

RIGHT: *Large birds with seven-foot wingspans, threatened brown pelicans have recently also made a strong comeback.*

BELOW: *The brilliant yellow flag iris, a swamp-loving Old World species, flaunts its showy blooms each spring.*

other species that brighten spring and summer days.

Just south of the suburb of Marrero on Route 45, the **Barataria Preserve Unit** of **Jean Lafitte National Historical Park and Preserve**❖ encompasses 8,600 acres. (Jean Lafitte, a French pirate, was active in the area around 1810–20.) Its excellent and easily accessible trail system vividly demonstrates how in this low-lying environment a small difference in elevation can cause a big change in habitat. The Bayou Coquille Trail begins on a natural levee of Bayou des Familles (once a channel of the Mississippi), where live oaks and sweet gums grow. As the path descends ever so slightly, palmettos and red maples appear, giving way to a swamp dominated by bald cypresses and water tupelos. Beyond the swamp is an extensive grassy marsh bordering Lake Salvador.

Two of the most noticeable plants in the Barataria preserve are not native species at all. Elephant's-ear, with its enormous leaves, is a pest in many Louisiana wetlands, but its impact is small compared with that of the water hyacinth. This tropical species, admired for its beautiful lavender-blue flowers, was introduced into Louisiana in 1884. In still or slow-moving water it spreads with incredible speed, clogging channels, displacing native vegetation, and depleting oxygen levels. Today, millions of dollars are spent yearly throughout the South on control efforts—a costly ecology lesson.

Barataria's wildlife includes alligators,

mink, otters, swamp rabbits, muskrat, ibis, mottled ducks, and king rail. Arachnophobes take note: Trails at the preserve are lined with the impressive webs of the golden silk spider, which, although harmless, is large enough—and abundant enough—to intimidate some people.

Farther south—at the southern terminus of Route 1—an eight-mile barrier island is home to **Grand Isle State Park❖,** famed for fine fishing. From the beach or from a 400-foot public pier, speckled trout, redfish, croaker, white trout, and Spanish mackerel are the most sought fish. Birding is excellent at Grand Isle, especially in spring and fall when plover, sandpipers, turnstones, avocets, stilts, and other shorebirds gather in the greatest numbers.

Not long ago, pesticides and persecution caused a sharp decline in the United States population of brown pelicans, putting Louisiana in the uncomfortable position of having extirpated its state bird as a

---

OVERLEAF: *When hopes for the survival of America's herons and egrets seemed dim, "Bird City" at Avery Island maintained a protected nesting area; today, thousands gather here to raise their young each spring.*

breeding species. In recent years, though, brown pelicans have made an encouraging comeback, and Grand Isle is one of the coastal spots where they can often be found.

SOUTHWEST LOUISIANA: THE GULF COAST

For most people, Louisiana's geology is less interesting than its always fascinating wildlife. One exception is **Avery Island,** southwest of New Iberia via Route 329, where what seems an anomalous low hill rises from the surrounding flat marshes and sugarcane fields. This "island," one of five in the area, is actually the tip of a gigantic dome of salt pushed up from several miles below the surface by the great weight of Mississippi River–deposited sediments.

Apart from its geologic distinction, Avery Island holds a unique place in culinary history—Tabasco sauce is produced here—as well as conservation history. Shortly before the turn of the century, E. A. McIlhenny, a businessman, naturalist, and traveler whose descendants still own the island, became alarmed by the plight of herons, egrets, and other wading birds, which were being slaughtered in staggering numbers to supply the decorative feather trade. He reestablished a small group of snowy egrets on an artificial lake, and they became the nucleus of a mixed colony of waders that today number in the thousands. Bird City is one of the attractions at the **Jungle Gardens**❖ of Avery Island, where picturesque native live oaks grow alongside all

196

LEFT: *It is easy to get complacent around the usually sluggish American alligator. The big reptile can move fast when it wants to, however—as many a rabbit, turtle, and snake has discovered just a bit too late.*

RIGHT: *Introduced from South America in the 1930s, the nutria is an important prey for alligators. Larger than a muskrat, the nutria is often trapped; its softer fur is used for coats, its coarser hairs for making hat felt.*

manner of exotic plantings, from camellias and wisterias to bamboos.

Near the garden's water hyacinths visitors may glimpse another introduced species: the nutria, a muskratlike rodent from South America. Brought to Avery Island in the 1930s, nutrias escaped to become abundant in much of the South and now constitute a commercially important source of fur. Their insatiable appetite for marsh plants is a contributing factor in coastal wetland loss. Some suggest that the recent recovery of the alligator population was aided by nutrias, which gators consider just the right size for a tasty mouthful.

Dotting the Gulf Coast from Louisiana west through Texas are a string of wildlife refuges established to protect the wintering grounds of ducks and geese. In addition, the refuges preserve the habitat of literally thousands of other species, from humble marsh plants to mink, foxes, and such spectacular wading birds as great egrets and roseate spoonbills. Four refuges totaling more than a quarter-million acres are clustered in southwestern Louisiana, encompassing freshwater, brackish, and saltwater marshes that together compose one of America's richest environments.

In 1912 E. A. McIlhenny of Avery Island bought the 84,000 acres of the state-owned **Rockefeller Refuge✥,** south of Route 82 and a few miles west of the town of Pecan Island, to create a protected home for wildlife in the days before effective game laws. As many as 400,000 ducks winter at Rockefeller, and alligators, raccoon, muskrat, and otters are common. Less obvious is the essential role the marsh environment plays as a "nursery" for marine creatures ranging from crabs to game fish. Many species caught for sport and food depend on estuarine habitats for part of their life cycle; if the marshes disappear, so will they.

Road access to Rockefeller Refuge is limited; most visitors are local residents who come by boat to fish and to harvest shrimp, crabs, crawfish, and oysters. The same is true of **Lacassine National Wildlife Refuge❖** and the fairly new **Cameron Prairie National Wildlife Refuge❖,** both located southeast of the city of Lake Charles. Although wildlife-watchers are welcome (and a recently opened road at Lacassine facilitates viewing of more of the refuge), neither offers the accessible introduction to the coastal environment provided by their expansive neighbor to the west.

Sabine National Wildlife Refuge❖, south of Hackberry off Route 27, covers more than 124,000 acres of marsh where freshwater from upland rivers mixes with the saline Gulf. Flanked by two large lakes, Sabine and Calcasieu, the refuge is truly one of Louisiana's great natural areas. Visitors should stop at headquarters, on Route 27, for a refuge guide and checklists of birds and other wildlife. Dioramas and audiovisual displays explain Sabine's ecological importance and introduce some of its residents. Four and a half miles south is the Marsh Trail, a levee and boardwalk path providing a close look at a habitat that from a distance seems a flat, monotonous sea of grass.

The refuge may be flat (nowhere is it more than two feet in elevation), but it is hardly boring. Those bulbous eyes breaking the water's surface beside the walkway belong to an alligator, the top of the marsh food chain. (Many people wildly overstate the size of the gators they see; for a reasonable guess, estimate the number of inches from the tip of the snout to the eyes and convert that number into feet.) Twittering calls from bordering grass reveal the presence of marsh wrens, while the "*witchety*" songs of common yellowthroats sound from nearby shrubs. Two of the most beautiful birds of the Gulf Coast may be seen here: the purple gallinule, with its red bill and blue forehead, and the shocking-pink roseate spoonbill, named for its strange spatulate bill. Cormorants, herons, egrets, bitterns, ibis, and rail appear at various times of year; nutrias and rabbits are the most commonly seen mammals.

In winter, Sabine hosts a large and diverse population of ducks and

ABOVE: *From alligators to mosquitoes, wildlife abounds along the Marsh Trail at the Sabine National Wildlife Refuge. Wax myrtle, groundsel tree, marsh elder, and bullwhip provide cover for wrens and warblers.*

geese; the most common species are snow goose, mottled duck, mallard, pintail, green-winged and blue-winged teal, shoveler, gadwall, and American wigeon. Birders should check flocks of snow geese for the rare Ross's goose, which looks much like a snow but is noticeably smaller and sports a stubbier bill.

On the coast off Route 82, west of the small town of Holly Beach, is one of Louisiana's most celebrated birding spots: the **Holleyman-Sheely and Henshaw Sanctuaries❖.** At certain times during spring migration the trees here teem with migrant songbirds seeking rest and food after their flight across the Gulf of Mexico. Ornithologists estimate that as many as two million birds pass through annually on their way north.

The sanctuary woods are a fine example of what Louisianans call a chenier, from *chêne,* the French word for oak. Live oaks predominate on these forested, slightly elevated coastal ridges, which are actually relict beaches formed over the past 3,000 years by the combined action of waves and Gulf currents depositing sediments from the Mississippi River.

CAJUN COUNTRY AND THE ATCHAFALAYA SWAMP

Away from the Gulf of Mexico, Louisiana is a potpourri of rivers, low-lying swamps, upland pine forests, and rolling terrace lands shaped by prehistoric streams and shorelines. In geologic terms the terrain is young and still changing—though not as rapidly as the coast. Quite often, disparate features occur side by side; at **Sam Houston Jones State Park❖,** just north of Lake Charles off Route 171, pine warblers and brown-headed nuthatches, both pinewoods birds, live next door to swamps frequented by prothonotary warblers and great blue herons. Nature trails here traverse mixed woodland and riparian areas; the main park road passes through bald-cypress–tupelo wetlands draped with Spanish moss.

A member of the pineapple family, Spanish moss is an epiphyte, not a parasite; it gets its food from tiny particles floating in the air and draws no nourishment from its host, which is used only for support. (This characteristic is readily apparent when the plant grows on telephone wires or dead trees.) Spanish moss occurs throughout the Deep South, and where it grows thickly its long strands add an exotic, almost dreamy atmosphere to swamps and woodlands.

Many people are surprised to learn that prairie grasses and wildflowers once covered 2.5 million acres of southwestern Louisiana. An impermeable layer of clay below the surface, in conjunction with frequent fires, suppressed tree and shrub growth, creating a vast grassland often called the Cajun Prairie. Little of this habitat remains today; rice cultivation has been the major factor in its loss.

Small tracts of prairie have managed to survive here and there, often along railroad rights-of-way. At one such site, the **Cajun Prairie Restoration Project❖** in Eunice at the corner of Magnolia Avenue and Martin Luther King Drive, conservationists are trying to re-create the natural environment settlers found in the nineteenth century. Along with such grasses as big and little bluestem, Indiangrass, and switchgrass, wildflowers in a rainbow array bloom throughout much of the year. Grass pink orchid, false indigo, blue-eyed grass, prairie parsley,

---

RIGHT: *With their fearsomely spiny leaves, thistles often multiply to become pests in farm pastures. Members of the sunflower family, they produce seeds relished by birds such as quail and goldfinches.*

LEFT: *In early spring water hyacinth, an alien plant that clogs waterways throughout the South, spreads quickly under still-leafless willows along the lower Atchafalaya River near Morgan City.*

RIGHT: *The venomous and aggressive cottonmouth snake feeds on fish, frogs, birds, and other snakes. When annoyed, it opens its mouth widely, exposing the "cotton" color that inspired its name.*

black-eyed Susan, ladies' tresses orchid, compass plant, liatris, butterfly weed, and coneflower are just a few of the dozens of types found here.

About 25 miles southeast, the city of Lafayette is proud to consider itself the Capital of Cajun Country—referring to the culturally distinct part of southern Louisiana settled by Acadians, French Canadians exiled from Nova Scotia in 1755. Travelers stopping to sample gumbo, boudin (sausage), and zydeco music can enjoy a taste of the local environment at the **Acadiana Park Nature Station❖,** in the northeastern part of the city south of Interstate 10 next to the Vermilion River. The park straddles the escarpment dividing higher terrace land from the Mississippi River floodplain; its nature trail is an easily accessible small-scale version of the nearby Atchafalaya Basin. Bald cypress, sugarberry, sycamore, green ash, American elm, sweet gum, and several oaks (live, water, swamp chestnut, and others) are typical trees. Breeding birds include Mississippi kites, red-shouldered hawks, Acadian flycatchers, northern parulas, hooded warblers, broadwinged hawks, and Swainson's warblers.

Without a doubt, the most renowned wild site on Louisiana's map is the **Atchafalaya River Basin,** the largest riverine swamp in the United States. Depending on who's measuring, estimates of its size range from a half-million acres to well over twice that. The untamed character of the Atchafalaya (its name is an Indian word meaning "long river") has suffered somewhat in modern times, primarily from levees that contain its once-expansive flooding and water-control structures that limit inflow from the Mississippi. Nevertheless, vast areas remain primeval-looking

and heavily forested, little visited except by Cajun trappers, hunters, and anglers familiar with the swamp's intricate maze of channels.

Access to Atchafalaya's interior is problematic. Many Louisiana outdoorspeople take canoes into the river's backwaters and bayous; a quiet, solitary paddle under towering bald cypresses is the ideal way to see the area—but maps, local advice, and prudence are essential. Several commercial tour companies, from Morgan City north to Henderson, take visitors into the swamp on barges; some are well versed in natural history, but others seem to specialize in far-fetched legends and tall tales.

Those who want to remain on dry land find Route 975, a gravel road that runs between Route 190 and Interstate 10 west of Baton Rouge, a good introduction to the Atchafalaya. Although the road is outside the main river levee, the environment is typical of much of the region. Just 2 miles south of Route 190, a nature trail in the **Sherburne Wildlife Management Area**❖ loops through bottomland forest; a walk along the levee can stretch for miles in either direction. **Lake Fausse Point State Park**❖, 20 miles southeast of St. Martinville, offers land and water access to typical Atchafalaya habitats.

What might a canoeist or hiker see in the Atchafalaya? Bald eagles,

LEFT: *Bald cypresses and live oaks frame a bayou scene in* Land of Evangeline, *an 1874 oil by the landscape painter Joseph Meeker (1827-89) based on a poem by Henry Longfellow.*
RIGHT: *Underlying Tunica Hills is fine wind-deposited sediment called loess. Although it supports a forest of oaks, magnolias, and beeches, loess-based soil does erode easily, exposing tree roots on slopes.*

ospreys, and even rare, exquisitely graceful swallow-tailed kites nest along its length; black bears roam the woods, but are glimpsed by only the luckiest visitors. Gators live here along with raccoon, mink, muskrat, and nutrias. Snakes are common; poisonous and sometimes aggressive cottonmouths make frequent appearances, but many so-called water moccasins (as cottonmouths are often called) are actually harmless water snakes of several varieties. Swainson's warblers, scarce birds over much of their range, may reach their greatest abundance in the Atchafalaya area. Prothonotary warblers, small golden birds locally called swamp canaries, vie with male wood ducks for sheer beauty. Both nest in tree holes; wood ducks often occupy cavities excavated by pileated woodpeckers, big black-and-white birds with red crests whose laughing calls echo through the swamp. The list could go on and would still be only a sampling of the life in this rich wilderness.

CENTRAL LOUISIANA: PINE HILLS AND RIVER TERRACES

A trip east of the Mississippi River leads to the Nature Conservancy's **Tunica Hills Wildlife Management Area❖,** off Route 66 in West

LEFT: *The tooting call of the ivory-billed woodpecker still sounded in southern forests when John James Audubon depicted it in 1810. Tragically, this spectacular bird disappeared along with the virgin woods it needed to survive. A few may remain alive in eastern Cuba.*

Feliciana Parish. The ridges here—topped with wind-deposited sediment called loess and dissected by stream-eroded ravines—are part of a strip of high ground that extends along the east side of the Mississippi Valley north to Illinois. (Clark Creek Natural Area, across the state line in Mississippi, is part of the same ecosystem.)

The Tunica Hills support a notable diversity of plants and animals, from black bears to worm-eating warblers, from pyramid magnolias to delicate little three-birds orchids. Beech, southern magnolia, cherrybark oak (a variety of southern red oak), water oak, tulip tree, and sweet gum are the dominant forest trees; in blooming season, dogwood, oak-leaf hydrangea, and two-winged silver bell punctuate the greenery.

About 15 miles southeast, near the historic town of Saint Francisville, is **Audubon State Commemorative Area❖,** centered on the 1799 Oakley plantation house. John James Audubon—artist, outdoorsman, adventurer, storyteller, entrepreneur, self-promoter, and eventual icon of bird lore—lived and worked here in 1821, having contracted to teach drawing to a daughter of the plantation owners. (He left four months later after a falling-out with the family, a common occurrence in the life of the temperamental Audubon.)

Several first-edition prints from the monumental *Birds of America* are displayed at Oakley. Visitors taking the nature trail through the surrounding woods may see many of the same species Audubon studied while he was here, including Mississippi kites, red-shouldered hawks, wood ducks, ruby-throated hummingbirds, yellow-throated warblers, and orchard orioles. An appropriate though possibly less welcome sighting would be a rattlesnake; here Audubon made a drawing of the serpent that he later incorporated into his famous painting of nesting mockingbirds.

RIGHT: *After catching a tasty crayfish, frog, turtle, or, in this case, a crab, the yellow-crowned night heron often tosses its hapless prey in the air repeatedly, making sure it is positioned properly for easy swallowing. Here, a breeding male prepares to dine.*

A fine mature forest is the main attraction at the **Louisiana State Arboretum❖**, on Route 3042 about seven miles north of Ville Platte. Natural vegetation and plantings on this 600-acre site encompass a good portion of the trees and shrubs found in the state; many are labeled for identification. Most impressive are the beeches, their smooth gray bark and columnar form creating a dramatic effect. Southern magnolias are common, but other types, including tulip trees (tulip magnolias) and the aptly named big-leaf magnolias, with leaves nearly three feet long, also grow here. Look for sassafras, which has variable leaves that can be elliptical, mitten-shaped, or mitten-shaped with two thumbs; ground-up young leaves of this tree make the filé powder used to thicken gumbo. Trails wind through a fern garden, along upland terraces, and down into low swampy spots. Although camping and picnicking are not allowed at the arboretum, both are available at adjacent **Chicot State Park❖,** where eight miles of backpacking trails trace the shoreline of a lake ringed by bald cypress trees.

Kisatchie National Forest❖ covers more than 600,000 acres of mostly pine woods, divided among six ranger districts in western and northwestern Louisiana. Several of the state's most popular and rewarding recreational sites are within the forest, including the 8,700-acre **Kisatchie Hills Wilderness,** south of Natchitoches off I-49. Within this area (which shows obvious effects of past logging, but will remain undisturbed in the future) is a region of sandstone bluffs sometimes called the Little Grand Canyon of Louisiana. Although the nickname will seem hyperbolic to visitors from western states, these hills boast rocky cliffs and elevations ranging from 120 to more than 300 feet.

For hikers, the **Backbone Trail** winds through the wilderness area

for 11 miles. The nearby **Longleaf Vista** picnic area offers fine views of hills and stream-cut valleys, as well as an excellent 1.5-mile self-guided nature trail that acquaints visitors with trees and other natural features. The **Longleaf Trail Scenic Byway** is a 17-mile auto-tour route providing access to the wilderness, the vista point, and Kisatchie Bayou, a state natural and scenic stream.

Burned areas along the byway are evidence of efforts to improve nesting conditions for the endangered red-cockaded woodpecker. Loss of habitat has caused a sharp decline in the population of this small black-and-white bird, which requires mature pine forest with an open understory and prefers very old trees with a fungal infection called red-heart disease. Especially in late afternoon, quiet watching may locate one or more of the birds; look for "candlestick" trees with extensive whitish flows of sap. Kisatchie National Forest hosts fairly healthy numbers of red-cockaded woodpeckers, and the **Longleaf Scenic Area,** southeast of Leesville, is another good place to find them.

The **Wild Azalea National Recreation Trail** is one of the forest's most popular natural attractions. From its southern terminus near Woodworth on Route 165, the path covers 31 miles north to Valentine Lake Recreation Area, traversing a pleasing variety of habitats along the way. As its name indicates, the trail is famed for azaleas, which display their pink flower clusters in early spring. About midway along the trail, **Castor Creek Scenic Area** features fine old-growth forest, including some very large loblolly pines. Those who don't want to hike that far can reach the area by walking a half-mile from Forest Road 273.

About 15 miles northeast of Natchitoches, **Saline Bayou National Wild and Scenic River❖** features a 10-mile canoe float between Routes 126 and 156, south of the town of Saline. The trip, a picturesque journey through bottomland forest, is feasible only with proper water conditions; check with the ranger station in Winnfield before starting.

Bordering Kisatchie National Forest, just south of Alexandria, 8,000-acre **Alexander State Forest❖** is mostly composed of mixed loblolly, slash, and longleaf pine forest. **Indian Creek Recreation Area,** accessed from Route 165 or I-49, includes camping areas and a good

---

LEFT: *Longleaf pines dominate the woods at the Kisatchie National Forest's Longleaf Vista. The adjacent wilderness area comprises deep valleys and sandstone bluffs—a most atypical Louisiana landscape.*

hiking trail; it is best known among birders as an excellent place to find red-cockaded woodpeckers. Cavity trees along the entrance road make seeing the birds easy; the best time is late in the day, when they return to their roost trees after foraging in nearby woodland.

Created by a dam on the Sabine River, the huge **Toledo Bend Reservoir,** the fifth-largest man-made lake in the country, covers 185,000 acres along the Texas-Louisiana line. Besides the bass, crappie, bream, and catfish that draw anglers throughout the year, the reservoir's greatest natural attraction is its wintering birdlife. Loons, grebes, ducks, and other waterbirds are visible from a number of parks and recreation areas along the shoreline, including **North Toledo Bend State Park❖,** southwest of Zwolle off Route 191 to Route 3229. Like many similar lakes, Toledo Bend hosts an increasing number of wintering bald eagles, which perch in tall waterside trees when not searching for food. (Belying their majestic image, bald eagles would rather scavenge a dead fish or wounded duck than hunt down a healthy prey animal.) The area around the dam, at the southern end west of Anacoco, is a productive place to seek the national bird.

Caroline Dormon is legendary among Louisiana conservationists. Born in 1888, she grew up loving nature and later wrote several books about the state's flora and fauna. She was the main force behind the establishment of the Kisatchie National Forest and helped found the Louisiana State Arboretum. Although she died in 1971, her legacy lives on at **Briarwood❖,** a nature preserve on Route 9 south of Saline.

Orchids, irises, rhododendrons, azaleas, pitcher plants, and other species from across the South, many of them very rare, testify to decades of cultivation and care. Among the impressively large trees at Briarwood, one longleaf pine, called Grandpappy, is thought to be more than 300 years old. Bald cypresses grow in swampy areas, and the preserve even includes baygalls, acidic habitats named for sweet bay magnolia and gallberry holly. Visitors with a botanical bent often consider Briarwood the highlight of a trip to Louisiana.

CLOCKWISE FROM TOP LEFT: *Growing mostly in wet areas, the southern blue flag iris varies in color from white to purple. Silvery white buds are distinctive to longleaf pines, lending a candlesticklike appearance to the treetop. The creamy white flowers of bigleaf magnolia can be a foot in diameter. Yellow pitcher plants trap insects in their hollow leaves.*

NORTHEAST LOUISIANA

Eastward toward the Mississippi floodplain, the terrain turns flatter and cropland dominates the landscape. Trees border fields and line many streams, but once-extensive bottomland hardwood forests have been decimated here, as they have elsewhere in the Delta. Perhaps as little as 15 percent remains of the original 25 million acres of woodland in the lower Mississippi Valley. The U.S. Fish and Wildlife Service has made acquisition of remaining tracts of this highly productive ecosystem one of its top priorities; as a result, eastern Louisiana is home to several new and still undeveloped refuges.

Neither new (established in 1958) nor particularly large (5,308 acres), **Catahoula National Wildlife Refuge❖,** about 25 miles northeast of Alexandria off Route 28, is worth a visit for its wetland areas and for the tens of thousands of ducks that winter here. The refuge auto-tour route passes swamps where bald cypresses, decorated with Spanish moss, rise from sluggish backwaters. Bald eagles are common in winter, herons and egrets are abundant, and anhingas, long-necked relatives of pelicans, are often seen perching on high branches. Anhingas are often called "snakebirds" for their long, slender necks; they use their sharp bills to spear fish while swimming underwater.

Flooding at Catahoula each winter, when large areas of the refuge are inundated for months at a time, makes access difficult or impossible; but it's also a vital part of the local ecological cycle. Dependent on the flooding at nearby Catahoula Lake, abundant wetland plants such as chufa (a sedge with edible tubers) and millet provide favored food for mallard and other ducks and help explain why Catahoula Lake ranks among Louisiana's most valuable waterfowl habitats.

About 50 miles northeast, **Tensas River National Wildlife Refuge❖** south of Route 80 protects one of the largest bottomland-hardwood forests in the Mississippi Alluvial Plain. Before the 64,000-acre refuge was established in 1980, this area was known as the Singer Tract because the famous sewing-machine company owned the land and harvested oak, walnut, cherry, and other hardwoods for its cabinetwork.

The Singer Tract is legendary among ornithologists as the home of the last known ivory-billed woodpeckers in the United States. Now extirpated in North America (a few may survive in Cuba), this huge bird disappeared as virgin southern forests were cut; controversy surrounds the ivory-bill's final years, but it definitely survived here into the 1940s.

Today, Tensas River supports a population of threatened Louisiana black bears (estimated at about a hundred individuals) and is among the best places in the state to see wild turkeys. Alligators float lazily in refuge lakes; manipulation of water levels on fields stimulates the growth of food plants for wintering ducks and geese. White-tailed deer, bobcat, otters, and mink are among the mammals found on the refuge.

A four-mile trail at Rainey Lake traverses a fine bottomland area, continuing alongside an oxbow lake lined with huge bald cypresses. The short Hollow Cypress Wildlife Trail at the refuge visitor center follows a boardwalk to a tower overlooking fields where waterfowl are common in winter and deer can usually be seen at dusk. Large sweet gums and white, water, willow, and overcup oaks dominate the wet woods, where barred owls and red-shouldered hawks hunt. Ruby-throated humming-birds, red-bellied woodpeckers, pileated woodpeckers (large, but not as awesomely so as ivory-bills), eastern wood-pewees, Acadian flycatchers, wood thrushes, red-eyed vireos, northern parulas, yellow-throated warblers, prothonotary warblers, and summer tanagers nest in the forest.

D'Arbonne National Wildlife Refuge❖ and **Upper Ouachita National Wildlife Refuge❖,** both north of Monroe off Route 143, encompass 17,421 and 21,000 acres, respectively, of mostly bottomland woods similar to those at Tensas River. Containing some upland woods and pine forest as well, both refuges include birds such as red-cockaded woodpeckers, brown-headed nuthatches, and pine warblers in their avifaunas. Upper Ouachita and the Felsenthal National Wildlife Refuge, which lies just to the north in Arkansas, create a large and important wintering ground for waterfowl.

Near the small town of Collinston, about 15 miles northeast of Monroe, **Kalorama Nature Preserve❖,** on Route 593, harbors a surprising diversity of native plants on its 40-acre grounds. The tract lies atop a geologic formation known as the Bastrop Ridge, where loess and other soil types support towering oaks, Florida sugar maples, papaws, sweetleaf (also known as horse sugar), green ashes, and both loblolly and shortleaf pines. In bottomland areas, massive grapevines wind into the trees, mayapples bloom in spring, and wood ducks nest. Wildflowers are varied and abundant, and small tracts of native prairie are being encouraged and restored.

MISSISSIPPI:
SEABIRDS, PINE WOODS, AND SAVANNA WILDFLOWERS

G eographically speaking, Mississippi surely ranks among the most misunderstood states. Too many people still view the South as a succession of Faulknerian cotton fields, punctuated by swampy bayous teeming with snakes and catfish. And too often, the archetype for this unenlightened image is the Magnolia State.

Travelers indeed find flat cropland and meandering backwaters here, but that landscape is only part of Mississippi's natural scene. Although located entirely within the Gulf Coastal Plain, the state encompasses a true diversity of habitats in its varied physiographic regions.

Mississippi's 88-mile-long Gulf of Mexico coastline is paralleled by some of America's most beautiful and unspoiled barrier islands; Gulf Islands National Seashore invites visitors to explore dunes and marshes little changed from the earliest days of European exploration. Inland from the coast's white-sand beaches, pine savannas are home to an array of fascinating wildflowers, as well as an endangered nonmigratory race of the sandhill crane.

A broad region of rolling pine forest occupies much of the southern half of the state. In the early decades of this century, these pinewoods were severely abused by "cut and run" logging, leaving many areas devastated both environmentally and economically. With the establish-

PRECEDING PAGES: *Just a short boat ride from coast resorts, Gulf Islands National Seashore offers the solitude of undeveloped white-sand beaches.*
LEFT: *On the Natchez Trace Parkway, alien kudzu competes with native vegetation—and serves as a warning of the danger of introduced species.*

ment of the De Soto, Bienville, and other national forests (there are six in the state) and the institution of sustained-harvest methods of timber cutting, the forest-products industry is once again an important force in the Pine Hills.

In the northwest, the Mississippi Alluvial Plain, often called the Delta, sprawls flat and broad alongside the river that gave it its name. Intensively exploited for agriculture, it can seem hot, featureless, and uninteresting to a summer visitor. But from fall through spring, tracts of bottomland-hardwood forest host mallard and other ducks; flocks of geese, increasing in number in recent years, feed in winter fields; and springtime brings waves of migratory songbirds to woodlands.

The Loess Hills, high ground built of eolian (wind-deposited) silt, form a thin strip along the eastern border of the Mississippi Alluvial Plain. They curve the length of the state, from Woodville to Memphis, Tennessee. Clark Creek Natural Area, at the southern end of the hills in the state's southwestern corner, is as ecologically important as it is scenic, providing habitat for several rare plants and animals.

The North Central Hills, Flatwoods, and Pontotoc Ridge regions of northeastern Mississippi, stretching from Ripley to Meridian, are distinguished by differences in geology and soil. Boundaries between them are not always distinct to the unpracticed eye, although, as its name implies, the narrow strip of the Flatwoods shows very little relief. In the hill regions, as elsewhere in Mississippi, low ridges called cuestas occur between river valleys. Sloping gently on one side and more steeply on the other, cuestas result from differing resistance to erosion of the underlying sedimentary formations.

Travelers in the northeast passing through the crescent-shaped Black Belt, or Black Prairie, extending from Corinth to Macon, can easily see the dark, fertile soil that made this area so valuable for cotton and later for cattle ranching. Much of Mississippi's prairie landscape, here and in the more southerly Jackson Prairie region running east-west from Jackson, has been lost to the plow, but wildflowers still create spring and summer color in a few scattered remnants.

In the northeastern corner of the state, an outlying region of the Appalachian Mountains (known variously as the Tombigbee Hills, the Tennessee River Hills, or the Fall Line Hills) creates a unique highland ecosystem containing the oldest geologic formations in Mississippi.

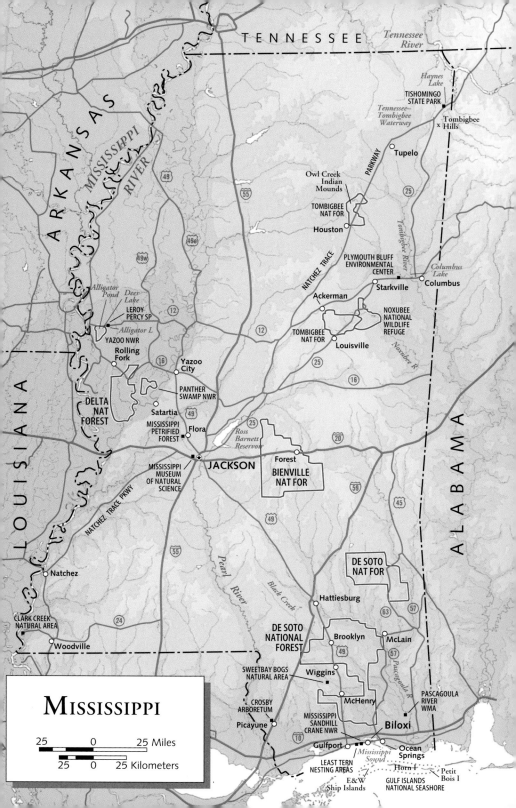

TENNESSEE

Tennessee River

ARKANSAS

MISSISSIPPI RIVER

Haynes Lake

TISHOMINGO STATE PARK

Tennessee–Tombigbee Waterway

Tombigbee Hills ×

Tupelo

49

55

PARKWAY

25

Owl Creek Indian Mounds

TOMBIGBEE NAT FOR

Houston

Tombigbee River

Columbus Lake

PLYMOUTH BLUFF ENVIRONMENTAL CENTER

Starkville

Columbus

49e

Ackerman

NOXUBEE NATIONAL WILDLIFE REFUGE

49w

Alligator Pond

Deer Lake

LEROY PERCY SP

Alligator L.

YAZOO NWR

Rolling Fork

12

12

TOMBIGBEE NAT FOR

Louisville

Noxubee R.

16

25

16

Yazoo City

PANTHER SWAMP NWR

DELTA NAT FOREST

Satartia

MISSISSIPPI PETRIFIED FOREST

49

Flora

Ross Barnett Reservoir

25

Forest

20

BIENVILLE NAT FOR

JACKSON

MISSISSIPPI MUSEUM OF NATURAL SCIENCE

NATCHEZ TRACE PKWY

59

45

49

DE SOTO NAT FOR

55

Natchez

Pearl River

Black Creek

Hattiesburg

63

57

CLARK CREEK NATURAL AREA

24

Woodville

DE SOTO NATIONAL FOREST

Brooklyn

McLain

Pascagoula R.

SWEETBAY BOGS NATURAL AREA

49

57

Wiggins

PASCAGOULA RIVER WMA

CROSBY ARBORETUM

McHenry

MISSISSIPPI SANDHILL CRANE NWR

Biloxi

Picayune

10

Gulfport

Ocean Springs

ALABAMA

LOUISIANA

LEAST TERN NESTING AREAS

Mississippi Sound

Horn I.

Petit Bois I.

E&W Ship Islands

GULF ISLANDS NATIONAL SEASHORE

MISSISSIPPI

25   0   25 Miles

25   0   25 Kilometers

The showcase for this rocky terrain is Tishomingo, the best of the state parks, whose creeks and hills are among the most inviting of Mississippi's habitats for natural-history exploration.

Human activities, from lumbering to plowing to draining of wetlands, have greatly altered Mississippi's environment. Several once-common species, including Florida panthers (mountain lions), black bears, and red-cockaded woodpeckers, have either disappeared or been much reduced in number. But Mississippians increasingly recognize the value of the state's remaining wild places. A number of new national wildlife refuges have been established to protect bottomland forests; additional areas have been safeguarded as state wildlife management areas. The Nature Conservancy has acted to save such important tracts as Sweetbay Bogs, nationally significant for its rare plants. The new (and as yet undeveloped) Grand Bay Savanna National Wildlife Refuge, on the Alabama border in southeastern Mississippi, aims to preserve the largest and least disturbed wet savanna in the United States. And the fine Mississippi Museum of Natural Science in Jackson is educating natives and visitors alike about the state's heritage.

A swallow-tailed kite soaring above a swamp, pitcher plants in a sphagnum-moss bog, tulip trees in full bloom, shorebirds feeding on a pristine sea island—all are part of that heritage, and for the traveler, part of a better understanding of the Magnolia State's varied landscape.

Beginning in the southeastern corner, this chapter moves west along the coastal area and continues north through the pine woods. The route then explores highlights of the Natchez Trace, loops west through the flatlands of the Mississippi Alluvial Plain to Greenville, then follows Route 82 east and concludes in the hills of the northeast.

THE GULF COAST

Few other natural places are as beautiful, inviting, and at times even exciting as a coastal barrier island. Near the mainland, but separated from it both physically and psychologically; exposed and vulnerable, yet often serene and calm; composed of solid ground, but dominated by the pervasive presence of the sea and its infinite possibilities for discovery—all these qualities are part of the experience at **Gulf Islands National Seashore❖,** which spans the coastline from Gulfport, Mississippi, 150 miles east into the Florida panhandle. Four major islands—East and West Ship, Horn, and Petit Bois—are contained within the Mississippi section of the seashore, along with a small area on the mainland near Ocean Springs, where the park headquarters is located.

Formed from rock washed down from the Appalachians and ground to dazzling white sand over the eons, the barrier islands are places of constant change. Littoral currents relentlessly move them westward: Petit Bois once stretched much farther east into Alabama, and nineteenth-century Fort Massachusetts, built 500 feet from the western tip of West Ship Island, is now more than a mile from the point. Ship Island was split into East and West parts by Hurricane Camille in 1969.

The great majority of island visitors see only West Ship Island; pas-

ABOVE: *Related to gulls and terns, black skimmers are graceful coastal birds with unusual long lower mandibles. They feed by "skimming" the water surface in flight, using their beak to snap up fish and invertebrates.*

senger boats make daily shuttle runs from Gulfport or Biloxi from March through October, filled in summer with vacationers seeking only a great beach and a tan. Travelers interested in the islands' natural history do well to visit in spring or fall, when both crowds and temperatures are down.

Atlantic bottlenosed dolphins often play in the ship's wake during the 12-mile trip across the shallow Mississippi Sound; hungry for handouts, laughing gulls follow close behind while least terns dive for small fish. On the island, a walk along the beach away from the busy swimming area may yield all sorts of surprises: the cast-off "skin" of a horseshoe crab or a variegated treasure of seashells (only empty shells may be collected). Reddish egrets dance crazily in the water as they feed, and alligators sun in marshes. West Ship has no large trees, but East Ship is partially wooded; ospreys nesting there often fly to West Ship to fish. Many kinds of shorebirds visit during migration, and a few stay to nest. Dolphins often swim off the point at the western end of the island.

The passenger-boat dock makes a good observation platform for seeing mullet, sea trout, and other fish; certain water conditions bring colorful tropical species such as sergeants major to the island. Rays are also commonly visible from the dock. To protect themselves from stingray stings, which are regular occurrences at West Ship Island, swimmers and waders can shuffle their feet in the sand as they walk.

ABOVE: *Artist Walter Anderson lived in Ocean Springs, but his spiritual home lay across Mississippi Sound.* Horn Island, *from about 1960, is one of hundreds of interpretations he painted of the lonely barrier island.*

"The world of man is far away and so is man," wrote the eccentric artist Walter Anderson of Horn Island, where he often camped alone to paint and draw. Thirty years after his death, his observation is still true—and that solitude, so rare today, attracts small numbers of visitors seeking a true island adventure. The only access to Horn is by private boat (charters are expensive unless shared by a group), and there are no facilities on the island except a ranger station. Campers must prepare for heat, insects, bad weather, and possible encounters with alligators and cottonmouths. As a reward, they experience a pristine wilderness with its own unique ecosystem, from sandy beach and dunes (held in place by picturesque, and strictly protected, sea oats) to pine-oak-palmetto forest and marsh. Thanks to a reintroduction program, bald eagles have returned to nest on Horn for the first time in 50 years. The island has also been the site of experimental releases of red wolves.

Although most certainly not for everyone, Horn Island is much beloved by those who know it. "It's a wonderful place for the senses because of the sights and the sounds and the smells," one park naturalist has said. "There are textures and patterns everywhere. It's just a very special place."

One reason the barrier islands are so popular with swimmers is that water off mainland Mississippi is often dingy and muddy. The island's white-sand shoreline should, in fact, be marshland instead of the world's

223

RIGHT: *In courtship, sandhill cranes "dance" by bounding into the air with wings half opened. The birds also bow to each other in their animated displays, which usually take place at dawn and dusk.*

largest artificial beach, covered with countless tons of hauled-in sand. Nature is reclaiming a little of its own, though, at the **Least Tern Nesting Areas❖** in Gulfport. Here, crowded between the Gulf and busy Route 90, the diminutive terns, threatened in parts of their range, are protected from sunbathers, over-served spring-breakers, and similar disturbances. They're joined by breeding black skimmers, attractive black-and-white birds with ungainly looking bills adapted for "skimming" fish from the water while in flight. Parking areas just off the highway make it easy to stop for a quick look.

A different sort of bird is the focus of protection efforts at **Mississippi Sandhill Crane National Wildlife Refuge❖,** off Interstate 10 east of Ocean Springs. Although sandhill cranes are common in western North America, the nonmigratory Mississippi subspecies is critically endangered, primarily by the loss of its wet savanna habitat. Much of this ecosystem has been drained and converted to pine plantations by timber companies, and additional habitat has been lost to residential and commercial areas.

Thanks to a captive-breeding program, about 130 of the four-foot-tall cranes live on or near the 19,000-acre refuge today. Refuge managers are working to raise the number of breeding pairs from fewer than 10 to 30. The refuge offers tours to see the cranes only in January

and February, and then by reservation only. The rest of the year visitors seldom see the birds. The refuge is worth a visit, though, for its informative visitor center and short nature trail, which leads by a pitcher-plant marsh and through a pine savanna where Bachman's sparrows sing their pretty trilling song in spring and summer.

Encompassing more than 40,000 acres in the southeastern corner of the state, the **Pascagoula River Wildlife Management Area❖** has been called Mississippi's finest natural area. Stretching for 30 river miles along the Pascagoula, the tract is the quintessential southern bottomland-hardwood ecosystem: a meandering river with dozens of oxbow lakes; bald cypresses and water tupelos hung with Spanish

225

LEFT: *Flooding carries the Pascagoula River over its banks in early spring, before water tupelos, bald cypresses, and other bottomland trees have put out new leaves. Receding waters leave layers of silt behind, enriching riverside soil.*

RIGHT: *A champion excavator, the gopher tortoise requires a habitat with sandy soil suited to digging. The stumpy-legged reptile, which excavates burrows 40 feet long or more, grows to just over a foot long on a diet of grass and fruit.*

moss; huge oaks, sweet gums, cottonwoods, sycamores, and a wide variety of other trees in often-flooded forest.

The Pascagoula tract is neither an untouched wilderness nor a strictly protected natural area: It has been selectively logged since the nineteenth century, and hunting and fishing are important focuses of its management plan. Even so, the state's goal—to maintain the natural diversity of the river and bottomland ecosystem—is an important conservation milestone for a type of habitat that has suffered tremendously throughout the South.

Black bears still live in the Pascagoula bottoms, as do rainbow snakes, gopher tortoises, and yellow-blotched sawback turtles—all threatened species. Among birders, the area is best known for its population of swallow-tailed kites, graceful hawks with long forked tails that are often ranked among the world's most beautiful birds. Special plants found here include green-fly orchids (epiphytes that can be hard to see on tree trunks), Florida flame (or orange-flowered) azaleas, Juneberry holly, and silky camellias.

Extensive exploration of the Pascagoula River area is difficult without a boat, a compass, and good local information. The paved Wade-Vancleave Road passes through the tract (turn left or west off Route 63 about 15 miles north of Interstate 10), offering an introduction to this environment. (The property can also be reached via Route 26.) The management-area office here can provide advice, especially important during hunting seasons, about conditions on access roads and suitable trails. Camping is allowed, but no developed facilities exist at this time.

THE PINE WOODS

By comparison, all sorts of facilities are available in the **De Soto National Forest❖,** the largest (more than half a million acres) and in many ways the most interesting of Mississippi's six national forests. Nine developed recreation areas are scattered through the forest, which lies mainly south of Hattiesburg, except for the outlying Chickasawhay Ranger District to the northeast. The major natural attraction in the De Soto forest is Black Creek, a name that applies to a float trip, a hiking trail, and a 5,050-acre wilderness area.

Aptly named Black Creek is a "blackwater" stream, stained the color of coffee by tannins leached from decaying vegetation. The dark, acidic water contrasts pleasingly with streamside sandbars, popular camping spots for canoeists on the 40-mile float through the national forest. Twenty-one miles of the creek are part of the national Wild and Scenic River system, including the stretch that passes through the **Black Creek Wilderness.** The float trip begins at Big Creek Landing, a few miles west of Brooklyn, and ends at Fairley Bridge Landing, east of Wiggins. Other takeout areas facilitate trips of varying lengths.

The **Black Creek National Recreation Trail** begins and ends at the same points as the float trip, mostly paralleling the creek for its 41-mile length. Most hikers' favorite part is the 11-mile section in the wilderness area. Here the woodland is presently little different from other areas of the forest, but because it is protected from future cutting, it will look more mature as time passes. Outfitters in Brooklyn will set up float trips of varying lengths and shuttle cars for hikers on the Black Creek Trail, making one-way backpacking possible. The Forest Service office in Wiggins can provide names of outfitting companies.

Lying within the Pine Hills region of Mississippi, De Soto is in many places dominated by longleaf, slash, and loblolly pines. Varying elevation and moisture create a woodland mosaic, so walkers and boaters can enjoy bald cypress, tupelo, river birch, oaks, magnolia, tulip tree, American holly, and dogwood, among many other trees. Some of the common shrubs found here are azalea, swamp cyrilla (a water-loving plant also known as titi), and several hollies including yaupon (its scientific name, *Ilex vomitoria,* refers to its one-time use as an emetic).

Travelers pressed for time will find the national forest's **Tuxachanie Trail,** just south of McHenry off Route 49, a convenient place to experience a little of the Mississippi Pine Hills. From a parking area on the east side of the highway, the trail follows the raised bed of an abandoned railroad line. The walking is straight and easy through (but comfortably above) a wet forest of large tulip trees and water oaks; log bridges cross creeks once spanned by substantial rail trestles. The trail soon rises to a higher pinewoods area, where summer tanagers sing from the treetops and rufous-sided towhees call "*chewink*" from the underbrush.

Although less well known than the much larger Black Creek Wilderness, the **Leaf Wilderness Area,** five miles south of McLain off Route 57, is well worth a visit. Small (only 940 acres) and mostly within the sound of log trucks on Route 57, this tract in the Leaf River bottoms is nonetheless full of interesting flora and fauna. Exotic-looking bigleaf magnolias, their huge leaves two feet long and a foot wide, stand out in a forest of beech, American holly, sweet gum, and various oaks. Bald cypress and tupelo grow in wet areas, along with spruce pine, a southeastern United States specialty. Barred owls shout their "*who cooks for you, who cooks for you-all?*" call, and gorgeous hooded warblers, in jet black and brilliant yellow, sing from low perches.

A 1.5-mile one-way trail begins on high ground and then drops slightly into the bottomland, where the going can be muddy at times and the mosquitoes dismayingly thick. Still, this trail, one of the state's most interesting, amply repays a visit any time of year.

The Nature Conservancy's **Sweetbay Bogs Natural Area❖,** about eight miles southwest of Wiggins off Route 26 and Smithtown Road, protects a hillside seepage bog where trumpet (also known as yellow) pitcher plants bloom in spring. Plants of this insectivorous species thrive in extremely poor conditions, where acidity and a high water table make life impossible for most other plants; they use nutrients from invertebrates' bodies trapped in their tubular leaves to supplement nourishment extracted from the soil. Sundews, smaller and less showy plants, similarly "eat" insects caught on their sticky leaves. Sweetbay Bogs (named for the sweet bay magnolias found here) hosts several extremely rare plants, including large-leaved grass of Parnassus and bog spicebush. Because of the area's vulnerable flora, those planning a trip to Sweetbay Bogs should first contact the Nature Conservancy office in Jackson.

Just off Interstate 59 at Picayune, the **Crosby Arboretum❖** is devel-

ABOVE: **Mimus polyglottos,** *the scientific name of the state bird, the northern mockingbird (left), means "mime of many tongues." The rufous-sided towhee (right) is sometimes called "ground robin" for its reddish breast.*

oping into one of the South's truly noteworthy public gardens. Devoting itself to the Pearl River ecosystem, the arboretum is headquartered at a 64-acre former strawberry farm called Pinecote; it also manages 11 nearby natural areas totaling 1,700 acres, encompassing pinewoods, swamps, pitcher-plant bogs, and beech-magnolia forest.

Trails and plant displays are still under construction at Crosby, following a master plan that will allow visitors to experience much of the diverse native flora of the region in a relatively small area. Prescribed burning is restoring tracts of longleaf pine savanna, mimicking lightning-caused fires that once regularly swept through the region. Wetlands patterned after beaver ponds display water lilies, pickerelweed, Louisiana irises, buttonbush, titi, and other aquatic or moist-soil plants.

Because many of the Crosby Arboretum's associated natural areas are extremely susceptible to disturbance, visitation is limited. The visitor center at Pinecote can provide information about tours to places such as Hillside Bog, an extremely diverse tract featuring pitcher plants and hardwood and savanna habitats.

One of Mississippi's remotest wild places is also one of its finest: **Clark Creek Natural Area❖,** 13 miles west of Woodville via Pinck-

RIGHT: *The De Soto National Forest's Tuxachanie Trail winds for 21 miles through stands of longleaf and slash pine as well as varied hardwoods. The westernmost five miles follow an abandoned rail line.*

ABOVE: *Found from Georgia to Louisiana, the attractive buckwheat tree is named for its winged fruit, which looks like that of the familiar grain plant. Racemes of showy creamy white flowers appear in early spring.*

neyville Road in the extreme southwestern corner of the state, protects a superb variety of flora and fauna within its 700 acres. It is undoubtedly the state's premier showcase for the Loess Hills physiographic region and its associated ecosystem.

The rugged terrain here is the result of the formation of a ridge of fine wind-blown sediment during an extremely dry climatic period; the dust was created by the grinding action of glaciers during Pleistocene epoch ice ages. In the millennia since, stream erosion has relentlessly cut into the earth, carving steep-sided gullies. (Loess has a tendency to erode along vertical splits, often forming sheer bluffs.) Within the Clark Creek area, the vagaries of geology and erosion have produced more than 40 waterfalls up to 40 feet high, which flow most impressively following spring rains.

Even those who give no thought to geology or biology will find a

LEFT: *A live oak supports lush growths of Spanish moss and ferns on its gnarled limbs at the Crosby Arboretum. An epiphyte that takes no nourishment from its host, this "moss" is related to the pineapple.*

visit to Clark Creek enjoyable. A trail from the parking area, near the small settlement of Pond, leads into a woodland of oak, hickory, and sweet gum, dominated in places by large beech trees and diversified by Southern magnolia, tulip tree, and American holly. The path continues along a streambed, where the walking is sometimes difficult but always rewarding. When the woods are loud with spring birdsong, the aesthetic experience needs no other dimension.

Those whose interest is more scientific might want to look for some of the area's special plants, such as Carolina magnolia vine (or climbing magnolia), and in summer the curiously attractive crested coralroot orchid, which lacks chlorophyll and gets its nourishment from decaying organic matter. Both Venus maidenhair fern and Alabama lipfern, unusual for Mississippi, grow here. A state-endangered fish, the southern redbelly dace, lives in the Clark Creek drainage, and black bears, threatened in Mississippi, prowl the forest, glimpsed only by the luckiest visitors.

Centered on the aptly named town of Forest, the 178,000-acre **Bienville National Forest**❖ is about 45 miles east of Jackson. Two recreation areas and the **Shockaloe National Recreation Trail,** a 23-mile route for horseback riders, are among its attractions. From a natural-history viewpoint, two special areas are particularly noteworthy; easily accessible, both are just a few minutes from Interstate 20 near Forest.

The largest remaining tract of old-growth pines in Mississippi, **Bienville Pines Scenic Area** comprises 189 acres of impressively tall shortleaf and loblolly pines, many 200 years old or more. A 1.8-mile trail through the trees often affords a glimpse of an endangered red-cockaded woodpecker; such species as downy woodpeckers, Carolina chickadees, and pine warblers are common throughout the year. The thick understory of hardwoods here is indicative of eventual succession to an oak-hickory forest. In the absence of naturally occurring fires (or artificial openings such as clear-cuts), sunlight-loving young pines are shaded out by hardwoods, which will eventually dominate the woodland—although the process will take decades.

Just two miles farther east, **Harrell Prairie Hill Botanical Area** is a

---

RIGHT: *Draining uplands of fine silty soil, streams in the Clark Creek Natural Area turn muddy after springtime rains. A diverse flora, from orchids to oaks, makes this one of the state's most important preserves.*

ABOVE: *Drive-by geology: At a roadside exhibit near Mississippi's southern terminus of the Natchez Trace Parkway, Loess Bluff exposes a vertical section of the wind-deposited soil that built the surrounding hills.*

rolling glade in the pines that stages a colorful show of wildflowers in spring and summer. This kind of alkaline-soil ecosystem, typical of the Jackson Prairie region, is now extremely rare. The Forest Service manages the area by cutting and burning to minimize intrusion of woody growth and preserve the grassy habitat.

NATCHEZ TRACE PARKWAY

From its beginning as a series of Indian trails, the path that was eventually called the Natchez Trace played a significant part in the development of the United States. Settlers traveled it from Nashville through the Chickasaw and Choctaw nations to Natchez; riverboatmen who floated down the Ohio and Mississippi to Natchez and New Orleans sold their boats in those cities for lumber, then followed the trace back north; Thomas Jefferson designated the route a post road; and Andrew Jackson marched his troops home along it after the Battle of New Or-

236

leans in 1815. When steamboat travel became common in the 1820s, use of the road declined.

In 1937 the National Park Service began construction of an auto parkway that more or less followed the legendary trace; building has continued ever since, and upon its completion (probably in the 1990s), the **Natchez Trace Parkway❖** will stretch along a 445-mile diagonal from Natchez to near Nashville, Tennessee. Although the parkway's genesis lies in its historical importance, its 310 Mississippi miles include many short nature trails and interpretative exhibits. Indeed, a trip up the Natchez Trace can provide an excellent series of introductory lessons in Mississippi's natural environment.

At mile 12, just north of Natchez, the Loess Bluff exhibit describes the formation of the Loess Hills physiographic region, where uplands were formed by the deposition of wind-blown sediment following the most recent ice age. These hills, bordering the Mississippi Alluvial Plain in a strip 3 to 30 miles wide, are capped with fine loess sediment to depths of 30 to 90 feet. Where the trace crosses this formation, the passage of feet, hooves, and wheels has sunk it into the soil as deep as 20 feet. The effect is easily visible at the Sunken Trace stop, at mile 41, and at Rocky Springs, a historic town site at mile 54. In both places, portions of the original trace have eroded so far down that the bases of trees along the path are higher than a walker's head.

The pretty Cypress Swamp Trail at mile 122, near Ross Barnett Reservoir, perfectly realizes many people's image of the natural South: bald cypress and tupelo rise from tannin-stained, duckweed-covered water; the air rings with the songs of tufted titmice and prothonotary warblers; and anoles, lizards that change color in the manner of Old World chameleons, skitter up tree trunks beside the path. Another fine trail, Hurricane Creek (mile 164, 4 miles north of Kosciusko) makes a short loop through woodland full of such wildflowers as jack-in-the-pulpit, bloodroot, Indian pink, false Solomon's seal, and mayapple; ferns abound, and sassafras and devil's walking-stick grow among the beech, oak, hickory, and pine.

Just outside Tupelo at mile 261, the Chickasaw Village exhibit preserves a small patch of the original Black Belt prairie. The bodies of countless small sea creatures, from periods when this region lay under the ocean, were compressed over millions of years into limestone. Exposed on the earth's surface, the rock eventually weathered into this rich, heavy black soil. Prairie grasses and wildflowers exist in a complex ecosystem that is destroyed by plowing; the remnant here is one of the few that have survived the demand for cropland.

Donivan Slough, at mile 283.3 about 20 miles north of Tupelo, is a low-lying woodland of impressive water oaks, sycamores, sweet gums, beeches, and bald cypresses. Tulip trees, a species of magnolia, display their beautiful flowers in April and May; their trunks rise in the forest as straight and round as marble columns. Trilliums grow here, as does American strawberry bush, whose reddish fruits inspired the colorful folk name "hearts a-bustin' with love."

The strange-looking half-height trees along the northern Mississippi section of the parkway are the result of a freakishly severe ice storm in early 1994, when the great weight of the accumulating ice bent small trees and snapped off the tops of many of them like a giant lawnmower. Although the damage was dismaying, in years to come motorists will be able to watch and appreciate the slow process of nature healing its wounds.

MISSISSIPPI RIVER BOTTOMLANDS

Jackson's **Mississippi Museum of Natural Science❖** on North Jefferson Street is well worth a visit for its dioramas interpreting the state's ecosystems. An attentive visitor will leave with new insight into such habitats as Gulf Coast marsh, Pearl River swamp, pitcher-plant bog, cypress swamp, old field, and longleaf pine forest. Aquarium tanks afford close looks at a wide variety of fish, from freshwater longnose gar to saltwater inhabitants of the barrier islands. The museum also offers checklists of Mississippi's birds, butterflies, fish, and mammals. Special exhibits focus on some of the state's threatened species, including black bears, sandhill cranes, and panthers.

Fifteen miles northwest of Jackson, off Route 49 near Flora, the privately operated **Mississippi Petrified Forest❖** displays its stone logs along a short, mostly paved trail through a pine-oak woodland. The

---

RIGHT: *Countless horses' hooves and human feet, combined with erosion, have worn the venerable Natchez Trace deep into the earth, forming a tunnel beneath overhanging branches of oaks and hickories.*

238

LEFT: *Common but rarely seen because of their nocturnal habits, flying squirrels use flaps of skin between their front and rear legs to glide like sailplanes from one tree to another.*

RIGHT: *Washed up as driftwood 36 million years ago, ancient logs at Mississippi Petrified Forest have weathered into a variety of shapes; this unusual example is fancifully known as the Frog.*

only one of its type in the eastern United States, the forest was designated a National Natural Landmark in 1966, and its presentation is admirably uncontrived. The petrified trees, many quite large, were deposited as driftwood here 36 million years ago. Covered by sand and silt, the wood was gradually replaced by silica and other minerals. Erosion has since exposed the logs—jumbled and broken, but showing amazingly fine details of grain, pores, and other markings in the original wood. The steep, eroded bluffs here are part of the Loess Hills region of Mississippi, a geologic feature easily observed along the trail.

Although the boundaries between some of Mississippi's physiographic regions are subtle, the transition from the Loess Hills to the Mississippi Alluvial Plain is not: Heading west in the vicinity of Yazoo City or Satartia, a traveler moves from rolling countryside to flatland with the abruptness of a door slamming. This area was once entirely wooded, subject to annual renewing floods, and as rich in wildlife as anyplace in North America. Like much of the rest of the great southern bottomland-hardwood region, however, the Mississippi Alluvial Plain has been largely deforested and devoted to agriculture. Happily for the nature lover, some shining exceptions endure.

Panther Swamp National Wildlife Refuge❖, a 28,611-acre tract just west of Yazoo City off Route 49W, provides outstanding woodland habitat for animals ranging from bobcat and alligators to mallard and wading birds. Public access is difficult, though, at least for those without all-terrain vehicles or boats. From two parallel levee roads that transect the refuge for about six miles, travelers can look down on

swampy forest and bald cypress sloughs. In the spring, side roads (when they're not flooded) lead to excellent birding. Wet fields in the center of the refuge often contain good numbers of great egrets and great blue herons. Visitors should be aware that Panther Swamp is a very popular hunting area and plan their visits accordingly.

About five miles west off Route 18, **Delta National Forest❖**—which is, rather surprisingly, the only bottomland-hardwood national forest in the United States—makes exploration easier, although it too floods annually. (Inquire locally about road conditions or call the national forest office in Rolling Springs before visiting.) Forest Roads 703 and 715, which loop through the northern part of the 59,000-acre refuge past the **Blue Lake Recreation Area,** make an excellent nature route on a spring day: Wild turkeys feed along the roadside; a coyote may jog ahead, glancing back over its shoulder before disappearing; pairs of wood ducks swim side by side in the swamp; beautiful prothonotary

LEFT: *Red-cockaded woodpeckers became rare after southern old-growth pinewoods were converted into tree farms. The Noxubee refuge provides them with protected habitat.*
RIGHT: *Young bald cypresses rise from the still water of Noxubee's Bluff Lake. Birds from hawks and herons to hummingbirds can be found in the surrounding bottomland.*

warblers, shining in the woods like brilliant golden lamps, sing their simple whistling songs everywhere. A walk down a side road in April or May will turn up a multitude of warblers, plus such other birds as pileated woodpeckers, barred owls, acadian flycatchers, red-eyed vireos, and summer tanagers. This area too can be positively crowded with hunters during the various game seasons.

Just off Route 1, about 10 miles northwest of Rolling Fork, **Yazoo National Wildlife Refuge❖** may be the best spot in the Mississippi flatlands for wildlife observation. Attracted by grain, acorns, and other food, as many as 35,000 snow geese, 10,000 Canada geese, and 100,000 ducks winter on the 13,000-acre refuge. Most ducks are dabblers such as mallard, pintail, and wigeon; the refuge hosts lesser numbers of scaup, buffleheads, ring-necked ducks, and other divers. A few bald eagles winter as well.

February and March are good months at Yazoo for seeing white-tailed deer and wild turkeys. In March and April wood ducks mate and alligators are active, their bellowing heard often around the refuge lakes. (Deer Lake and Alligator Pond are the best places to see gators.) Many typical southern wetland birds are common at Yazoo, including pied-billed grebes, anhingas, snowy egrets, great egrets, great blue herons, little blue herons, green herons, and common moorhens. Mississippi kites, graceful raptors that feed mostly on insects, nest here and soar overhead in spring and summer. Shorebirds are abundant in managed areas during late August and early September. Visitors should stop at the refuge office for a bird list and information on roads and the best spots for wildlife viewing.

ABOVE: *A white-tailed deer looks after two fawns whose spotted coats camouflage them from predators in sun-dappled woods.* RIGHT: *Canada geese feed in a muddy field at Noxubee National Wildlife Refuge. Each autumn, such northern migrants join resident species for the winter.*

Just a few miles north of the Yazoo refuge off Route 12, **Leroy Percy State Park❖** is a pleasant wooded retreat from the denuded farmland surrounding it. Abundant Spanish moss decorates the large oaks along the entrance road; a fine nature trail passes alongside Black Bayou, and another circles Alligator Lake. At Alligator Pond, warm artesian springs feed a small pool where gators are easily observed from a boardwalk.

NORTHEAST HILLS

The two sections of the 66,000-acre **Tombigbee National Forest❖** are about 45 miles apart in northeastern Mississippi. One area is just north of Louisville off Route 25; the other is southwest of Tupelo. **Choctaw Lake Recreation Area,** in the southern section near Ackerman off Route 15, is one of the state's prettiest campgrounds. A three-mile nature trail here leads visitors through a forest of oaks, pines, tulip trees, and hickories. Near the lake, shagbark hickory, with its peeling bark

and thick-shelled nuts, is common along the trail.

The Natchez Trace Parkway passes through the Tombigbee National Forest east of Houston, where the rolling highway is especially attractive. In spring, overarching trees form a lush green tunnel, and in autumn, their foliage can be breathtaking. A short detour from the parkway toward **Davis Lake Recreation Area** passes the Owl Creek Indian Mounds, which date from the Mississippian Period, about A.D. 1000–1300. Riders enjoy the Tombigbee's Witch Dance Horse Trail, a 15-mile route with its trailhead at a rest area on the parkway.

Noxubee National Wildlife Refuge❖, adjoining the southern portion of Tombigbee National Forest south of Starkville off Route 12, is a highlight of any Mississippi nature tour. Its 47,000 acres encompass an impressive range of habitats, from bottomland hardwoods and pine forests to marshes and fields.

Egrets and herons decorate cypresses at Bluff Lake, where raccoon hunt frogs and crayfish around the water's edge (and try to avoid becoming a meal themselves for the refuge's alligator population, estimated at about a hundred). The Beaver Dam Trail and the Trail of Big Trees, both across the dike from the lake, are excellent walks through low forest, especially during the spring songbird migration. Wild turkeys are regulars here, and hens with young can be seen in late spring. Swamp-loving red-shouldered hawks give their two-syllable screams as they fly just above the treetops.

At the end of Keaton Tower Road, the Sierra Club has constructed a three-mile loop trail through a refuge wilderness area. Beginning at a log crossing of the Noxubee River, the trail traverses beech-magnolia forest and bottomland, including a bald-cypress oxbow slough. Both the entrance road and the trail are sometimes muddy; check with refuge personnel for current conditions.

Near headquarters, an observation deck overlooks a field where resident Canada geese breed and deer feed on fall mornings. Just across the road, a short trail winds through a parklike stand of pines where red-cockaded woodpeckers roost; although they can be inconspicuous in the treetops, their shrill calls often attract the birders' attention.

The red-cockaded woodpecker is found only in pinelands in the southern United States. Within that habitat, it nests only in mature pine forest with an open understory and almost always excavates its cavities in trees with a fungal rot called red-heart disease. Modern forestry practices, including the suppression of fire (which once restrained undergrowth in pine woods) and cutting trees at an early age, have played a major role in the steep decline in red-cockaded woodpecker numbers. At Noxubee, which hosts more than 30 active woodpecker clusters (the current term for colonies), suitable pine stands are managed to create and maintain favorable conditions. Efforts here seem to be succeeding because red-cockaded numbers have been climbing in recent years. Another good place to spot the little black-and-white bird is the large pines just south of Bluff Lake.

Life of a more ancient variety inspired the Nature Conservancy in 1963 to buy the land that has evolved into the **Plymouth Bluff Environmental Center❖,** just west of Columbus via Route 82 and Old West Point Road. An exposed bluff here contains abundant fossils dating from the Upper Cretaceous period, including sharks' teeth, spiral-shelled cephalopods called ammonites, and oysters of the genus *Exogyra*. The bluff is downstream from Columbus Lake on the old channel of the Tombigbee River, now bypassed by the newly constructed Tennessee-Tombigbee Waterway. Because the high water that once regularly scoured the channel no longer occurs, vegetation is encroaching on the bluff, but fossils are still visible in the Selma Chalk sedimentary formation.

The environmental center, operated by the Mississippi University for Women, is at the heart of 190 acres of varied woodland, where trails wind through cypress lowlands and higher oak-hickory-cedar forest. Bois d'arc, red buckeye, and immense post oaks are common on the property, as are some remarkably large fire-ant mounds—walkers beware.

Ask a Mississippian to name his or her favorite state park, and the answer will almost always be **Tishomingo State Park❖**, in the Tombigbee Hills 48 miles northeast of Tupelo off the Natchez Trace Parkway. Geologically unique—more like part of Appalachia than the rest of Mississippi—Tishomingo was carved from Paleozoic sandstone by the meanderings of Bear Creek, which flows north as part of the Tennessee River system. Boulders and limestone and sandstone outcrops are common on steep hillsides. The existence of this habitat explains the presence in the park of a small fern called lobed spleenwort, which prefers crevices in rock ledges and is found nowhere else in the state.

A picturesque swinging footbridge, built by the Civilian Conservation Corps in the 1930s, crosses Bear Creek near the park swimming pool. On the east side of the bridge, one of the park's best nature trails follows bluff lines in one-to-three mile loops. In all, the park contains 13 miles of trails, including a circle around Haynes Lake, where there are primitive tent campsites as well as developed sites for recreational vehicles.

For a closer look at Bear Creek, the park offers eight-mile float trips from April until mid-October. The route passes beneath sandstone bluffs, past bald cypress, water tupelo, and river birch, in a trip that lasts about three hours and is gentle enough for beginning canoeists.

OVERLEAF: *Bear Creek flows mud-brown beneath river birch in Tishomingo State Park, carrying runoff from bordering hills. Tishomingo's sandstone bluffs make it unique among Mississippi's natural areas.*

FURTHER READING ABOUT THE SOUTH-CENTRAL STATES

FAULKNER, WILLIAM. *Big Woods: The Hunting Stories of William Faulkner.* New York: Random House, 1955. This collection from the Nobel Prize–winning Mississippi novelist includes the classic story "The Bear."

FLORES, DAN. *Caprock Canyonlands.* Austin: University of Texas Press, 1990. Natural and cultural history of the often-overlooked region where East meets West in Texas.

FRITZ, EDWARD C. *Realms of Beauty: A Guide to the Wilderness Areas of East Texas.* Austin: University of Texas Press, 1993. A very detailed guide for hikers and backpackers to national forest wildernesses in the Piney Woods.

GRAHAM, GARY L. *Texas Wildlife Viewing Guide.* Helena, MT: Falcon Press, 1992. Brief but thoughtful descriptions of 142 natural areas around the state, listing resident species and giving hints for seeing them.

HARINGTON, DONALD. *The Architecture of the Arkansas Ozarks.* Boston: Little, Brown, 1975. Architecture is only one of the themes of this wonderful (and misleadingly titled) novel by an Arkansas writer.

HOLT, HAROLD R. *A Birder's Guide to the Texas Coast.* Colorado Springs: American Birding Association, 1993. The Texas Gulf Coast is one of America's famed birding hot spots; this guide is essential for anyone who wants to find the greatest number of species there. The equally valuable companion *A Birder's Guide to the Rio Grande Valley* (Holt, 1992) covers the lower Valley, the Hill Country, and Big Bend National Park.

LANCASTER, BOB. *The Jungles of Arkansas.* Fayetteville: University of Arkansas Press, 1989. History, both natural and un-, by an observer who can be simultaneously very funny and dead serious, and who is nothing if not trenchant.

LOCKWOOD, C. C. *Discovering Louisiana.* Baton Rouge: Louisiana State University Press, 1986. An overview of the state by a fine writer-photographer intimately familiar with its varied habitats.

MCALISTER, WAYNE, AND MARTHA MCALISTER. *Matagorda Island, A Naturalist's Guide.* Austin: University of Texas Press, 1993. Excellent ecological informa-

ABOVE: *Lined up to cross the Salt Fork River, some 4,000 wagons prepare*

tion on a seldom-visited area; much of the material in this book is applicable to all Texas barrier islands.

NUTTALL, THOMAS. *A Journal of Travels into the Arkansas Territory During the Year 1819.* 1821. Reprint, Norman: University of Oklahoma Press, 1980. Writings on nature, geology, and native peoples by a curious and adventurous botanist. Nuttall traveled across Arkansas into what is now Oklahoma and down the Mississippi River to New Orleans.

Oklahoma Watchable Wildlife Viewing Guide. Oklahoma City: Oklahoma Department of Wildlife Conservation. Very brief descriptions of 126 wildlife-viewing sites around the state, with directions.

PARENT, LAURENCE. *The Hiker's Guide to Texas.* Helena, MT: Falcon Press, 1992. Maps, directions, and descriptions encompassing a wide variety of trails, from long backpacking hikes to short nature walks.

SCHUELER, DONALD G. *Adventuring Along the Gulf of Mexico.* San Francisco: Sierra Club Books, 1986. Varied and useful information on parks, refuges, and other areas on and near the Gulf shore.

SEVENAIR, JOHN P., ED. *Trail Guide to the Delta Country.* New Orleans: New Orleans Group of the Sierra Club, 1992. Hikes, bike rides, and canoe trips in southern Louisiana and southern Mississippi, with maps, detailed descriptions, and other information useful for visitors.

SPEARING, DARWIN. *Roadside Geology of Texas.* Missoula, MT: Mountain Press, 1991. A guide to the varied landforms of Texas, where travelers can walk on some of the oldest and youngest ground in North America.

SUGG, REDDING S., JR. *The Horn Island Logs of Walter Inglis Anderson.* Memphis: Memphis State University Press, 1973. Paintings and observations on the environment by a solitary, eccentric artist who often visited this Gulf Coast barrier island, and who sought in his work to bring "nature and art to one thing."

WAUER, ROLAND H. *Naturalist's Big Bend.* College Station: Texas A&M Press, 1980. An introduction to the plants and animals of Big Bend National Park, an International Biosphere Reserve, from a former chief naturalist there.

for Oklahoma's famed land run for prairie homesteads in April 1889.

GLOSSARY

alluvial fan deposit of alluvium: gravel, sand, and smaller materials that have formed a fan shape, usually at the base of mountains; created by water rushing down a mountain

badlands barren, arid area in which soft rock strata are eroded into varied, fantastic forms

barrier island narrow island of sediment—sand, silt, and gravel—that protects the coast from direct battering by storm waves and wind

batholith large mass of igneous rock that has melted into surrounding strata and lies a great distance below the earth's surface

bayou marshy creek or swampy backwater of a lake or river, generally occuring in flat, low-lying areas with poor drainage

biotic pertaining to plants and animals

bluff cliff or steep wall of rock or soil that borders a river or floodplain; created as the water erodes the riverbank

butte tall, steep-sided tower of rock formed from an eroded plateau

conglomerate rock composed of rounded, water-eroded fragments of older rock, usually in combination with sand

deciduous describing trees that shed leaves seasonally and remain leafless for part of the year

delta flat, low-lying plain that forms at the mouth of a river as the river slows and deposits sediment that it gathered upstream

diurnal describing animals that are active by day

endemic originating in and restricted to one particular environment

escarpment cliff or steep rock face, formed by a faulting or fracturing of the earth's crust that separates two comparatively level land surfaces

floodplain flat area along the course of a stream that is subject to periodic flooding and deposition of the sediment the stream has been carrying

flowstone calcite mineral deposited by a thin sheet of flowing water along the floor or walls of a cave

gypsum very common calcium sulfate mineral used in plaster of Paris and as a fertilizer

hoodoo natural column of rock often formed into fantastic shapes; these volcanic intrusions are found in western North America

igneous referring to rock formed by cooled and hardened lava or magma

lek assembly area where birds, especially prairie chickens, carry on courtship behavior

mesa isolated, relatively flat-topped elevation more extensive than a butte and less extensive than a plateau

monadnock height of land containing more erosion-resistant rock than the surrounding area

oxbow lake that forms where a meandering river overflows and creates a crescent-shaped body of standing water; called an oxbow because its curved shape looks like the U-shaped harness frame that fits around an ox's neck

pictograph prehistoric painting or drawing on rock created with natural pigments applied with animal-hair brushes

rapids broken, fast-flowing water that tumbles around boulders; classified from I to VI according to increas-

ing difficulty of watercraft navigation
riparian relating to the bank of a natural watercourse, lake, or tidewater
sandstone sedimentary rock composed of sand grains
savanna tropical grassland with
clumps of grasses and widely scattered tree growth; occurs in areas
where a prolonged dry season alter-
nates with a rainy season
sedimentary rocks formed from deposits of small eroded debris such as
gravel, sand, mud, silt, or peat
slough swampy, backwater area;
inlet on a river or creek in a marsh or
tidal flat
speleothem any structure that forms
within a cave

stalactite icicle-shaped piece of
dripstone formed when water containing dissolved limestone drips
from the roof of a cave and evapo-
rates, leaving the mineral formation
on the roof
stalagmite spire formed as water
drips onto a cave floor and deposits minerals that were dissolved
in the water
talus accumulated rock debris at
the base of a cliff
tectonic referring to changes in the
earth's crust, the forces involved,
and the resulting formations
wetland area of land covered or
saturated with groundwater; includes swamps, marshes, and bogs

ABOVE: *In the 1920s a group of moonshiners pose with their still in a secluded "holler" of the Ouachita Mountains in southwestern Arkansas.*

LAND MANAGEMENT RESOURCES

The following public and private organizations are among the important administrators of the preserved and protected areas described in this volume. Brief explanations of the various legal and legislative designations of these areas follow.

MANAGING AGENCIES

Arkansas National Heritage Commission
Manages 54 natural areas totaling approximately 16,856 acres, which protect rare plants, animals, and ecological communities. Agency of the Department of Arkansas Heritage.

Arkansas State Parks
Manages 50,904 acres within 48 state parks, including natural, recreational, and cultural sites. Division of Arkansas Department of Parks and Tourism.

Houston Audubon Society
Local chapter of the National Audubon Society owns and manages 13 sanctuaries in Texas, totaling 1,360 acres. Protects critical habitats for birds.

Louisiana Department of Wildlife and Fisheries
Manages 50 wildlife management areas and 10 wildlife refuges totaling 1.3 million acres. Also regulates state hunting and fishing licensing.

Louisiana Office of State Parks
Manages 15 state parks and recreation areas, 13 commemorative sites, and 1 preservation area, totaling approximately 30,000 acres open to the public. Part of the Department of Culture, Recreation, and Tourism.

Mississippi Department of Wildlife, Fisheries, and Parks
Manages 28 state parks and 38 wildlife management areas. Regulates hunting and fishing licensing. Includes Division of Parks and Recreation.

National Park Service (NPS) Department of the Interior
Regulates the use of national parks, monuments, and preserves. Resources are managed to preserve and protect landscape, natural and historic artifacts, and wildlife. Also administers historic and national landmarks, national seashores, wild and scenic rivers, and the national trail system.

The Nature Conservancy (TNC) Private organization
International nonprofit organization that owns the largest private system of nature sanctuaries in the world, some 1,300 preserves. Aims to preserve significant and diverse plants, animals, and natural communities. Some areas are managed by other private or public conservation groups, some by the Conservancy itself.

Oklahoma Department of Wildlife Conservation
Manages about 900,000 acres in 60 wildlife management areas. Regulates and licenses all hunting and fishing within these areas.

Texas Parks and Wildlife Department
Manages 137 state parks totaling 519,000 acres and 52 wildlife management areas totaling 730,756 acres. Wildlife division also regulates hunting and fishing licenses.

U.S. Fish and Wildlife Service (USFWS) Department of the Interior
Principal federal agency responsible for conserving, protecting, and enhancing the country's fish and wildlife and their habitats. Manages national wildlife refuges and fish hatcheries as well as programs for migratory birds and endangered and threatened species.

U.S. Forest Service (USFS) Department of Agriculture
Administers more than 190 million acres in the national forests and national grasslands and is responsible for the management of their resources. Determines how best to combine commercial uses such as grazing, mining, and logging with conservation needs.

LAND DESIGNATIONS

National Forest
Acreage managed for the use of forests, watersheds, wildlife, and recreation by both the public and private sectors. Managed by the USFS.

National Grassland
Federal land where more than 80 percent of the canopy cover is dominated by grasses or grasslike plants. May encompass private holdings. Managed by the USFS.

National Monument
Nationally significant landmark, structure, object, or area of scientific or historic significance. Managed by the NPS.

National Park
Spacious primitive or wilderness land area that contains scenery or natural wonders so outstanding that it has been preserved by the federal government. Managed by the NPS.

National Recreation Area
Site established to conserve and develop for recreational purposes an area of national scenic, natural, or historic interest. Powerboats, dirt and mountain bikes, and ORVs allowed with restrictions. Managed by the NPS.

National Seashore
Area of pristine, undeveloped seashore designated to protect its natural state and provide public recreation in a natural setting. Camping and ORVs allowed with restrictions. Managed by the NPS.

National Wild and Scenic River System
National program set up to preserve selected rivers in their natural free-flowing condition; stretches are classified as wild, scenic, or recreational, depending on the degree of development on the river, shoreline, or adjacent lands. Management shared by the BLM, NPS, and USFWS.

National Wildlife Refuge
Public land set aside for wild animals; protects migratory waterfowl, endangered and threatened species, and native plants. Managed by the USFWS.

Natural Area
Area designated and preserved in its natural state for its exceptional value as an example of the natural history of the United States. Managed by individual states.

Wilderness Area
Area with particular ecological, geological, or scientific, scenic, or historic value that has been set aside in its natural condition to be preserved as wild land; limited recreational use is permitted. Managed by the BLM.

Wildlife Management Area
Land managed or owned by the state to protect wildlife. Aside from seasonal restrictions, hunting, fishing, and public access are allowed. Managed by individual states.

NATURE TRAVEL

The following is a selection of national and local organizations that sponsor nature-related travel activities or can provide specialized regional travel information.

NATIONAL

National Audubon Society
700 Broadway
New York, NY 10003
(212) 979-3000
Offers a wide range of ecological field studies, tours, and cruises throughout the United States

National Wildlife Federation
1400 16th St. NW
Washington, D.C. 20036
(703) 790-4363
Offers training in environmental education, wildlife camp and teen adventures, conservation summits with nature walks, field trips, and classes

The Nature Conservancy
1815 North Lynn St.
Arlington, VA 22209
(703) 841-5300
Offers a variety of excursions from regional and state offices. May include hiking, backpacking, canoeing. Contact above number to locate state offices

Sierra Club Outings
730 Polk St.
San Francisco, CA 94109
(415) 923-5630
Offers tours of different lengths for all ages throughout the United States. Outings may include backpacking, hiking, biking, skiing, and water excursions

Smithsonian Study Tours and Seminars
1100 Jefferson Dr. SW
MRC 702
Washington, D.C. 20560
(202) 357-4700
Offers extended tours, cruises, research expeditions, and seminars throughout the United States

REGIONAL

Arkansas Department of Parks and Tourism
1 Capitol Mall, 4th Fl.
Little Rock, AR 72201
(800) 828-8974
(501) 682-7777
Provides brochures and travel-related material. Can also answer specific questions regarding travel within the state

Louisiana Office of Tourism
P.O. Box 94291
Baton Rouge, LA 70804
(800) 334-8626
(504) 342-8119
Distributes maps, state brochures, and vacation planning guides. Can also answer specific questions

Mississippi Division of Tourism
P.O. Box 1705
Ocean Springs, MS 39566
(800) WARMEST (927-6378)
Provides highway maps, travel planners, and brochures, and answers specific travel and accommodation queries

Oklahoma Department of Tourism and Recreation
2401 N. Lincoln, Rm. 505
Oklahoma City, OK 73105
(800) 652-6552
Publishes vacation guide with maps and state brochures. Operator can answer travel-related questions

Texas Travel and Information Center
P.O. Box 5064
Austin, TX 78763
(800) 888-8TEX (8839)
(800) 452-9292
Call to order state travel-guide packet with maps and accommodation listings, or to ask specific travel questions

How to Use This Site Guide

The following site information guide will assist you in planning your tour of the natural areas of Arkansas, Louisiana, Mississippi, Oklahoma, and Texas. Sites set in boldface and followed by the symbol ❖ in the text are here organized alphabetically by state. Each entry is followed by the mailing address (sometimes different from the street address) and phone number of the immediate managing office, plus brief notes and a list of facilities and activities available. (A key appears on each page.)

Information on hours of operation, seasonal closings, and fees is often not listed, as these vary from season to season and year to year. Please bear in mind that responsibility for the management of some sites may change. Call well in advance to obtain maps, brochures, and pertinent, up-to-date information that will help you plan your adventures in the South Central region.

Each site entry in the guide includes the address and phone number of its immediate managing agency. Many of these sites are under the stewardship of a forest or park ranger or supervised from a small nearby office. Hence, in many cases, those sites will be difficult to contact directly, and it is preferable to call the managing agency.

The following umbrella organizations can provide general information for individual natural sites, as well as the area as a whole:

REGIONAL
U.S. Fish and Wildlife Service
Southeast Regional Office
1875 Century Blvd.
Atlanta, GA 30345
(404) 679-4000

ARKANSAS
Arkansas Natural Heritage Commission
1500 Tower Bldg.,
323 Center St.
Little Rock, AR 72201
(501) 324-9619

Arkansas Dept. of Parks and Tourism
1 Capitol Mall
Little Rock, AR 72201
(501) 682-7743

LOUISIANA
Louisiana Dept. of Agriculture and Forestry
PO Box 631
Baton Rouge, LA 70821
(504) 922-1234

Louisiana Dept. of Wildlife and Fisheries
PO Box 98000
Baton Rouge, LA 70898
(504) 765-2800

Louisiana Office of State Parks
PO Box 44426
Baton Rouge, LA 70804
(504) 342-8111

MISSISSIPPI
Mississippi Dept. of Wildlife, Fisheries, and Parks
PO Box 451
Jackson, MS 39205
(601) 362-9212
(601) 364-2010 (Parks and Rec. Division)

OKLAHOMA
Oklahoma Dept. of Wildlife Conservation
PO Box 53465
Oklahoma City, OK 73152
(405) 521-3851

Oklahoma Division of State Parks
PO Box 52002
Oklahoma City, OK 73105
(405) 521-3411

TEXAS
National Park Service
Southwest System Support Office
PO Box 728
Santa Fe, NM 87504
(505) 988-6011

Texas Parks and Wildlife Dept.
4200 Smith School Rd.
Austin, TX 78744
(512) 389-4800

257

ARKANSAS

BAKER PRAIRIE NATURAL AREA
Arkansas Natural Heritage Commission
1500 Tower Bldg., 323 Center St.
Little Rock, AR 72201
(501) 324-9619 (ANHC)
(501) 663-6699 (TNC) **BW**

BIG LAKE NATIONAL WILDLIFE REFUGE
U.S. Fish and Wildlife Service
PO Box 67
Manila, AR 72442
(501) 564-2429 **BW, F, I**

BLACK FORK MOUNTAIN WILDERNESS
Ouachita National Forest
PO Box 1270
Hot Springs, AR 71902
(501) 321-5202 **BW, C, F, H, MT**

BLANCHARD SPRINGS CAVERNS
Ozark National Forest
PO Box 1279
Mountain View, AR 72560
(501) 757-2211
Entry fee; Dripstone Tour accessible to wheelchairs with strong assistance; Discovery Tour not for those with health or walking problems; call for hours of operation **BW, C, F, GS, H, I, MT, PA, RA, S, T, TG**

BUFFALO NATIONAL RIVER
National Park Service
PO Box 1173
Harrison, AR 72602
(501) 741-5443
Lodging at Buffalo Point; ranger-led activities summer only **BW, C, CK, F, H, HR, I, L, MT, PA, RA, S, T**

CHEROKEE PRAIRIE NATURAL AREA
Arkansas Natural Heritage Commission
1500 Tower Bldg.
323 Center St.
Little Rock, AR 72201
(501) 324-9619 **BW**

COSSATOT RIVER STATE PARK AND NATURAL AREA
Arkansas Parks Div. and
Natural Heritage Commission
960 Rte. 4 East
Wickes, AR 71973
(501) 385-2201
(501) 387-3141 (24-hour recorded river stage information)
Tours by prearrangement; no glass containers within 50 feet of river; no firearms; primitive camping **BW, C, CK, F, H, MT, PA, RA, S, T, TG**

CRATER OF DIAMONDS STATE PARK
Arkansas Parks Div.
Rte. 1, Box 364
Murfreesboro, AR 71958
(501) 285-3113 **C, F, GS, H, I, MT, PA, RA, T**

DEVILS DEN STATE PARK
Arkansas Parks Div.
11333 West AR Hwy. 74
West Fork, AR 72774
(501) 761-3325
Cabins available **BT, BW, C, F, GS, H, HR, I, L, MB, MT, PA, RA, S, T, TG**

FELSENTHAL NATIONAL WILDLIFE REFUGE
U.S. Fish and Wildlife Service
PO Box 1157
Crossett, AR 71635
(501) 364-3167
Primitive camping **BW, C, F, H, I**

HOLLA BEND NATIONAL WILDLIFE REFUGE
U.S. Fish and Wildlife Service
Rte. 1, Box 59
Dardanelle, AR 72834
(501) 229-4300 **BW, F, H, MT, PA, T**

HOT SPRINGS NATIONAL PARK
National Park Service
PO Box 1860
Hot Springs, AR 71902
(501) 624-3383, ext. 640 **BW, C, GS, H, HR, I, MT, PA, RA, T, TG**

LAKE CHICOT STATE PARK
Arkansas Parks Div.
2542 Rte. 257
Lake Village, AR 71653
(501) 265-5480
Cabins available **BW, C, CK, F, GS, H, I, L, MT, PA, RA, S, T, TG**

BT Bike Trails	**CK** Canoeing, Kayaking	**F** Fishing	**HR** Horseback Riding
BW Bird-watching		**GS** Gift Shop	
C Camping	**DS** Downhill Skiing	**H** Hiking	**I** Information Center

LOUISIANA PURCHASE NATURAL AREA
Arkansas Natural Heritage Commission
1500 Tower Bldg., 323 Center St.
Little Rock, AR 72201
(501) 324-9619; (501) 682-1191   **BW, MT**

OUACHITA NATIONAL FOREST
U.S. Forest Service
PO Box 1270, Hot Springs, AR 71902
(501) 321-5202
   Some recreation areas have day-use fees
                      **BT, BW, C, CK, F, H, HR,
                      I, MB, MT, PA, RA, S, T**

OZARK NATIONAL FOREST
U.S. Forest Service
PO Box 1008, Russellville, AR 72811
(501) 968-2354
   Includes an archaeological museum
                      **BT, BW, C, CK, F, GS, H, HR, I, L, MB,
                      MT, PA, RA, RC, S, T, TG**

PETIT JEAN STATE PARK
Arkansas Parks Div.
Rte. 3, Box 340
Morrilton, AR 72110
(501) 727-5441   **BW, C, F, GS, H, I, L,
                      MT, PA, RA, S, T, TG**

RAILROAD PRAIRIE NATURAL AREA
Arkansas Natural Heritage Commission
1500 Tower Bldg., 323 Center St.
Little Rock, AR 72201
(501) 324-9619   **BW**

ROTH PRAIRIE NATURAL AREA
Arkansas Natural Heritage Commission
1500 Tower Bldg., 323 Center St.
Little Rock, AR 72201
(501) 324-9619   **BW**

SAINT FRANCIS NATIONAL FOREST
U.S. Forest Service
PO Box 1008, Russellville, AR 72801
(501) 968-2354; (501) 295-5278
   Horses and mountain bikes allowed on
   roads only   **BW, C, F, H, HR,
                      I, MB, PA, S, T**

VILLAGE CREEK STATE PARK
Arkansas Parks Div.
201 CR 754, Wynne, AR 72396
(501) 238-9406
   Cabins available   **BW, C, CK, F, GS, H,
                      I, L, MT, PA, RA, S, T, TG**

**WAPANOCCA NATIONAL
WILDLIFE REFUGE**
U.S. Fish and Wildlife Service
PO Box 279
Turrell, AR 72384-0279
(501) 343-2595   **BW, F, I**

WARREN PRAIRIE NATURAL AREA
Arkansas Natural Heritage Commission
1500 Tower Bldg.
323 Center St.
Little Rock, AR 72201
(501) 324-9619   **BW**

**WHITE RIVER NATIONAL
WILDLIFE REFUGE**
U.S. Fish and Wildlife Service
PO Box 308
DeWitt, AR 72042
(501) 946-1468
   Seasonal primitive camping   **BW, C, F**

LOUISIANA

ACADIANA PARK NATURE STATION
City of Lafayette, Div. of Arts and Culture
Lafayette Natural History Museum
637 Gerard Park Drive
Lafayette, LA 70503
(318) 261-8448
   Camping at adjacent Acadiana Park
                      BW, C, H, I, MT, PA, T, XC

ALEXANDER STATE FOREST
Louisiana Dept. of Agriculture and Forestry
PO Box 298
Woodworth, LA 71485
(318) 487-5172   **BW, C, F, H,
                         MT, PA, S, T**

AQUARIUM OF THE AMERICAS
Audubon Institute
1 Canal St.
New Orleans, LA 70130
(504) 565-3033
   Entry fee; handicapped-accessible; self-
   guided tours   **GS, I, T, TG**

AUDUBON STATE COMMEMORATIVE AREA
Louisiana Dept. of Culture,
Recreation and Tourism
PO Box 546
Saint Francisville, LA 70775
(504) 635-3739
   Entry fee   **BW, I, PA, T, TG**

L	Lodging	**PA**	Picnic Areas
MB	Mountain Biking	**RA**	Ranger-led Activities
MT	Marked Trails		

RC	Rock Climbing	**TG**	Tours, Guides
S	Swimming	**XC**	Cross-country Skiing
T	Toilets		

BRIARWOOD
PO Box 226
Natchitoches, LA 71458
(318) 576-3379
Open weekends March, April, May, August, and November; by appointment rest of year   **BW, H, I, MT, PA, T, TG**

CAJUN PRAIRIE RESTORATION PROJECT
Louisiana State
University at Eunice
Eunice, LA 70535
(318) 457-7311, ext. 245   **BW, H**

CAMERON PRAIRIE NATIONAL WILDLIFE REFUGE
U.S. Fish and Wildlife Service
1428 Rte. 27
Bell City, LA 70630
(318) 598-2216 (visitor information)
(318) 598-4235 (Boat Bay openings)
Refuge permits as well as state licenses required for fishing
BW, CK, F,H, I, MT, T

CATAHOULA NATIONAL WILDLIFE REFUGE
U.S. Fish and Wildlife Service
PO Drawer Z
Rhinehart, LA 71363-0201
(318) 992-5261   **BW, F, H**

CHICOT STATE PARK
Louisiana Office of State Parks
Rte. 3, Box 494
Ville Platte, LA 70586
(318) 363-2403
(318) 363-2503 (recorded information)
Entry fee   **BW, C, F, H, I, L, MT, PA, S, T**

D'ARBONNE NATIONAL WILDLIFE REFUGE
U.S. Fish and Wildlife Service
Rte. 2, Box 401B
Farmerville, LA 71241
(318) 726-4222
No ATVs; special-use permit required for horseback riding
BW, CK, F, H, HR, MT

FONTAINEBLEAU STATE PARK
Louisiana Office of State Parks
PO Box 8925
Mandeville, LA 70470-8925
(504) 624-4443
Entry fee; group lodge available
BW, C, F, I, L, PA, S, T

GRAND ISLE STATE PARK
Louisiana Office of State Parks
PO Box 741, Grand Isle, LA 70358
(504) 787-2559
Entry fee; seniors free
BW, C, F, PA, S, T

HOLLEYMAN-SHEELY AND HENSHAW SANCTUARIES
Baton Rouge Audubon Society
PO Box 82525
Baton Rouge, LA 70884
(504) 768-9874
Entry fee or annual permit
BW, F, H, I, T

JEAN LAFITTE NATIONAL HISTORICAL PARK AND PRESERVE
National Park Service
Barataria Preserve Unit
7400 Rte. 45
Marrero, LA 70072
(504) 589-2330
Sunday ranger-led tour by reservation; two moonlight tours per week; no cars
BW, CK, F, GS, H, I, MT, PA, RA, T, TG

JOYCE WILDLIFE MANAGEMENT AREA
Louisiana Dept. of
Wildlife and Fisheries
PO Box 98000
Baton Rouge, LA 70898
(504) 765-2360
Except for boardwalk, most of area is inaccessible   **BW, F**

JUNGLE GARDENS
Avery Island, LA 70513
(318) 369-6243
Includes Bird City; entry fee
BW, GS, H, I, MT, PA, T, TG

KALORAMA NATURE PRESERVE
Kalorama Foundation
PO Box 126
Collinston, LA 71229-0126
(318) 874-7777   **BW, I, MT, TG**

KISATCHIE NATIONAL FOREST
U.S. Forest Service
2500 Shreveport Hwy.
Pineville, LA 71360
(318) 473-7158   **BT, BW, C, CK, F, H, HR, MB, MT, PA, S, T**

BT	Bike Trails	**CK**	Canoeing, Kayaking	**F**	Fishing	**HR**	Horseback Riding
BW	Bird-watching			**GS**	Gift Shop		
C	Camping	**DS**	Downhill Skiing	**H**	Hiking	**I**	Information Center

LACASSINE NATIONAL WILDLIFE REFUGE
U.S. Fish and Wildlife Service
HCR 63, Box 186
Lake Arthur, LA 70549
(318) 774-5923
Tours for groups on request; best access by boat; boats permitted in Lacassine Pool mid-March to mid-October; December and January view waterfowl flights from road   **BW, C, F, H, TG**

LAKE FAUSSE POINT STATE PARK
Louisiana Office of State Parks
5400 Levee Road
Saint Martinville, LA 70582
(318) 229-4764
Entry fee; no horses   **BW, C, CK, F, H, I, L, MB, MT, PA, T**

LOUISIANA NATURE CENTER
Audubon Institute
PO Box 870610
New Orleans, LA 70187-0610
(504) 246-9381 (recorded information)
(504) 246-5672 (administration)
(504) 243-3395 (reservations)
(504) 246-STAR (planetarium)
      BW, GS, I, MT, PA, T, TG

LOUISIANA STATE ARBORETUM
Louisiana Office of State Parks
Rte. 3, Box 489
Ville Platte, LA 70586
(318) 363-6289; (318) 363-2403
No fee; self-guided tours   **BW, H, MT**

NORTH TOLEDO BEND STATE PARK
Louisiana Office of State Parks
PO Box 56
Zwolle, LA 71486
(318) 645-4715
Entry fee; boat launch; tours by pre-arrangement   **BW, C, F, H, I, L, MB, MT, PA, RA, S, T, TG**

PEARL RIVER WILDLIFE MANAGEMENT AREA
Louisiana Dept. of
Wildlife and Fisheries
PO Box 98000
Baton Rouge, LA 70898
(504) 765-2360
North end off Rte. 11 accessible by foot; southern ⅔ accessible only by boat
      BW, C, CK, F, H

POVERTY POINT STATE COMMEMORATIVE AREA
Louisiana Office of State Parks
PO Box 276
Epps, LA 71237
(318) 926-5492
Entry fee; children and seniors free; Easter to Labor Day motorized tram tours; self-guided tours rest of year
      BW, H, I, MT, PA, TG

ROCKEFELLER REFUGE
Louisiana Dept. of
Wildlife and Fisheries
5476 Grand Chenier Hwy.
Grand Chenier, LA 70643
(318) 538-2165; (318) 538-2276   **BW, F, I**

SABINE NATIONAL WILDLIFE REFUGE
U.S. Fish and Wildlife Service
Rte. 27 S., 3000 Main St.
Hackberry, LA 70645
(318) 762-3816   **BW, F, I, MT, T**

SALINE BAYOU NATIONAL WILD AND SCENIC RIVER
Kisatchie National Forest
2500 Shreveport Hwy.
Pineville, LA 71360
(318) 473-7158   **BT, C, CK, F, H, MT, PA, T**

SAM HOUSTON JONES STATE PARK
Louisiana Office of State Parks
107 Sutherland Rd.
Lake Charles, LA 70611
(318) 855-2665
Entry fee   **BT, BW, C, CK, F, H, I, L, MT, PA, T**

SHERBURNE WILDLIFE MANAGEMENT AREA
Louisiana Dept. of
Wildlife and Fisheries
PO Box 98000
Baton Rouge, LA 70898
(504) 765-2360   **BW, C, F, H**

TENSAS RIVER NATIONAL WILDLIFE REFUGE
U.S. Fish and Wildlife Service
Rte. 2, Box 295
Tallulah, LA 71282
(318) 574-2664
Tours available during scheduled events
      BW, CK, F, H, I, MT, T, TG

L	Lodging	**PA**	Picnic Areas	**RC**	Rock Climbing	**TG** Tours, Guides
MB	Mountain Biking	**RA**	Ranger-led Activities	**S**	Swimming	**XC** Cross-country Skiing
MT	Marked Trails			**T**	Toilets	

**TUNICA HILLS WILDLIFE
MANAGEMENT AREA**
Louisiana Dept. of Wildlife and Fisheries
PO Box 98000
Baton Rouge, LA 70898-9000
(504) 765-2360
    Primitive trail system   **BW, H**

**UPPER OUACHITA NATIONAL
WILDLIFE REFUGE**
U.S. Fish and Wildlife Service
c/o D'Arbonne National Wildlife Refuge
Rte. 2, Box 401 B
Farmerville, LA 71241
(318) 726-4222
    Marked trails for ATVs; bike and hiking
    trails unmarked; special-use permit re-
    quired for horseback riding
        BT, BW, CK, F, H, HR, MT

WHITE KITCHEN PRESERVE
The Nature Conservancy
PO Box 4125, Baton Rouge, LA 70821
(504) 338-1040   **BW, CK, H, PA**

MISSISSIPPI

BIENVILLE NATIONAL FOREST
U.S. Forest Service
Rte. 2, Box 1239
Forest, MS 39074
(601) 469-3811
    Entry fees to some areas   **BT, BW, C, F,
        H, HR, I, MB, MT, PA, S, T**

CLARK CREEK NATURAL AREA
Mississippi Dept. of Wildlife,
Fisheries and Parks
PO Box 451
Jackson, MS 39205
(601) 888-4426   **BW, H**

CROSBY ARBORETUM
PO Box 190
Picayune, MS 39466
(601) 799-2311   **BW, GS, I, MT, T**

DELTA NATIONAL FOREST
U.S. Forest Service
Sharkey-Ag Bldg.
402 Rte. 61 N
Rolling Fork, MS 39159
(601) 873-6256
    Primitive camping
    BT, BW, C, F, GS, H, HR, I, MB, MT, PA

DE SOTO NATIONAL FOREST
U.S. Forest Service
PO Box 248
Wiggins, MS 39577
(601) 928-5291; (601) 928-4422
    Some handicapped-accessible trails and
    campsites; information center at district
    ranger office in Wiggins
        **BT, BW, C, CK, F, H,
        HR, I, MB, MT, PA, T**

GULF ISLANDS NATIONAL SEASHORE
National Park Service
3500 Park Rd.
Ocean Springs, MS 39564
(601) 875-0821; (601) 875-3962
        **BT, BW, C, CK, F,
        GS, H, I, PA, RA, S, T**

LEAST TERN NESTING AREAS
Harrison County Sand Beach Authority
842 Commerce St.
Gulfport, MS 39507
(601) 896-0055   **BW**

LEROY PERCY STATE PARK
Mississippi Parks and Recreation Div.
PO Box 176
Hollandale, MS 38748
(601) 827-5436
    Entry fee; swimming in pool only, not in
    lake; tours by prearrangement; no pets
    in cabins   **BW, C, F, GS, H, L,
        MT, PA, RA, S, T, TG**

**MISSISSIPPI MUSEUM OF
NATURAL SCIENCE**
Mississippi Dept. of Wildlife,
Fisheries and Parks
111 North Jefferson St.
Jackson, MS 39202
(601) 354-7303   **I, PA, T, TG**

MISSISSIPPI PETRIFIED FOREST
PO Box 37, Flora, MS 39071
(601) 879-8189   **BW, C, GS, MT, PA, T**

**MISSISSIPPI SANDHILL CRANE
NATIONAL WILDLIFE REFUGE**
U.S. Fish and Wildlife Service
7200 Crane Lake
Gautier, MS 39553
(601) 497-6322
    Tours for groups by prearrangement
        BW, H, I, MT, T, TG

BT	Bike Trails	**CK**	Canoeing, Kayaking	**F**	Fishing	**HR** Horseback Riding
BW	Bird-watching			**GS**	Gift Shop	
C	Camping	**DS**	Downhill Skiing	**H**	Hiking	**I** Information Center

NATCHEZ TRACE PARKWAY
National Park Service
Tupelo, MS 38801
(601) 680-4025; (800) 305-7417
BW, C, CK, H, HR, I,
MT, PA, RA, S, T

NOXUBEE NATIONAL WILDLIFE REFUGE
U.S. Fish and Wildlife Service
Rte. 1, Box 142
Brooksville, MS 39739
(601) 323-5548   BW, F, I, MT, T

**PANTHER SWAMP NATIONAL
WILDLIFE REFUGE**
U.S. Fish and Wildlife Service
Rte. 1, Box 286
Hollandale, MS 38748
(601) 839-2638
    Wet swampy conditions during winter
    can make area difficult to traverse
                        BW, F, H

**PASCAGOULA RIVER WILDLIFE
MANAGEMENT AREA**
Mississippi Wildlife
and Fisheries Div.
PO Box 451
Jackson, MS 39205
(301) 947-6376; (601) 588-3878
                  BW, C, CK, F, H

**PLYMOUTH BLUFF
ENVIRONMENTAL CENTER**
Mississippi University for Women
Columbus, MS 39701
(601) 329-7376   BW, F, H, I, L, MT, T

SWEETBAY BOGS NATURAL AREA
Mississippi Chapter of
The Nature Conservancy
PO Box 1028
Jackson, MS 39215-1028
(601) 355-5357
    Call in advance; tours by prearrange-
    ment   BW, TG

TISHOMINGO STATE PARK
Mississippi Parks and Recreation Div.
PO Box 880
Tishomingo, MS 38873
(601) 438-6914
    Cabins and group huts available
                      C, CK, F, GS, H,
                      I, L, PA, S, T

TOMBIGBEE NATIONAL FOREST
Tombigbee Ranger District
Rte. 1, Box 98 A
Ackerman, MS 39735
(601) 285-3264   BW, C, F, H, HR,
                      MB, MT, PA, S, T

YAZOO NATIONAL WILDLIFE REFUGE
U.S. Fish and Wildlife Service
Rte. 1, Box 286
Hollandale, MS 38748
(601) 839-2638   BW, H, I, MT

OKLAHOMA

ALABASTER CAVERNS STATE PARK
Oklahoma Div. of State Parks
Rte. 1, Box 32, Freedom, OK 73842
(405) 621-3381
    Not recommended for those with mobil-
    ity or breathing problems
                  BW, C, GS, H, I, MT, PA, T, TG

**ARKANSAS RIVER LEAST
TERN PRESERVE**
The Nature Conservancy
23 W. 4th St., Ste. 200
Tulsa, OK 74103
(918) 585-1117   BW

**BEAVER RIVER WILDLIFE
MANAGEMENT AREA**
Oklahoma Dept. of Wildlife Conservation
Rte. 1, Box 94
Forgan, OK 73938
(405) 259-6281
    Primitive camping   BW, C, H, HR

BEAVERS BEND RESORT PARK
Oklahoma Div. of State Parks
PO Box 10, Broken Bow, OK 74728
(405) 494-6300
    Includes Beavers Bend and Hochatown
    state parks; cabins available; trout fish-
    ing year-round   BW, C, CK, F, GS, H,
                    I, L, MT, PA, RA, S, T, TG

**BEECH CREEK NATIONAL
SCENIC AND BOTANICAL AREA**
Ouachita National Forest
PO Box 1270
Hot Springs, AR 71902
(501) 321-5202
    Horses restricted to trails only
                  BT, BW, HR, I, MT, PA

L	Lodging	**PA**	Picnic Areas	**RC**	Rock Climbing	**TG**	Tours, Guides
MB	Mountain Biking	**RA**	Ranger-led Activities	**S**	Swimming	**XC**	Cross-country Skiing
MT	Marked Trails			**T**	Toilets		

BLACK FORK MOUNTAIN WILDERNESS
Ouachita National Forest
PO Box 1270
Hot Springs, AR 71902
(501) 321-5202   **BW, C, F, H, MT**

BLACK KETTLE NATIONAL GRASSLAND
U.S. Forest Service
Rte. 1, Box 55B
Cheyenne, OK 73628
(405) 497-2143
          BT, BW, C, CK, F, H, HR, I, MB, MT, PA

BLACK MESA NATURE PRESERVE
c/o Black Mesa State Park
HCR 1, Box 8
Kenton, OK 73946-9704
(405) 426-2222
          Allow 4–6 hours to hike trail to monu-
          ment and back; register at park before
          hiking; no motorized vehicles   **BW, H**

**BOEHLER SEEPS AND
SANDHILLS NATURE PRESERVE**
The Nature Conservancy
23 W. 4th St.
Ste. 200
Tulsa, OK 74103
(918) 585-1117   **BW, H**

BOILING SPRINGS STATE PARK
Oklahoma Div. of State Parks
PO Box 965
Woodward, OK 73802
(405) 256-7664; (405) 256-8307
          **BW, C, F, GS, H, I,
          L, MT, PA, S, T**

CHARONS GARDEN WILDERNESS AREA
c/o Wichita Mountains
National Wildlife Refuge
RR 1, Box 448
Indiahoma, OK 73552
(405) 429-3222
          Reservation and permit required for
          backcountry camping
          BW, C, H, I, MT

**CHICKASAW NATIONAL
RECREATION AREA**
National Park Service
PO Box 201
Sulphur, OK 73086
(405) 622-3165   **BT, BW, C, CK, F,
          GS, H, I, MT, PA, RA, S, T**

**GEORGE MIKSCH SUTTON
URBAN WILDERNESS PARK**
Norman Parks and Recreation Dept.
PO Box 370, Norman, OK 73070
(405) 366-5472   **BW, F, H, I, MT**

**LITTLE RIVER NATIONAL
WILDLIFE REFUGE**
U.S. Fish and Wildlife Service
PO Box 340, Broken Bow, OK 74728
(405) 584-6211   **BW, F**

LITTLE SAHARA STATE PARK
Oklahoma Div. of State Parks
RR 2, Box 132, Waynoka, OK 73860
(405) 824-1471   **C, H, I, PA, T, TG**

MARTIN PARK NATURE CENTER
Oklahoma City Parks and
Recreation Dept.
5000 W. Memorial Rd.
Oklahoma City, OK 73142
(405) 755-0676
          No entry fee; call for hours and days of
          operation   **BW, GS, H, I,
          MT, PA, RA, T, TG**

**McCURTAIN COUNTY
WILDERNESS AREA**
c/o Broken Bow
Wildlife Management Area
HC 75, Box 308-12
Broken Bow, OK 74728
(405) 241-7875   **BW, C**

**McGEE CREEK NATURAL
SCENIC RECREATION AREA**
c/o McGee Creek State Park
HC 82, Box 572, Atoka, OK 74525
(405) 889-5822
          Pets allowed on leashes
          **BT, BW, C, CK, F, H, HR,
          I, MB, MT, PA, RA, S, T, TG**

OUACHITA NATIONAL FOREST
U.S. Forest Service
PO Box 1270, Hot Springs, AR 71902
(501) 321-5202   **BT, BW, C, F, H, HR,
          I, MB, MT, PA, RA, S, T**

OXLEY NATURE CENTER
Tulsa Parks and Recreation Dept.
5701 East 36th St. N.
Tulsa, OK 74115
(918) 669-6644

BT	Bike Trails	**CK**	Canoeing, Kayaking	**F**	Fishing	**HR**	Horseback Riding
BW	Bird-watching			**GS**	Gift Shop		
C	Camping	**DS**	Downhill Skiing	**H**	Hiking	**I**	Information Center

(918) 669-6646 (Oklahoma Rare Bird
Hotline)   **BW, F, GS, H, I, PA, RA, T**

**QUARTZ MOUNTAIN
STATE RESORT PARK**
Oklahoma Div. of State Parks
Rte. 1, Box 40, Lonewolf, OK 73655
(405) 563-2238
                BW, C, F, GS, H, I, L, PA, S, T

REDBUD VALLEY NATURE PRESERVE
Tulsa Parks and Recreation Dept.
5701 E. 36th St. N.
Tulsa, OK 74115
(918) 669-6644   **BW, H, I, PA, RA, T, TG**

RED ROCK CANYON STATE PARK
Oklahoma Div. of State Parks
PO Box 502, Hinton, OK 73047
(405) 542-6344   **BW, C, MT, PA, RC, S, T**

RITA BLANCA NATIONAL GRASSLAND
U.S. Forest Service
714 Main St.
Clayton, NM 88415
(505) 374-9652
    Picnic area and toilets at Felt Camp-
    ground   **BW, C, H, MB, PA, T**

**ROBERT S. KERR NATURE CENTER AND
BOTANICAL AREA**
Ouachita National Forest
PO Box 1270, Hot Springs, AR 71902
(501) 321-5202   **BW, H, I**

ROMAN NOSE STATE PARK
Oklahoma Div. of State Parks
Rte. 1, Box 2-2
Watonga, OK 73772-9701
(405) 623-7281
            **BT, BW, C, CK, F, GS, H, HR
            I, L, MB, MT, PA, RA, S, T, TG**

**SALT PLAINS NATIONAL
WILDLIFE REFUGE**
U.S. Fish and Wildlife Service
Rte. 1, Box 76
Jet, OK 73749
(405) 626-4794   **BW, C, F, I, MT, PA, T**

SEQUOYAH NATIONAL WILDLIFE REFUGE
U.S. Fish and Wildlife Service
Rte. 1, Box 18A
Vian, OK 74962
(918) 773-5251   **BW, F, H, I, MT, T**

**SPARROWHAWK WILDLIFE
MANAGEMENT AREA**
Oklahoma Dept. of Wildlife Conservation
1801 N. Lincoln
Oklahoma City, OK 73105
(405) 521-4616   **BW, H**

TALLGRASS PRAIRIE PRESERVE
The Nature Conservancy
PO Box 458
Pawhuska, OK 74056
(918) 287-4803   **BW, GS, H, I, PA, TG**

**TISHOMINGO NATIONAL
WILDLIFE REFUGE**
U.S. Fish and Wildlife Service
Rte. 1, Box 151
Tishomingo, OK 73460
(405) 371-2402   **BW, F, H, T**

UPPER KIAMICHI RIVER WILDERNESS
Ouachita National Forest
PO Box 1270
Hot Springs, AR 71902
(501) 321-5202   **C, H, MT**

VANN'S MARSH
Oklahoma Dept. of Wildlife Conservation
Rte. 1, Box 75-B
Porter, OK 74454
(918) 683-1031; (918) 683-0098
                BW, F, I, MT, TG

WASHITA NATIONAL WILDLIFE REFUGE
U.S. Fish and Wildlife Service
Rte. 1, Box 68; Butler, OK 73625
(405) 664-2205
    October through February best time to
    view waterfowl   **BW, F, T, TG**

**WICHITA MOUNTAINS NATIONAL
WILDLIFE REFUGE**
U.S. Fish and Wildlife Service
RR 1, Box 448; Indiahoma, OK 73552
(405) 429-3222   **BT, BW, C, CK, F, H,
                    I, MT, PA, RC, T**

TEXAS

**ALIBATES FLINT QUARRIES
NATIONAL MONUMENT**
National Park Service
PO Box 1460
Fritch, TX 79036
(806) 857-3151   **BW, MT, RA, T, TG**

L	Lodging	**PA**	Picnic Areas	**RC**	Rock Climbing	**TG**	Tours, Guides
MB	Mountain	**RA**	Ranger-led	**S**	Swimming	**XC**	Cross-country
	Biking		Activities	**T**	Toilets		Skiing
MT	Marked Trails						

265

**AMISTAD NATIONAL
RECREATION AREA**
National Park Service
HCR 3, Box 5J
Del Rio, TX 78840-9350
(210) 775-7491
　　Three boat ramps　　　**BW, C, F, GS,
　　　　　　　　　　　　H, I, L, MT, PA, S, T**

ANAHUAC NATIONAL WILDLIFE REFUGE
U.S. Fish and Wildlife Service
PO Box 278
Anahuac, TX 77514
(409) 267-3337
　　Horses on roads only; no potable water;
　　primitive camping
　　　　　　　　　BW, C, F, H, HR, I, T

ANGELINA NATIONAL FOREST
U.S. Forest Service
PO Box 756
Lufkin, TX 75901
(409) 639-8620
　　Vehicle parking permit required for
　　those fishing by boat; ORVs restricted to
　　certain areas　　　**BW, C, CK, F, H, I,
　　　　　　　　　　　L, MB, MT, PA, S, T**

ARANSAS NATIONAL WILDLIFE REFUGE
U.S. Fish and Wildlife Service
PO Box 100
Austwell, TX 77950
(512) 286-3559
(512) 286-3409 (TDD)
　　Includes wildlife interpretative center;
　　day use only; registration required
　　　　　　　　　BW, GS, I, MT, PA, T

ARMAND BAYOU NATURE CENTER
PO Box 58828
Houston, TX 77258
(713) 474-2551
　　Open Wednesdays through Sundays;
　　trails are primitive and often wet
　　　　　　　　　**BW, CK, H, I, MT,
　　　　　　　　　　PA, RA, T, TG**
**ATTWATER PRAIRIE CHICKEN NATIONAL
WILDLIFE REFUGE**
U.S. Fish and Wildlife Service
PO Box 519
Eagle Lake, TX 77434
(409) 234-3021
　　Day use only; auto-tour route may be
　　closed following heavy rains
　　　　　　　　　　BW, I, MT, TG

**BALCONES CANYONLANDS NATIONAL
WILDLIFE REFUGE**
U.S. Fish and Wildlife Service
20171 Burnet Rd., Ste. 201
Austin, TX 78758
(512) 339-9432
　　Closed to public use except by special
　　permit or guided tour; contact refuge
　　　　　　　　　　BW, H, RA, TG

BALMORHEA STATE PARK
Texas Parks and Wildlife Dept.
PO Box 15, Toyahvale, TX 79786
(915) 375-2370
(512) 389-8900 (reservations)
　　　　　　　BW, C, GS, L, PA, S, T, TG

BASTROP STATE PARK
Texas Parks and Wildlife Dept.
PO Box 518, Bastrop, TX 78602
(512) 321-2101
　　Entry fee　　　　**BW, C, F, GS, H, I,
　　　　　　　　　　L, MT, PA, RA, S, T**

**BENTSEN–RIO GRANDE
VALLEY STATE PARK**
Texas Parks and Wildlife Dept.
PO Box 988, Mission, TX 78573
(210) 585-1107
(210) 585-0902
(210) 519-6448
　　Entry fee; self-guided nature trail
　　　　　　　　**BT, BW, C, CK, F, GS,
　　　　　　　　H, I, MT, PA, RA, T, TG**

BIG BEND NATIONAL PARK
National Park Service
PO Box 116
Big Bend National Park, TX 79834
(915) 477-2251　　　**BW, C, CK, F, GS, H,
　　　　　　　　　I, L, MB, MT, PA, RA, T, TG**

BIG BEND RANCH STATE PARK
Texas Parks and Wildlife Dept.
PO Box 1180, Presidio, TX 79845
(915) 229-3416　　　**BT, BW, C, CK, F, GS,
　　　　　　　　　H, HR, I, L, RA, T, TG**

BIG CREEK SCENIC AREA
Sam Houston National Forest
Sam Houston Ranger District
PO Box 1000
New Waverly, TX 77358
(713) 592-6461
　　No dogs or hunting　　　**BW, H, MT**

266

BT Bike Trails	**CK** Canoeing,	**F** Fishing	**HR** Horseback
BW Bird-watching	Kayaking	**GS** Gift Shop	Riding
C Camping	**DS** Downhill	**H** Hiking	**I** Information
	Skiing		Center

BIG THICKET NATIONAL PRESERVE
National Park Service
3785 Milam St., Beaumont, TX 77701
(409) 246-2337 (visitor information)
(409) 839-2689 (headquarters)
       **BT, BW, C, CK, F, H,
       HR, I, MT, PA, RA, S, T, TG**

BLACK KETTLE NATIONAL GRASSLAND
U.S. Forest Service
Rte. 1, Box 55B, Cheyenne, OK 73628
(405) 497-2143   **BT, BW, C, CK, F, H,
       HR, I, MB, MT, PA**

**BOLIVAR FLATS
SHOREBIRD SANCTUARY**
Houston Audubon Society
440 Wilchester Blvd.
Houston, TX 77079
(713) 932-1639   **BW**

BRAZORIA NATIONAL WILDLIFE REFUGE
U.S. Fish and Wildlife Service
1212 N. Velasco, Ste. 200
Angleton, TX 77515
(409) 849-6062
    Open to public first full weekend of each
    month; group tours by prearrangement;
    auto-tour route; bring mosquito repellent
                    BW, F, T

BRAZOS BEND STATE PARK
Texas Parks and Wildlife Dept.
21901 FM 762
Needville, TX 77461
(409) 553-5112   **BT, BW, C, F, GS, H,
       I, L, MT, PA, RA, T**

BUESCHER STATE PARK
Texas Parks and Wildlife Dept.
PO Box 75
Smithville, TX 78957
(512) 237-2241
    Entry fee; no motors on lake; size of
    boats restricted; no horses
        BW, C, F, H, I, MT, PA, S, T

**BUFFALO LAKE NATIONAL
WILDLIFE REFUGE**
U.S. Fish and Wildlife Service
PO Box 179
Umbarger, TX 79091
(806) 499-3382
    Entry fee; permit required; auto-tour
    route   **BW, H, I, MT, PA, T**

CADDO LAKE STATE PARK
Texas Parks and Wildlife Dept.
Rte. 2, Box 15
Karnack, TX 75661
(903) 679-3351
(512) 389-8900 (reservations)
        BW, C, CK, F, H, I, MT, PA, S, T

CADDO NATIONAL GRASSLAND
U.S. Forest Service
PO Box 507, Decatur, TX 76234
(817) 627-5475
        BW, C, CK, F, H, HR, PA, T

CAPROCK CANYONS STATE PARK
Texas Parks and Wildlife Dept.
PO Box 204
Quitaque, TX 79255
(806) 455-1492
(512) 389-8900 (reservations)
    Bring drinking water
             **BT, BW, C, F, GS, H, HR,
           I, L, MB, MT, PA, RA, S, T, TG**

CAVERNS OF SONORA
PO Box 1196
Sonora, TX 76950
(915) 387-3105; (915) 387-6507
             **BW, C, GS, H, I,
           MT, PA, T, TG**

CLYMER MEADOW
The Nature Conservancy of Texas
PO Box 1440
San Antonio, TX 78295
(903) 568-4139   **BW, I, T, TG**

COPPER BREAKS STATE PARK
Texas Parks and Wildlife Dept.
Rte. 2, Box 480
Quanah, TX 79252
(817) 839-4331
    Horses restricted to certain areas
             **BW, C, CK, F, GS, H,
          HR, I, MT, PA, RA, S, T, TG**

CROSS TIMBERS TRAIL
Army Corps of Engineers
Rte. 4, Box 493
Denison, TX 75020
(903) 465-4990; (903) 463-2860
    Primitive camping; no vehicles; wilder-
    ness camping permits required; informa-
    tion at Texas Travel Information Center
    in Denison   **BW, C, F, H, I, MT**

L	Lodging	**PA**	Picnic Areas	**RC**	Rock Climbing	**TG**	Tours, Guides
MB	Mountain Biking	**RA**	Ranger-led Activities	**S**	Swimming	**XC**	Cross-country Skiing
MT	Marked Trails			**T**	Toilets		

DAVIS MOUNTAINS STATE PARK
Texas Parks and Wildlife Dept.
PO Box 1458
Fort Davis, TX 79734
(915) 426-3337   **BW, C, GS, H, I, L,**
                         MT, PA, RA, T

DAVY CROCKETT NATIONAL FOREST
U.S. Forest Service
PO Box 130, Apple Springs, TX 75926
(409) 544-2046 (Crockett)
(409) 831-2246 (Apple Springs)
    Includes Four C Trail and Piney Creek
    Horse Trail (50-mile loop) for horses
    and hikers   **BW, C, CK, F, H,**
                    HR, I, MT, PA, S, T

DEVILS RIVER STATE NATURAL AREA
Texas Parks and Wildlife Dept.
HCR-1, Box 513
Del Rio, TX 78840
(210) 395-2133
(512) 389-8900 (reservations)
    Texas Conservation Passport required age
    17 and over; group barracks available
        BT, BW, C, H, L, MB, T, TG

DEVILS SINKHOLE STATE NATURAL AREA
Kickapoo Cavern State Park
PO Box 705, Brackettville, TX 78832
(210) 563-2342
    Tours by reservation only   **BW, TG**

DINOSAUR VALLEY STATE PARK
Texas Parks and Wildlife Dept.
PO Box 396, Glen Rose, TX 76043
(817) 897-4588   **BT, BW, C, F, GS, H,**
                  I, MB, MT, PA, T, TG

ECKERT JAMES RIVER
BAT CAVE PRESERVE
The Nature Conservancy of Texas
PO Box 164255
Austin, TX 78716
(512) 327-9472 (year-round)
(915) 347-5970 (seasonal)
    Call in advance for time of bat emergence
              BW, H, MT, TG

ENCHANTED ROCK STATE NATURAL AREA
Texas Parks and Wildlife Dept.
Rte. 4, Box 170
Fredericksburg, TX 78624
(915) 247-3903
    BW, C, F, GS, H, I, MT, PA, RC, T

FORT WORTH NATURE
CENTER AND REFUGE
Fort Worth Parks and
Community Services Dept.
9601 Fossil Ridge Rd.
Fort Worth, TX 76135
(817) 237-1111
    BW, CK, H, I, MT, PA, RA, T, TG

FRANKLIN MOUNTAINS STATE PARK
Texas Parks and Wildlife Dept.
PO Box 200, Canutillo, TX 79835
(915) 566-6441
    Tent camping only
              BW, C, GS, H, HR, I,
           MB, PA, RA, RC, T, TG

GALVESTON ISLAND STATE PARK
Texas Parks and Wildlife Dept.
14901 FM 3005, Galveston, TX 77554
(409) 737-1222
(512) 389-8900 (reservations)
    Reservations needed for camping
           BW, C, F, MT, PA, S, T

GOOSE ISLAND STATE PARK
Texas Parks and Wildlife Dept.
HCO 1, Box 105, Rockport, TX 78382
(512) 729-2858
(512) 389-8900 (reservations)
        BW, C, F, GS, H, MT, PA, T

GUADALUPE MOUNTAINS NATIONAL PARK
National Park Service
HC 60, Box 400
Salt Flat, TX 79847
(915) 828-3251
    Free permits required for backcountry
    camping   **BW, C, H, HR, I, MT,**
                    PA, RA, T, TG

GUADALUPE RIVER STATE PARK
Texas Parks and Wildlife Dept.
3350 Park Rd. 31
Spring Branch, TX 78070
(210) 438-3422   **BW, C, CK, F, GS, H,**
                  I, MT, PA, RA, S, T, TG

HAGERMAN NATIONAL WILDLIFE REFUGE
U.S. Fish and Wildlife Service
Rte. 3, Box 123, Sherman, TX 75092
(903) 786-2826
    Horses allowed on roads only; boating
    April through September
            BW, CK, F, GS, H, HR,
                I, MB, MT, PA, T

BT Bike Trails	**CK** Canoeing,	**F** Fishing	**HR** Horseback
BW Bird-watching	Kayaking	**GS** Gift Shop	Riding
C Camping	**DS** Downhill	**H** Hiking	**I** Information
	Skiing		Center

268

**HEARD NATURAL SCIENCE MUSEUM
AND WILDLIFE SANCTUARY**
One Nature Place, McKinney, TX 75069
(214) 562-5566   **BW, CK, GS, H, I,
MT, PA, RA, T, TG**
HIGH ISLAND
Houston Audubon Society
440 Wilchester Blvd.
Houston, TX 77079
(713) 932-1639
  Includes Boy Scout Woods and Smith
  Oaks; tours by prearrangement March
  through May   **BW, I, MT, T, TG**

HILL COUNTRY STATE NATURAL AREA
Texas Parks and Wildlife Dept.
4200 Smith School Rd.
Austin, TX 78744
(210) 796-4413
  Park closed Tuesdays and Wednesdays
  year-round; during hunting season (No-
  vember to March) park open to public
  Fridays, Saturdays and Sundays only
      **BW, C, F, H, HR, I, L,
MB, MT, PA, RA, S, T**

HUECO TANKS STATE HISTORICAL PARK
Texas Parks and Wildlife Dept.
6900 Hueco Tanks Rd. #1
El Paso, TX 79938
(915) 857-1135   **BW, C, GS, H, I, MT,
PA, RA, RC, T, TG**

INDIAN MOUNDS WILDERNESS AREA
Sabine National Forest
201 S. Palm
Hemphill, TX 75948
(409) 787-3870
  Primitive camping   **BW, C, H, HR**

KICKAPOO CAVERN STATE PARK
Texas Parks and Wildlife Dept.
PO Box 705, Brackettville, TX 78832
(210) 563-2342
  Tours by reservation only; Texas Conservation Passport required for ages 17
  and over (annual fee)   **BW, TG**

**LAGUNA ATASCOSA NATIONAL
WILDLIFE REFUGE**
U.S. Fish and Wildlife Service
PO Box 450, Rio Hondo, TX 78583-0450
(210) 748-3607
  Daily entry fee or seasonal pass required
      BW, GS, H, I, MT, T

**LAKE MEREDITH NATIONAL
RECREATION AREA**
National Park Service
PO Box 1460, Fritch, TX 79036
(806) 857-3151
      BW, C, F, GS, H, HR, I, PA, S, T

LITTLE LAKE CREEK WILDERNESS AREA
Sam Houston National Forest
Sam Houston Ranger District
PO Box 1000, New Waverly, TX 77358
(409) 344-6205   **BW, C, H, HR, MB, MT**

LONGHORN CAVERN STATE PARK
Texas Parks and Wildlife Dept.
Rte. 2, Box 23, Park Rd. 4
Burnet, TX 78611
(512) 756-4680
(512) 756-6976 (recorded message)
      **BW, GS, H, I,
MT, PA, RA, T, TG**

LOST MAPLES STATE NATURAL AREA
Texas Parks and Wildlife Dept.
HCO 1, Box 156, Vanderpool, TX 78885
(210) 966-3413
(512) 389-8900 (reservations)
      BW, C, F, GS, H, I, MT, PA, S, T

**LYNDON B. JOHNSON
NATIONAL GRASSLAND**
USFS; PO Box 507, Decatur, TX 76234
(817) 627-5475
  Includes Cottonwood–Black Creek Trail;
  entry fee; view migratory Neotropical
  birds in spring; vehicle travel restricted;
  fire precautions especially when grasslands are dry
      BW, C, CK, F, H, HR, MT, PA, S, T

MATAGORDA ISLAND STATE PARK
Texas Parks and Wildlife Dept.
PO Box 117, Port O'Connor, TX 77982
(512) 983-2215   **BT, BW, C, CK, F, GS,
H, I, L, MB, PA, RA, S, T, TG**

**McCLELLAN CREEK
NATIONAL GRASSLAND**
U.S. Forest Service
c/o Black Kettle National Grassland
Rte. 1, Box 55B, Cheyenne, OK 73628
(405) 497-2143
(806) 779-2590 (reservations)
      **BT, BW, C, CK,
F, H, MB, MT, PA, T**

L	Lodging	**PA**	Picnic Areas	**RC**	Rock Climbing	**TG**	Tours, Guides
MB	Mountain Biking	**RA**	Ranger-led Activities	**S**	Swimming	**XC**	Cross-country Skiing
MT	Marked Trails			**T**	Toilets		

269

MCDONALD OBSERVATORY
University of Texas–Austin
PO Box 1337, Fort Davis, TX 79734
(915) 426-3640
"Star Parties" on Tuesdays, Fridays, and
Saturdays **I, T, TG**

MONAHANS SANDHILLS STATE PARK
Texas Parks and Wildlife Dept.
PO Box 1738, Monahans, TX 79756
(915) 943-2092
Horses restricted to certain areas
BW, C, GS, H, HR, MT, PA, RA, T, TG

MULESHOE NATIONAL WILDLIFE REFUGE
U.S. Fish and Wildlife Service
PO Box 549, Muleshoe, TX 79347
(806) 946-3341 **BW, C, I, PA, T**

**NATIONAL WILDFLOWER
RESEARCH CENTER**
4801 LaCrosse Ave., Austin, TX 78739
(512) 292-4100 (recorded information);
(512) 292-4200 **GS, H, I, MT, PA, T, TG**

NATURAL BRIDGE CAVERNS
26495 Natural Bridge Caverns Rd.
San Antonio, TX 78266
(210) 651-6101
Open every day except Thanksgiving,
Christmas, and New Year's Day
GS, I, MT, PA, T, TG

**OLD TUNNEL WILDLIFE
MANAGEMENT AREA**
Texas Parks and Wildlife Dept.
4200 Smith School Rd.
Austin, TX 78744
(210) 868-7304
(Pedernales Falls State Park)
Call for times of bat sightings and to reserve for tour; Texas Conservation Passport required to participate in tours; no
admission fee for overlook; handi-
capped accessible **BW, MT, T, TG**

PADRE ISLAND NATIONAL SEASHORE
National Park Service
9405 South Padre Island Dr.
Corpus Christi, TX 78418
(512) 949-8068 (visitor center)
(512) 949-8175 (weather and beach
conditions recording)
Entry fee (7-day pass)
BW, C, F, GS, I, MT, PA, RA, S, T, TG

PALMETTO STATE PARK
Texas Parks and Wildlife Dept.
Rte. 5, Box 201
Gonzalez, TX 78629
(210) 672-3266 **BW, C, CK, F, GS,
H, I, MT, PA, S, T**

PALO DURO CANYON STATE PARK
Texas Parks and Wildlife Dept.
Rte. 2, Box 285
Canyon, TX 79015
(806) 488-2227
(512) 389-8900 (reservations) **BT, BW,
C, GS, H, HR, I, L, MB, MT, PA, T**

PANTHER CAVE
Texas Parks and Wildlife Dept.
c/o Seminole Canyon State Historical Park
PO Box 820, Comstock, TX 78837
(915) 292-4464
Viewing site for Pecos River–style pictographs; accessible by boat only; overlook located in park

PARKHILL PRAIRIE PRESERVE
Collin County Open Space Plan
700A West Wilmeth Rd.
McKinney, TX 75069
(214) 548-3739
Day use only; no pets; call for map
BW, F, H, I, PA, T

PEDERNALES FALLS STATE PARK
Texas Parks and Wildlife Dept.
Rte. 1, Box 450
Johnson City, TX 78636
(210) 868-7304 **BT, BW, C, F, GS,
H, I, MB, PA, S, T**

**RED-COCKADED WOODPECKER
INTERPRETIVE SITE**
Sam Houston National Forest
Sam Houston Ranger District
PO Box 1000
New Waverly, TX 77358
(409) 344-6205
Area bordered by Rte. 1375, FM 2025,
and FR 215 **BW, C**

**RIO GRANDE NATIONAL
WILD AND SCENIC RIVER**
c/o Big Bend National Park
PO Box 116
Big Bend National Park, TX 79834
(915) 477-2251 **CK, F**

BT	Bike Trails	**CK**	Canoeing,	**F**	Fishing	**HR**	Horseback
BW	Bird-watching		Kayaking	**GS**	Gift Shop		Riding
C	Camping	**DS**	Downhill	**H**	Hiking	**I**	Information
			Skiing				Center

**RITA BLANCA
NATIONAL GRASSLAND**
U.S. Forest Service
714 Main St.
Clayton, NM 88415
(505) 374-9652   **BW, C, H, MB, PA, T**

**ROY E. LARSON
SANDYLAND SANCTUARY**
The Nature Conservancy of Texas
PO Box 909
Silsbee, TX 77656
(409) 385-0445; (409) 385-4135
                    BW, CK, H, MT, T

SABAL PALM GROVE SANCTUARY
National Audubon Society
PO Box 5052, Brownsville, TX 78523
(210) 541-8034
    Entry fee; tours by prearrangement for
    groups of ten or more
                    BW, GS, MT, PA, T, TG

SABINE NATIONAL FOREST
U.S. Forest Service
201 S. Palm, Hemphill, TX 75948
(409) 787-3870
    BW, C, CK, F, H, HR, I, MB, MT, PA, S, T

SAM HOUSTON NATIONAL FOREST
Sam Houston Ranger District
PO Box 1000, New Waverly, TX 77358
(409) 344-6205
    BT, BW, C, CK, F, H, HR, MB, MT, PA

**SAN BERNARD NATIONAL
WILDLIFE REFUGE**
U.S. Fish and Wildlife Service
1212 N. Velasco, Ste. 200
Angleton, TX 77515
(409) 849-6062
    Day use only; bring mosquito repellent
                    BW, H, I, MT, T

SANTA ANA NATIONAL WILDLIFE REFUGE
U. S. Fish and Wildlife Service
Rte. 2, Box 202A, Alamo, TX 78516
(210) 787-3079   **BW, GS, I, MT, T, TG**

SEA RIM STATE PARK
Texas Parks and Wildlife Dept.
PO Box 1066
Sabine Pass, TX 77655
(409) 971-2559   **BW, C, CK, F, PA, S, T**

**SEMINOLE CANYON STATE
HISTORICAL PARK**
Texas Parks and Wildlife Dept.
PO Box 820, Comstock, TX 78837
(915) 292-4464
    BW, C, GS, H, I, MB, MT, PA, RA, T, TG

TEXAS STATE AQUARIUM
PO Box 331307
Corpus Christi, TX 78463
(512) 881-1200; (800) 477-4873   **GS, T, TG**

TRAIL BETWEEN THE LAKES
Sabine National Forest
201 S. Palm, Hemphill, TX 75948
(409) 787-3870   **BW, C, F, H, MT**

WELDER WILDLIFE FOUNDATION
PO Drawer 1400
Sinton, TX 78387
(512) 364-2643
    No entry fee; tours Thursday afternoons;
    tours for groups over 15 can be pre-
    arranged   **BW, I, MT, T, TG**

WILD BASIN WILDERNESS PRESERVE
The Committee for
Wild Basin Wilderness, Inc.
805 N. Capital of Texas Hwy.
Austin, TX 78746
(512) 327-7622
                    BW, GS, H, I, MT, PA, RA, T, TG

L	Lodging	**PA**	Picnic Areas	**RC**	Rock Climbing	**TG**	Tours, Guides
MB	Mountain Biking	**RA**	Ranger-led Activities	**S**	Swimming	**XC**	Cross-country Skiing
MT	Marked Trails			**T**	Toilets		

PHOTOGRAPHY CREDITS

All photographs in the Texas, Oklahoma, and Arkansas chapters are by Jim Bones except for the following; all photographs in the Louisiana and Mississippi chapters are by Tria Giovan except for the following:

Front cover: Tria Giovan
i: Tom Vezo/The Wildlife Collection, Brooklyn, NY
iv: Tria Giovan
viii, left: Jim Bones
viii, right: Jim Roetzel/Dembinsky Photo Associates (DPA), Owosso, MI
ix, left: Tria Giovan
ix, right: Tom Vezo/The Wildlife Collection
x–xi: Jim Bones
xiv–xv: Jim Bones
xvi: Bill Lea/DPA
xx–xxi: Earl Nottingham, Temple, TX
3, 4: Jim Bones
5: Laurence Parent, Manchaca, TX
6–7: Jim Bones
8: Earl Nottingham, Temple, TX
9: Clay Myers/The Wildlife Collection
11, left: Gary Meszaros/DPA
11, top right: Anthony Mercieca/DPA
11, bottom right: Dan Dempster/DPA
20: Jim Battles/DPA
21: Stan Osolinski/DPA
27: Byron Jorjorian, Antioch, TN
28: John Mielcarek/DPA
31, left: Stan Osolinski/DPA
31, right, 34: Rod Planck/DPA
37: Collection of the New-York Historical Society, New York, NY
43: Bill Lea/DPA
45: Mark J. Thomas/DPA
48: Dominique Braud/DPA
55, top left: Charles Melton/The Wildlife Collection
55, top right: Anthony Mercieca/DPA
55, bottom left: Skip Moody/DPA
55, bottom right: Jim Battles/DPA
61: Jim Roetzel/DPA
65: Charles Melton/The Wildlife Collection
68: Stan Osolinski/DPA
71, left: Michael H. Francis/The Wildlife Collection
71, right: Lorri Franz/The Wildlife Collection
77, top: John Mielcarek/DPA
77, bottom: Jim Roetzel/DPA
82, top: Bill Lea/DPA
82, bottom: Jim Battles/DPA
84–85: Adam Jones/DPA
89: The Museum of Fine Arts, Houston archives; Private Collection of Ms. Jane Smith, Houston, TX
96, left: Stan Osolinski/DPA
96, right: Mark J. Thomas/DPA
97, 116: Anthony Mercieca/DPA
123, left: Barbara Gerlach/DPA
123, right: Adam Jones/DPA
132: Dominique Braud/DPA
135, top left: John Cancalosi, Tucson, AZ
135, top right, bottom right: Robert Lankinen/The Wildlife Collection
135, bottom left: Henry Holdsworth/The Wildlife Collection, Brooklyn, NY
137, left: Rod Planck/DPA
137, right: Barbara Gerlach/DPA
140: Center for Creative Photography, Tucson, AZ
144: Rod Planck/DPA
145: Jim Roetzel/DPA
146–147: Matt Bradley, Little Rock, AR
152: Tom Till, Moab, UT

158: Earl Nottingham, Temple, TX
159: Michael H. Francis/The Wildlife Collection
162: Tom Vezo/The Wildlife Collection
163: Greg Ryan and Sally Beyer, North Oaks, MN
166, right: Carl R. Sams II/DPA
168–169: Matt Bradley, Little Rock, AR
176: Tom Coker, Fayetteville, AR
177, top: Tom Vezo/The Wildlife Collection
177, bottom: Martin Harvey/The Wildlife Collection
181, left: Robert Lankinen/The Wildlife Collection
181, right: C.C. Lockwood, Baton Rouge, LA
192, top: John Shaw, Colorado Springs, CO
193: Carl R. Sams II/DPA
196: Michael H. Francis/The Wildlife Collection
203: Mark J. Thomas/DPA
204: The Saint Louis Art Museum, Gift of Mrs. W. P. Edgerton
206: Houghton Library, Harvard University, Cambridge, MA (pf MS Am 21)
207: George E. Stewart/DPA
220: Michael H. Francis/The Wildlife Collection
222: C. C. Lockwood, Baton Rouge, LA
223: Courtesy of the Family of Walter Anderson, Joan Gilley, Curator, Ocean Springs, MS
224–225: Henry Holdsworth/The Wildlife Collection
227, 230, left: Clay Myers/The Wildlife Collection
230, right: Johann Schumacher Design, Ridgewood, NY
240: Byron Jorjorian, Antioch, TN
242: C.C. Lockwood, Baton Rouge, LA
244, left: Len Rue, Jr., Blairstown, NJ
250–251: Cunningham-Prettyman Collection/Western History Collections, University of Oklahoma, Norman, OK
253: Arkansas History Commission, Little Rock, AR
Back cover: Jim Bones (cactus); Adam Jones/DPA (painted bunting); Henry Holdsworth/The Wildlife Collection (armadillo)

Acknowledgments

The editors gratefully acknowledge the professional assistance of Susan Kirby and Patricia Woodruff. We wish to thank those site managers and naturalists whose time and commitment contributed to this volume. The following consultants also helped in the preparation of this volume: Ian Butler, Oklahoma Biological Survey and Natural Heritage Inventory; Walter Davis, Director, Panhandle-Plains Historical Museum; Dr. Sidney McDaniel, Mississippi State University, Institute for Botanical Exploration; Dallas Rhodes, Professor and Chair of Geology, Whittier College; William Shepherd, Arkansas Natural Heritage Commission; Keith P. Tomlinson, Principal Naturalist, Biogeographic, Inc.; and James Whelan, Lafayette Natural History Museum.